To Roger,

One of a rare breed — a serious chukar hunter. i.e. both passionate and crazy. Hope you enjoy the book.

Mitch Rohlfs

COTTONTAILS TO KUDU

A HUNTER'S JOURNEY

By
W. Mitchell Rohlfs, Ph.D.

COTTONTAILS TO KUDU

A HUNTER'S JOURNEY

By
W. Mitchell Rohlfs, Ph.D.

ISBN 1-931291-67-5

Library of Congress Control Number: 2007932333

Published in the United States of America

First Edition

STONEYDALE PRESS PUBLISHING COMPANY
523 Main Street • P.O. Box 188
Stevensville, Montana 59870
Phone: 406-777-2729

DEDICATION

To the game, both furred and feathered,
that have enriched my life immeasurably.

ACKNOWLEDGMENTS

I would first like to acknowledge my father, Walter Mitchell Rohlfs, Jr. It was he who saw a son with a genuine interest in the natural world, and created an environment that allowed that interest to develop. He helped with my first butterfly collection, caught frogs for my aquarium, taught me to fish and ultimately opened my eyes to the mysteries of hunting. My debt to him can never be repaid.

To my mother, Doris Leigh, a city girl from Philadelphia who tolerated snakes, mice, toads, frogs, iguanas, guinea pigs and homing pigeons in the house; all for the purpose of nurturing a son whose interests were completely different from her own, I am eternally grateful. I also thank her for urging me to write this book, I can only say that I never would have completed it without her encouragement.

To my wife, Claudia Wilson Rohlfs, the love of my life since high school and forever, for understanding my passion for the hunt and all the time away from home that entails. I am also grateful for the many hours she spent critiquing this manuscript. Without her intelligence and insight, there would be no book.

To my hunting buddies, whose good nature and enthusiasm enriched my life. It would have been a poorer life without your friendship.

To my daughters and grandson, for whom this book was written.

CONTENTS

INTRODUCTION

Lou Gehrig once said that he felt like the luckiest man on the face of the earth. He was. From his earliest youth he loved playing baseball; loved the game; loved the fans; loved his team mates; loved the feel of wood striking horsehide and of horsehide striking leather. He loved it so utterly that the years of sweat and practice were labors of joy rather than work.

Despite the remorseless disease that cut short his life, he knew that a life blessed with such passion was anything but tragic. So many men live their lives without a center; with nothing more or less important than anything else. They search for meaning; for their reason for being. The lucky ones find it or delude themselves into thinking they have. The others substitute society's values for their own; or if they are less noble, bounce from one thrill to another.

Some men however are truly blessed by being born with a center. Somewhere deep in their genetic code, the direction of life seems preordained. They know what they were meant to do and never doubt it. Men with this inborn center are not to be admired for they did nothing to earn it, but they are to be envied for as Lou Gehrig said, they are the luckiest people on the face of the earth.

Hunting is my center; my reason for being. A renewable source of existential joy, hunting draws me back again and again; an irresistible force. Ortega y Gasset in _Meditations on Hunting_ manages to sum up the indescribable: "It has always been at man's disposal to escape from the present to that pristine form of being a man, which, because it is the first form, has no historical suppositions. History begins with that form. Before it, there is only that which never changes: that which is permanent, Nature. 'Natural' man is always there, under the changeable historical man. We call him and he comes – a little sleepy, benumbed, without his lost form of instinctive hunter, but after all, still alive."

The escape that Ortega y Gasset described captivated me before I was five years old and it captivates me still. My daily life has been organized around the hunting seasons, but more than that, hunting has factored into every major decision of my life: Where to go to school; What to study; Who to marry; Where to live; When to have children and how many; and Whether to seek promotions. Without giving hunting full consideration in those decisions, I would have jeopardized the greatest gift I possess: my center.

In this book, I am speaking to those who share my passion for the hunt. This is the story of my journey. It is not the story of a rich boy who had it all handed to him, but of a middle class kid from Pennsylvania who wanted to experience everything hunting could offer. It is a story about discovery, and about ever-changing horizons. It is a story without an end.

Certainly, I hope the reader will enjoy sharing my journey, but more than that, I hope he will see his own hunting experience as part of a journey. I hope the reader will come to realize that modest means don't have to impede the search for new adventures; that his own journey will only be limited by the strength of his passion.

Chapter One

OPENED EYES

The vinyl soles of my Lone Ranger pajamas scratched on the cold concrete as I scurried across the garage. Laying on old newspapers spread in my maroon wagon were two ring necked pheasants and three cotton tailed rabbits. My eyes grew wide and I froze like a pointer pup smelling his first bird. A magical glow surrounded the creatures; a glow of life even in death, of hidden lives spent in a foreign world. I knelt in the early morning chill and stroked the brilliantly hued feathers on the pheasant's back. I lifted the green head, examined his red cheeks, pulled back the eyelids, and stared into his orange eyes.

The rabbits were already drawn, and blood stained the blackish brown fur. The long ears felt almost paper like between my fingers. Their brown eyes remained opened and glazed. I opened the mouth to see if they really did have teeth like Bugs Bunny, and I was pleased to learn that they did. They had a smell, not at all unpleasant; as if plucked from the soil itself.

I was intrigued at the idea of possessing them. How was it possible to capture such elusive wildness and to hold it in your hands?

"Please, please can I come too," I begged.

"I'm sorry, Buddy. You just aren't big enough yet," answered Dad.

"Yes I am. I could keep up."

"Not this time. Maybe *in* a few years."

The same discussion was repeated a hundred times. Just after my ninth birthday, the outcome finally changed.

I sat in the back seat of the '56 Chevy listening to Dad chat with his old hunting buddy. Mr. Nichol was a big man; six foot three and 230 lbs. He had a pointed nose and jolly, pink face. A cigar was clamped tightly between his teeth and he nearly always smiled when he spoke.

The weather on this final Saturday in October was crisp and bright. Frost had turned the grass to seas of silver and the woods were made resplendent by golden hickories and flaming orange sugar maples. We pulled into the drive of a three story, stone farm house with white shutters and a flat roof. Milling about the huge red barn were six men dressed in bright plaid, flannel shirts, duck cloth pants and red hats.

Feeling both excited and nervous, like an athlete about to enter the big game, I remained quiet by Dad's side as we waded into the group, exchanging greetings. The men were in fine spirit; joking and telling stories. Several asked about me, shook my hand and welcomed me as though I were a member of the group. A mysterious grown-up game seemed about to begin and I felt honored to be included.

A gray-haired man in a sports jacket and khaki pants called out loudly to get everyone's attention. "I believe everyone is here," he began. "John here will get you all started," he said pointing to his farm foreman. "I've asked him to take you down to the standing corn below the chestnut grove. We've been seeing a lot of birds in there and I believe you fellows ought to have a pretty good shoot. We have a good sized qroup, so everybody be careful."

"Thanks, Cal," a number of fellows called out. The men pulled shotguns from cases and we followed John down the dirt farm road.

"I'd suggest that you send three fellows down to the end of this field before you do anything else," drawled John as he stuck his hands deep into his overalls. "Maybe you can keep those roosters from running into the weed field over on Ol' Johnson's place. He doesn't allow any hunting at all, so stay out of there. OK?"

Dad cautioned me to stay close, and not to get in front of the line of hunters. The men separated to keep about 30 yards apart and began the drive. The corn stalks towered above me as I apprehensively walked down a row. Wide-eyed with anticipation, I wondered what would happen next. There was a sudden whir of wings to my right. Mr. Nichol hollered, "Hen! hen! hen!" to warn everyone to hold their fire. Halfway down the field two more hens flushed, both receiving the same hail from the nearest hunter as they flew out of sight.

A shot rang out from one of the blockers at the end of the field. "Those roosters are running," said Dad. I could now see a hunter standing quietly at the far end of my row. Another bird flushed to Mr. Nichols right. I caught a glimpse of purple and green. I was startled by the thunderous roar of the close quarter discharge. Another shot rang out and Mr. Nichol called out, "Good shot, Stan." Two more steps and immediately beneath my feet, the grass shook. For a split second, there he was standing right in front of me, a peacock of a bird. We momentarily froze; staring into each others eyes. He exploded into the air with a clamorous cackle, and I fell backward in slack-jawed amazement. Flaring to my right, the rooster crossed in front of Mr. Nichol. At the now expected bark of the gun, the big bird crashed to earth.

Mr. Nichol trotted forward to pick up his prize, and there was pandemonium. Four roosters and two hens, unnerved by the big man's sudden approach, burst into flight. A barrage opened from all directions.

"Attaboy," yelled one blocker to his comrade. By the time the downed birds were retrieved, we were a scant 30 yards from the end of the field. "Wow there were a lot of birds in that field," said a blocker to Dad.

"It may not be over yet," responded Dad.

No sooner were the words out of his mouth, than three pheasants that had held their ground, rocketed out of the end of the rows. The blockers blazed away, but missed cleanly.

We gathered together at the corner of the field. The grown-ups were as wound up as children. They proudly displayed the colorful roosters and described their view of the proceedings. One final bird, with nerves of steel, suddenly exploded from the shin-high weeds right in our midst. Caught totally off guard, we stood with our mouths gaping. One fellow recovered *in* time to fire at the departing bird, but he never cut a feather. The whole group burst into laughter.

"Talk about the guts of a burglar," laughed Dad.

Dad hadn't shot a bird yet and it was all I could do to keep from squirming in frustration. I wanted one of those magnificent gems and I wanted it now. In the next field Dad switched jobs with one of the blockers. He took up a position at the corner.

"I want you to stand right behind me," directed Dad. Birds might come out the end or from the side of the field, and I want to be able to shoot in either direction. If we stay quiet maybe a rooster will think that he can sneak off by coming this way."

We waited in silence, unsure if the drivers had begun their march. Our first indication that the drive was in progress came when dozens of sparrows and juncos winged out of the rows. In the distance, we heard the now familiar, "hen, hen, hen!" call. A rooster sailed from our side, but Dad didn't shoot. "Too far," he whispered.

I caught a glimpse of a driver, then saw a corn stalk shake where another hunter passed. Four shots popped from the field, but I couldn't discern what they shot at. A cock flushed out of the end of the field in plain site. The blocker to Dad's right dropped him and I saw the rooster flapping his death dance on the plowed ground. A green envy bubbled in my guts. Would our chance never come. My frustration turned into a whine, but Dad sternly hushed me.

The drivers were now a scant thirty yards away. My hopes began to fade once more. My pessimism was unwarranted, however, because a big cock bird flushed out the side. I could see the purple feathers on his upper breast, his brilliant green head, and the striking white neck ring. Dad swung his little .410 double and the bird folded in mid air. I began to run before he hit the ground, charging across the plowed field. He was still flopping about, and I dropped to my knees as I pounced upon him like an eager puppy. I pinned him to the ground and felt his struggles cease. Lifting the bird by the neck, I proudly showed everyone what Dad had accomplished.

"Can I carry him Dad," I asked hopefully.

"Sure," he agreed and slipped the pheasant into the game pouch of my boy's-sized hunting coat. The weight of the bird at the small of my back was utterly joyful. With each step, the rhythmic bump rekindled the thrill he had been. His long tail extended from the pouch, and I repeatedly stroked it as I walked.

We spread out across a field of alfalfa and hunted it toward a bare field recently prepared for wheat. No need to block this field; we hiked in a skirmish line. Three more roosters fell to the guns as we pushed onward. Where alfalfa met plowed ground, a final rooster thundered skyward. Mr. Nichol fired quickly and down tumbled the cock. With one bounce, the bird regained equilibrium and tore away on foot. Mr. Nichol, not willing to let the bird escape, charged across the barren field.

"Go George, Go!" shouted the entire group; amused at seeing the big man put on his burst of speed. His noble attempt at retrieving the wounded bird seemed in vain as he was unable to gain on the hard-running rooster. He screeched to a halt and fired at the fleeing cock. At the sound of the gun another rooster, which apparently had sneaked out of the alfalfa and crouched behind a dirt clod, took flight. Mr. Nichol shot and missed.

Returning to his initial objective, he charged off once again after the wing-tipped escapee. Ten yards into his sprint, a cock and two hens took off from the barren ground to his right. Mr. Nichol was beginning to resemble a pinball in an arcade as he skidded to a stop and missed again. His dignity was taking a terrible beating, and the screams of laughter from the other hunters were getting to be too much. Laughing at grown ups was a new experience for me, but nobody seemed to mind and it made me feel like I was one of the guys.

The wounded bird was going to win the foot race, so Mr. Nichol stopped and stood in a panic-stricken crouch ready for the next opportunity. Two more birds flushed but they were out of range. With a shrug and a shake of his head he returned to his still highly amused partners.

"That will teach us," he muttered upon his return. "Every field needs blockers."

"You're right about that, several guys said in unison, as they slapped his back in consolation.

John returned just before lunch, driving a tractor that towed a flat bed hay wagon. Each hunter dug into his jacket to extricate his catch. I proudly added our bird to the row of fourteen beautiful cocks.

"We'll give Cal a couple of birds, give one to John and just divide up the rest," suggested Mr. Nichol.

"Sounds fine," everyone agreed.

"One bird is plenty for me," said Dad. "I'm going to hunt this afternoon."

We rode the wagon back to the barn where everyone thanked our host and said their goodbyes. We returned to Mr. Nichols' house for lunch and a siesta.

"Are you going to join us this afternoon, George," asked Dad.

"I don't think so, Walter. I've got some errands that I really ought to take care of. Why don't you two guys see what you can do?" he replied.

The camaradarie and excitement of the morning were replaced by a quiet serenity in the afternoon as Dad and I had the entire farm to ourselves.

"I want to try the woods above the barn," said Dad. "When the birds get chased a bit, they usually end up there."

I walked along at Dad's right, less concerned about staying by his side now that it was just us.

"Kick into every brush pile that you come across," Dad instructed.

I was anxious to actually be of help, so I kicked all likely looking cover with gusto. Popping out of one brush pile came a rabbit streaking through the trees. My eyes followed the cottontail, wishing that I had a gun. I turned my head in time to see Dad shoot. The rabbit did a summersault and landed dead on his back.

"Wow, great shot Dad," I cheered.

I picked up the warm animal, stroked his fur, and felt the meat on his hind legs. Dad took the rabbit from me and said, "Let me show you a little trick".

He unsheathed his knife and slit open the belly. Grabbing the head and front legs in one hand and the hind legs in the other, he rapidly swung the rabbit. Virtually the entire viscera flew out and landed on the leafy ground. Dad then pulled the bladder, lungs and kidneys which remained and slid the bunny into my game pouch.

"There is another place that I want to try," said Dad, "and you might be able to help me on this one."

"Great, what do I do?"

"The ditch running between those plowed fields is deeper than it looks, and I've had shots in there before. What I want you to do is to walk all the way down to that big tree and stand in the middle of the ditch. You are going to be the blocker, but it will be a little different

My father, Walter M. Rohlfs, Jr., during a pheasant hunt in 1967.

than when we had the big group. This time, I want you to make enough noise to let the birds know that you are there. Maybe you can hold them in and I can get a shot."

Dad waited patiently as I got into position. I hummed a song while I watched him zigzag through the ditch. Still one hundred yards distant, I saw a rabbit streak away as Dad walked through a clump of weeds. Dad rolled the cottontail. I could see him drawing it as he had done before and stowing the rabbit in his jacket. Closer and closer he came. After the morning's lessons, I was a believer in blocking the escape routes, and I was cautiously optimistic that the strategy would pay off once more. Two hens flushed from the thick grass, followed a few seconds later by a cock. Dad was shooting well this day, and he dropped the bird cleanly. Only slightly less enthusiastically than before, I trotted out to collect the beautiful rooster.

"I never would have gotten that bird if you hadn't blocked for me," said, Dad.

"Maybe I did help out, huh?" I answered proudly.

"That makes for a pretty fine day. Are you tired out by now?"

"I am a little pooped," I responded honestly.

"Well I'm real proud of you. That was a lot of walking for a nine year old. You know something, I believe you are going to be a hunter."

Chapter Two

CANVASBACKS

We waited, duffels in hand, as Dad unlocked the door of the white, asbestos shingled house. Clouds of frozen breath billowed in our wake as we climbed the frigid stair well into the second floor apartment. A blocky, pine table complete with cigarette burns, ashtrays and poker chips occupied the living room along with a tattered, faded-blue sofa. Scattered throughout the remainder of the flat were eight bunks, each with attending foot locker, lending a barracks-like atmosphere.

Dad fiddled with the heater while I returned to unpack the car. Pausing in the oyster shell driveway; I inhaled the fragrance of brackish water, marsh mud and sea weed. From the distance, the squeals, whistles and honks of swans and geese jumbled together in a hauntingly wild serenade reminiscent of a full orchestra in warm up. Ten thousand stars twinkled in the icy, moonless sky and a stiff breeze cut through my wool sweater. I shivered from cold and excitement.

For years, I had been curious about Dad's duck and goose club. I had been allowed to tag along on day trips for pheasants and rabbits for two seasons, but until now, I had been denied the longer, over-night trips down to the Chesapeake. Each opening day of goose season, I anxiously awaited Dad's call. "Did you get any?" was always my opening question. I would struggle to envision the scenes Dad described of big honkers dropping into the decoys. I would desperately wish that I could see them myself, but Dad had not wanted a kid to intrude upon the other men's weekend. Besides, club members usually filled the available blind space, so there was no room for a non-shooting kid.

It was late December, the season was nearly over, and none of the other members planned to hunt, so Dad had invited me and his friend Mr. Roth to join him for the weekend. Mr. Roth was about 20 years Dad's senior. He had a full head of gray hair combed back at the sides. He wore a brown leather jacket and a western string tie cinched about his neck. During the drive south, he had regaled us with fascinating tales of deer and antelope hunts in Montana and Wyoming. He was one of my favorites among Dad's friends and I was glad that Dad had

17

asked him to come along.

Only a few stars peeked through the rapidly advancing clouds as we walked to the wharf restaurant for breakfast. The cafe was steamy warm, and I wiped the condensation from the windows to view the skipjacks tied to the docks. Loud, male voices filled the room as weather-beaten oysterman, crabbers, and fisherman devoured eggs and flapjacks in preparation for another day on the water. A middle-aged waitress in a short sleeved, white uniform poured us scalding coffee and took our order. The only female in this enclave of masculinity, she seemed totally at ease as she swapped wisecracks with the watermen. We wolfed down our breakfasts, hopped into the car and headed down Peninsula Road. I felt somewhat disoriented as we stood by the old dairy barn which was silhouetted against the still dark sky. A stiff breeze blowing off the bay caused a loose tin wall on a tractor shed to bang loudly. A cat scampered across the corral. What did this place look like during the day? With shotgun in hand, Dad led us toward the bay.

"I can hear the water, but where is the beach?" I asked. "There isn't much of a beach," answered Dad. "The soil around here is sort of a sandy loam without many rocks and the bay is eroding it away in a lot of places. The water is about thirty feet below this path."

Just over the edge of the embankment, perched on a mound of crumbling soil sat our blind. Broom sedge tacked to the walls and roof of the little plywood and scrap lumber structure, camouflaged it beautifully. The roof extended beyond the back wall until it met the cliff face; creating a back room ideal for storing decoys and equipment.

Dad pulled the waders from the cache and all three of us toted the decoys down to water's edge. Mostly, we had diver decoys: blackheads, wiflers, and canvasbacks, but there were a few black ducks and a couple of geese thrown in. The solid cedar dekes were wrapped with green cords attached to a half-pound lead weights. Dad waded into the shallow bay with a half dozen decoys tucked beneath his arms, and tossed them into the swells. The blackheads and canvasbacks were placed to the left of the blind, and the black ducks and geese on the right. The wiflers were strewn on the periphery of the set.

"Why aren't you putting any right in front of the blind," I asked.

"That's where we want the ducks to land," answered Dad.

18

"See, your old man knows what he's doing," said Mr. Roth, smiling.

Mr. Roth and I, being waderless, served as bearers, shuttling up and down the cliff with more decoys. The eastern sky was lightening as we completed our task and crawled into the blind.

The warm glow resulting from our exercise began to dissipate as we watched the day come to life. Rising with the sun, the stiff breeze grew to a full-fledged gale. White caps replaced the gentler swells on the brown-green bay. Our faces became pasty white as the capillaries on our cheeks shrank to prevent heat loss. Drops hung from our noses, as the icy wind cut through us.

"Ought to be a great day for ducks,!' chuckled Mr. Roth.

"Three o'clock, Tom, low on the water!" hissed Dad.

"I see them. Looks like baldpate."

Buffeted by the wind, five ducks hovered just off the narrow beach slowly heading upwind toward our blind. They began to rise up, but quickly dropped low where the air remained more navigable. We crouched behind the front wall and peered out through the wind-whipped sedge. The white skullcap of the drake was clearly visible when Dad blurted out, "Take' em."

We rose in unison and guns spoke on either side of me. I cheered as a pair of drakes tumbled from the sky and splashed into the icy water.

"We shouldn't have to wade for those," said Dad. "The wind will drive them into shore. Why don't you collect them for us, and pick up those two decoys that are floating away. The cords must be too short to hold them in this surf."

I scampered down the cliff, happy to be moving once again. Both birds floated, white bellies up, a few feet from one another. The wind was carrying them down as well as in, and I trotted along the dark, wet sand to keep up. I reached out with a branch of driftwood to direct the birds the final few feet into the beach.

Immediately, I was impressed by the thickness of their plumage, so different from the more familiar pheasants. On the breast, the snow-white feathers were nearly an inch deep. The widgeon, while not a gaudy bird, had an elegant array of colors. Through the eye was a streak of emerald green capped by a buff colored patch on top of the head.

The gently streaked neck gave way to a tweedy brown on the back and flanks. The speculum of the out-stretched wings presented another splash of emerald to match the eye.

The brace of ducks bumped against my knee as I headed back toward the blind. "Mitch, Get down!" Dad called from above. I scurried to the base of the embankment and crouched behind a clump of broom sedge. Driving toward us on rapidly pulsating wings came about twenty blackheads flying mere feet above the white caps. They banked right and buzzed directly over the decoys. A report sounded from above, and from my front row seat,I saw the shot splash directly behind the lead duck. A barrage of shots followed the first, and three ducks cart wheeled into the surf.

Before the triplet had floated into shore, three more shots popped from the blind. I turned just in time to see a lone duck falling from the sky. I fulfilled my duty as retriever and returned laden with ducks.

"That last one, was a different kind of duck; real pretty," I said.

"Let me see him," responded Dad, taking the birds from my hand. "These first three are scaup. We usually call them blackheads because of the coloration of the males, but the females are mostly brown with a half moon of white directly behind the bill. The one with the red head is a canvasback."

"A canvasback!" enthused Mr. Roth. "I haven't shot a can' for twenty years."

"Sometimes we get quite a few of them here," said Dad, "and this is just about the time of year and the kind of weather we usually get them in."

"You know, we already have six ducks and it is only eight o'clock. With a six duck limit, we are going to be all done in a couple of hours. Why don't we pass up everything but drake canvasbacks," suggested Mr. Roth.

"That sounds like a helluva idea," agreed Dad.

The icy wind showed no signs of letting up, and actually seemed to be gaining ferocity as the morning progressed. The ducks, unable to remain comfortable in the choppy waves, were constantly on the move as they searched for quieter, resting water. Flock after flock of scaup whizzed over the dekes, twice landing in their midst. They milled about, uncomfortable with their rigid hosts, and burst back into flight. Bright white golden eyes, usually alone or in pairs, skirted the decoys, but rarely landed within the set. Dad and Mr. Roth held their fire, determined to wait out the canvasbacks.

"OK! Here we go! Ten o'clock. About 15 cans' heading our way," said Mr. Roth.

The powerfully built ducks raced toward our decoys, scarcely slowed by the gale.

"They're a little bit far. Should we take 'em?" asked Dad.

"No. I think they'll make another pass."

"Darn, I don't think they're coming back," moaned Dad as we watched the flock wing off down the bay.

"Wait a minute," I said. "I think they're turning."

"Sure are," cackled Mr. Roth as the birds headed back. "They're in range now," said Dad.

"No, no. Let's give 'em one more pass. They're coming in for sure now."

Once again the wavering line of ducks hurtled away, seemingly for good, only to turn at the last minute. "Here they come!" hissed Mr. Roth as the birds set their wings and banked into the wind. "Take 'em."

With fingers in ears, I peered out from the blind as the grown-ups blasted away on either side of me. Two drakes dropped instantly and a third was hit. He towered straight up and both men used their remaining shells to finish him. By the time I was able to make the retrieve, brackish ice had covered all unsubmerged portions of the ducks.

"Well, we only have three more to go," said Dad. "Let's make this really sporting. Only one guy shoots and he only gets one shell."

"Damn! That is sporting," laughed Mr. Roth. "Okay Hotshot, you go first."

We waited out several flights of lesser ducks, which would gladly have been shot at on most days, until a pair of cans' raced by about 40 yards distant. Dad rose up and shot without result. We all stood and laughed as the drake shifted into high gear and departed unscathed. Mr. Roth had the next opportunity and knocked down one of five cans' that decoyed in. The bird hit the water swimming but Dad was prepared for that eventuality and came to the rescue. Both men missed their next shots before Dad finally connected on a lone drake crossing in front of the blind.

"I don't know," said Dad. It's getting a little late.

"Do you think we're going to get that last bird?"

"Wow! Look at that!" I uttered in astonishment.

"There must be sixty of them."

"Where did they come from?" asked Mr. Roth.

"From behind us, over land, I think," I answered.

"I'll bet they're redheads coming off the river instead of canvasbacks. I've never seen cans' come from that direction. Do you want to shoot them?" asked Dad.

"I can't think of a better way to end the day," smiled Mr. Roth, "but right now they're too high. Maybe they'll decoy."

"It's pretty tough to get that big a bunch to decoy," answered Dad.

"Well maybe so. But they sure are looking us over."

"Those son of a guns are coming in, Tom! It's your shot," said Dad.

"The heck with that!" answered Mr. Roth. This is going to be the last shot of the day. Let's both shoot, but let's be sure we shoot at the same bird."

"This ought to be the last pass. They're looking serious this time. Let's both take the closest bird," said Dad.

The red heads of the drakes were vivid dashes of color in the slate gray interface of sky and sea. Wings cupped and feet out-stretched, the flock prepared to light at the edge of the set. Both men's guns spoke at once and a lone bird plunged into a white cap.

Mr. Roth removed his glove and extended his hand to Dad. Beaming, he said, "Walter, Thanks for the best day of duck hunting I've ever enjoyed. The only problem is that you might have ruined your boy there, because he may never see another day as good as this one."

Chapter Three

BASIC TRAINING

Christmas, but not just any Christmas. This was the year Dad promised me a shotgun. Although only eleven, I would be old enough for my first hunting license next fall. Dad decided on a single shot 20 gauge with a boy's length stock. He said that a single shot would be safer, and it would teach me the importance of the first shot. The picture in the Sears catalogue was torn out and hung on my bedroom wall. Before bed each night, I gazed at the boy holding my shotgun under his arm. Would Christmas never arrive? I crossed another day from the calendar.

After dinner, Dad called me into the living room. "I've got some bad news for you", he began. "Your shotgun is back ordered and it might be another month before you get it."

"Ahh Jees!," I cried in anguish. "I can't believe it!"

"It might still arrive in time," he said. "I just wanted you to be prepared in case it doesn't."

Each afternoon I rushed home from school to ask Mom if Sears had called, but I remained disappointed.

On Christmas Eve, Dad promised to drive to the store after we went to bed just in case my gun had arrived. I fell asleep with only a glimmer of hope remaining. I awoke to my sister's shrieks, "It's Christmas! It's Christmas!" I jumped out of bed and raced to Dad and Mom's room.

"Did it come?" I cried anxiously.

Dad let out a devilish laugh.

"You had it all the time, didn't you?"

He laughed even harder. I felt like a real sucker; hooked, reeled in, and flopping in the net. I laughed at my gullibility and in relief as I realized that I was about to receive my first gun. No longer would I be relegated to game cleaning and brush stomping chores. Now I would join the ranks of the hunters.

The trap and skeet range was too small to be considered a club. It was more of a back yard hobby range. Two skeet towers and a single trap were situated behind a one room, cinder block structure. Dad had met Mr. Merkel at work, and he invited us to shoot with his friends one Sunday.

"Are you ready to shoot a round of skeet?" asked Mr. Merkel.

"I'd love to," said Dad. "I'd like my son to sit out for right now. This will be his first shooting experience, and if you don't mind, I'd like to let him shoot a round by himself when everyone else is finished."

"Sure! No problem at all. Darn good idea as a matter of fact," answered Mr. Merkel.

I sat in a blue and green lawn chair on the concrete porch watching the men take their turns at the first station. At each 'pull' command, yellow and black clay pigeons streaked from the high tower, then the low tower, and finally from both towers at once. I wondered if I would hit any at all when my turn came, and I was sure that I had no chance at making a double. All the shooters were doing pretty well, but Mr. Merkel and Dad were the best shots. Dad missed for the first time at station four and didn't miss again until station eight where he missed twice. Mr. Merkel only missed one target at station five.

The men shot one additional round and retired to the porch for a cool drink. After a few minutes of conversation, Dad could see that I was beginning to chomp at the bit in anticipation. "Go get your gun," he commanded, "but don't load it."

"Have you checked the boy's eye dominance?" asked Mr. Merkel.

"No, I haven't," answered Dad, "and I'm not sure exactly how to go about it."

Mr. Merkel returned from the house with a sheet of paper. He poked a hole through the paper and handed it to me. "Hold this paper at arm's length, and look through the hole with both eyes open. See the light bulb on the wall over there?" he said. "Now, pull the paper all the way to your face, but keep looking at the light."

I pulled the paper directly toward my left eye. "You are left eye dominant", he proclaimed. "Are you right or left handed?"

"Right," I replied.

"Oh boy!" he sighed. "You have cross dominance. Unless you can learn to shoot left handed, you will have to close your left eye when you shoot. Once you get some experience, you might learn to wink when you shoot."

"What is that?" I asked, not sure I wasn't being kidded.

"You keep both eyes open until you overtake the target. Then you wink your dominant eye, line up the bead, fire, and open both eyes again."

It sounds awfully difficult."

"It does take a bit of practice and you shouldn't worry about it. For now, just close your left eye and you will do fine."

"I appreciate you checking that for us," said Dad. "Okay Bud, are you ready to give it a whirl?"

"I sure am," I responded enthusiastically.

"OK, first of all you never load-the gun until you are in the station," he began. "We aren't going to worry about shooting a regulation round of skeet. We won't shoot any doubles, and we will concentrate on certain stations more than others. Go ahead and load the gun.

"The first target will fly out of the high tower right next to us and it will sail straight away. You don't have to worry about any lead with this shot. Simply aim right at it and shoot."

"Sort of like when I shot cans at home?"

"Exactly. Go ahead and pull the hammer back and put the gun to your shoulder. When you are ready say 'pull'."

The target sailed away and I missed.

"Don't worry about it. Bend your knees a little. Just take your time and get on it."

Twice more I missed. "Let's try again. Keep your face on the stock."

Determined to do better, I tracked the clay bird as it sailed from the tower. For a second the bead hovered around the pigeon. I waited until it settled directly on the target and fired. The target disintegrated.

"That a boy! Let's try to do that again."

Four of the next five pigeons broke.

"Being close isn't good enough is it? I have to be right on 'em," I said.

"You seem to have that shot down pretty well. Why don't we try station two. The target will cross at an angle, and if you aim directly at it, you will end up shooting behind.

You will have to lead the clay bird."

"How much do I lead it?" I asked.

"From here, I would say a foot or two."

I had trouble controlling the swing of the gun and I missed the first five in a row. On the sixth shot, I extended my lead and connected. I missed on the seventh shot and then broke number 8, 9 and 10.

We moved onto station three. "From here, you are more perpendicular to the line of flight, so you will have to lead more. Make sense?" he asked.

"Yeah, I know what you mean."

Once again, I started out missing, but it took less time for me to compensate for my errors. I broke two of six targets.

"That's enough for a first lesson," said Dad. "If you think back to most of the shots that you've seen me take on pheasants, I'll bet 90 percent came from one of the three angles that you just practiced."

I left the range with visions of opening day shots dancing through my mind.

Mitch Rohlfs with a black duck and bobwhite quail, standing near Chesapeake Bay at low tide.

Chapter Four

THE WATERMAN

The rotten, elastic, brackish ice that had covered the Northern Chesapeake for the last four weeks was breaking up in the warm rainstorm pushing in from the south. Raindrops splattered audibly against the waterman's quilted nylon jacket as he stood on the cliff silently observing the spectacle. The prospect of returning to the bay that provided his livelihood cheered him. Ice up had put his life on hold for the past month and he had become restless, puttering around the farm without really accomplishing much. Ice out was a sign of renewal, of spring, of the start of his own life's cycle.

Nature gives and nature takes away. The great shifting slabs of ice had sucked the support-pilings of the duck blind from the sand. The collapsed heap of plywood and brush rested on the ice like a bludgeoned heifer. With luck, he could salvage the pilings from shore in a few days. He shrugged, returned to the Chevy pick-up still idling in the barnyard, and whistled for his black Labrador who bounded into the truck bed.

The Waterman inched the heavy, square-bowed, wooden boat across the sand toward the recently opened but still frigid water. Hiking up his hip boots which had been folded bell bottom style around his ankles, he waded into the icy, green bay to attach the 10 horse power Johnson outboard. The flat-bottomed skiff slapped down on the choppy, bay surf lifting a pungent mist that dampened his face. His destination was the underwater rock piles that remained so secret that he didn't risk marking them with a buoy, lest one of the big commercial rigs sail in and obliterate his oyster bed. His equipment was simple but adequate. The oyster tongs consisted of thirty foot long, wooden handles pinned at the middle like a pair of giant scissors. To each handle, a five foot wide, wire scoop with long claws was attached.

The gentle swells rocked the boat beneath his feet as he manipulated the handles, causing the scoops to mesh like the jaws of an old fashioned steam shovel. Opening and closing the tongs, the Waterman broke loose the submerged rocks and then pinched the handles together in his clenched fists. Hand over hand he pulled up the jagged rocks and the oysters that were glued tenaciously to them. He dislodged the oysters with a rusty hammer, tossing the rocks over board and the oysters into the bushel baskets.

The oysters provided his family with a good living over the winter, but he was glad for the change when the weather warmed enough to roll the tractor from the shed and help his father turn the sandy-loam soil. The newly warmed earth smelled pungent and rich as he slowly dragged first the plow, then the harrow, and finally the seeder across the flat fields that his father and grandfather had tended. By the first of May, the year's corn was safely on its way.

In May through August, being months without R's in their names, the oysters were unfit for harvesting. The Bay harbored many riches however, and the Waterman had no difficulty in locating them. Taking advantage of the cool mornings, he cruised the marshes and river mouths, his skiff stacked with wire crab pots. The traps were designed with funnel shaped openings, which allowed the fat, blue clawed crabs in to feast on the chicken necks or other offal, but made escape impossible. He dropped each trap overboard and marked it with an empty Chlorox bottle buoy painted to identify it as his. Returning the next day, he simply unlatched one wall of the trap and dropped the scurrying crabs into white plastic buckets for a trip to the wharf where colored ladies, with flying fingers, stripped them of their delicate flesh.

After dinner, while his wife washed the dishes, he took his children out to play in the yard while he puttered about building a boat that he planned to sell to one of the local charter captains. The craft was his first effort and he was not a professional carpenter, but he managed to do a creditable job on the hull that was water tight. He then roughed out the cabin and sold it unfinished at about the time the corn was dry enough for harvesting.

Driving the combine back and forth, picking four rows on each pass, he couldn't help but wonder at the familiar, age-old scene that was unfolding around him. Great flocks of ducks and geese, driven by their destiny and cold winds, began dropping from the sky into the Chesapeake. He rejoiced at the sight of the new arrivals, which appeared at incredible altitudes with light clouds often passing beneath them. From the heights, they honked in celebration at arriving safely at their wintering grounds. He couldn't help but wonder about the far away places where they had lived since he had seen them last.

The waterfowl were not merely an aesthetic experience for the Waterman. For a number of years, his father had leased the hunting rights on the farm to a club of about a dozen Philadelphia businessmen and he hired himself out as guide and caretaker. Without him, the club could scarcely function. There were too many tasks for the men in Philadelphia to tackle.

Largest of the chores was the rebuilding the bay duck blind (locally referred to as a "booby" blind) that had been destroyed by the outgoing ice. Friends from a local construction firm that specialized in building piers placed eight new pilings; two rows of three to support the shooting platform, and two in the rear for a boat slip. He nailed two by sixes to the pilings about four feet above the water and laid plywood onto the supports to form the platform which was easily large enough for four shooters. He attached additional sheets of plywood directly to the pilings to form walls, and then built a half roof over the platform to protect the hunters from the rain and the peering eyes of the waterfowl. When completed, he totally covered the structure and the boat slip in cedar boughs which held their needle all season and transformed the blind into an apparent island.

In the center of his farm, in the largest cornfield was a man-made pond which was a favorite dropping-in spot for the Canada geese that frequented the bay. The pond held water but was low after the dry summer, so he hooked up a ten horse power pump to a long section of rubber hose which ran across the field and into the Bay. He ran the pump continuously for three weeks until the pond was finally filled with brackish water.

Some of the cedar decoys were beginning to show their age, so he carried them down to Mr. Jesse in town who repainted them for two dollars apiece. He had been dissatisfied with the anchor shaped decoy weights used the year before. Too often they failed to hold the decoys in place in rough weather necessitating retrieval by boat or sometimes they were lost entirely. He rectified the problem by melting lead and pouring it into old pop cans from which the tops had been removed. Wires hooks sunk into the liquid lead served as attachment for the green, braided, nylon decoy ropes.

All was in place for the hunters when the season opened in the

29

first week of November. It was then, as the first junior member of the club, that I met the Waterman. Mr. Ross, Mr. Marsh, Dad and I were seated at the marina cafe just finishing our breakfast in the predawn darkness when the Waterman strode in.

Whisker stubble, a week old, and a Kent cigarette dangling precariously from the corner of his mouth couldn't disguise his boyish face-cheeks somewhat chubby, eyes a brilliant blue. Close cropped above the ears, his hair burst into a tousle of blond curls that poked out beneath a blue vinyl, insulated cap with the name Hubbard's Marina stitched on the front. His black, quilted jacket with a tear beneath the right arm, stretched over his slightly round torso. Baggy gray pants stained with oil rode low on his hips and disappeared into black, Red Ball, hip waders which were folded down at the knee and hung loose above his feet like a sailor's bell bottoms.

Mr. Marsh, Mr. Ross and Dad leaped up and pumped his hand energetically and then introduced me.

"Do you want any breakfast?" asked Mr. Marsh.

"Well, I don't know. Are you paying?" he asked and then broke into a giggling, Andy Devine, chuckle which caused us all to laugh with him.

"Sure! sit down. Got to feed a growing boy," said Mr. Ross, who had a daughter about the Waterman's age.

"Yeah, I'm still growing all right, but lately it seems like I'm growing in the wrong direction," he said patting his belly.

"Have the ducks come down yet?" asked Dad.

"Umhum," he mumbled between bites of pancakes. "Geese too. Last week we had geese landing in the corn when we were still pickin'. I finished up the booby blind a few weeks ago and the divin' ducks have been moving off shore in some nice bunches. Looks like your only problem is going to be to hunt geese in the fields or ducks on the bay."

"I'd just as soon hunt geese," said Mr. Ross. "Me too," said Mr. Marsh.

"Mitch and I will hunt the booby blind then," said Dad.

"All right," drawled the Waterman. "I better go with you two fellows then. The geese decoys are already on the pond and in the corn fields, but you might need help with the decoys and boat in the bay."

With the outboard attached, he guided the little craft into the cedar shrouded slip where Dad scrambled into the blind.

"Why don't you give me a hand putting out the dekes," suggested the Waterman. Glad to be of help, I manned the bow while the Waterman navigated around the blind expertly directing me in the placement of the decoys – divers, tightly packed, to the right, geese and black ducks to the left and goldeneyes on the periphery.

The set complete, the Waterman and I tied up the boat and climbed into the blind – he with his rusty, Browning and I with my new Ithaca pump. His vision was uncanny and he was able to spot and identify ducks for us at incredible distances. The names he used for the various species were local creations rather than official nomenclature – widgeons were baldpates, scaup were blackheads, golden eyes were wiflers, buffleheads were butterballs, grebes were pigwitches and canvasbacks were cans, but he knew them all.

When a lone wifler drake raced along the outer edge of the set, the Waterman held his fire, allowing Dad and I to shoot. After my opening miss, Dad's shot sent the duck somersaulting to the water where it floated belly up just beyond the decoys. "Are we going to pick it up?" I asked.

"It's not goin' anywhere. We'll just let it sit for a little while." The Waterman's logic was soon vindicated when three baldpates passed behind the blind and then swung into the decoys with wings set. I managed to drop the lead bird as his feet stretched for the water and Dad folded a hen a half-second later.

"There's a gull looking that wifler over," commented the Waterman. "I better go pick 'em up before he eats the breast clean out." He descended the short ladder to the boat and raced toward the fallen birds, a long handled crab net tucked beneath his arm. He barely slowed down while he deftly scooped the duck from the water and gently dropped it on the seat in front of him. He repeated the maneuver with the remaining baldpates and returned to the concealment of the boat slip.

"Mark! Nine o'clock," hissed the Waterman, again the first one to spot the ducks. "About 30 blackheads comin' our way." Crouched behind the cedar-shrouded walls, we peered at the thin, wavering line that was racing toward us. "Let 'em go past," ordered the Waterman. "They'll come back around."

Just as he predicted, the big flock banked hard to the right, this time passing behind the blind in an ever tightening circle. When they next swung to the front, the Waterman called out "Take 'em" and we rose in unison.

The ensuing barrage left five ducks laying on the water and the Waterman had knocked down three of them. Two of the birds were not dead and were swimming quickly away from the blind. "You want to give me a hand?" he asked.

"Sure," I answered as I grabbed a handful of shells and scrambled into the boat. We cast off and raced toward the first of the escaping blackheads. As we approached, the drake dived beneath the surface. The Waterman circled with the boat while I stood at port arms in the bow. Seriously wounded, the bird didn't stay under for long and I finished him when he surfaced about twenty yards to my right.

The second fugitive was a hen with plenty of life left in her. Each time she dived, she managed to swim forty or fifty yards before emerging for air. We circled, vigilant for where she would pop up next. Twice she was up and down so quickly that I was unable to get off a shot. On the third opportunity, I snapped a shot at her and pellets sprayed all around but failed to finish her at that distance. The Waterman raced ahead trying to guess where she would next appear. His guess was a good one; too good in fact. She came up only five yards from the boat and I refrained from shooting for fear of destroying all the meat. From behind me I heard a quiet, silly giggle as the Waterman realized the absurdity of the situation. Dad, who had remained in the blind, must have thought we'd cracked up as our laughter floated across the Bay. Finally, on the fifth emergence, the hen was close enough. I managed to pull myself together and ended the chase.

By late afternoon, after we had shot three limits of ducks, we retrieved the decoys, stowed them in the blind, and motored toward shore. Four geese hung from the clubhouse door when we arrived and Mr. Marsh and Mr. Ross were just waking up from mid-day naps. They explained how they had shot all four birds by about ten o'clock but had then decided to take a siesta when the action slowed down. Dad and I packed up the car in preparation for our trip home.

Another group of hunters would be arriving in three days and the Waterman would provide the same service to them. Faced with another week of school, I envied the Waterman, and I suspected that even Dad, when he considered the pressures at work, felt a touch of envy. As we drove down the oyster shell lane, we knew that we were waving good-by to the freest man alive.

The auhor with some geese taken on the Chesapeake Bay in 1967.

Chapter Five

SCHOOL DAYS

The most mystifying dilemma of my youth had nothing to do with how much to lead a duck or how to prevent being scared to death by a close-flushing pheasant. It wasn't even how to talk to girls, although that was a close second. My biggest problem was figuring out how to withstand my education. By the ninth grade, I decided that school was not only boring but utterly inane.

Biologically, our planet was among the crown jewels of the universe, and nobody seemed to even notice. To my classmates and teachers, nature was superfluous beyond the immediacies of how to dress for the weather. Each day, they droned on about Shakespeare or European history or some other human contrivance, and I couldn't have cared less. Forlornly, I stared for hours out the classroom windows like a prisoner doing time. If I could somehow survive until college, maybe then I could put all this crap behind me and finally learn what I wanted to know: zoology. At fourteen years old however, college seemed a depressingly long way off.

In the meantime, my only exposure to nature was confined to weekend hunting trips to the Chesapeake Bay. But what an exposure it was! The bay country literally teemed with life. Crabs, oysters, striped bass and bluefish crowded the nutrient rich waters. Corn and bean fields, all neatly divided by brushy hedgerows, were home to myriad quail and cottontail rabbits while the occasional forest patch held some of the biggest, corn-fed white-tailed deer in the East.

But mostly, the Bay was waterfowl. Each autumn, hundreds of thousands of Canada geese, ducks and Tundra swans came to winter. At times, the sky would almost darken and the air would reverberate with cacophony as flocks commuted from feeding to resting areas.

The land leased by Dad's club was a bay-front farm near Rock Hall on Maryland's Eastern Shore. A small, working farm, usually planted in corn or occasionally soybeans; it was tailor-made for wildlife. Two man-made ponds attracted mallards, black ducks, green winged teal, and geese, while rafts of canvasbacks, redheads, scaup, goldeneyes and widgeon ferried off shore. Fences, overgrown with honeysuckle, separated the ten to twenty acre crop fields and provided ample cover for small game and songbirds.

For several years, the club members had rented some rooms in town which served as home base during the hunting season, but they were less than perfect: There was no kitchen, so we had to eat all of our meals in restaurants. More importantly, when the weather was particularly nasty, or when the ducks quit flying at mid-day, there was no convenient place to warm up or take a nap. We finally decided to build a new clubhouse in the old dairy barn right there on the farm.

Mr. Roth had enjoyed hunting with us as a guest over the years, and he offered to ramrod the building of the clubhouse in exchange for a membership. He was retired and his wife had passed away, so he had plenty of time to tackle the job. He parked his little trailer next to the barn and set up shop. All he had to start with was a sound roof and four concrete walls.

The barn was too wide to use the whole area, so he planned to build a wall down the middle and use only half of the space. A plywood floor would have to be laid over the concrete slab and an insulated ceiling nailed to the exposed rafters. The space would be divided into two rooms and a bathroom. The front room would be the living room/kitchen and the back a sleeping quarters.

My parents had recently remodeled our kitchen, so we saved the old sinks and cabinets for the clubhouse. About a month before the season opened, Dad rented a trailer to haul the fixtures down to the Bay. We planned to spend the weekend helping Mr. Roth plumb the kitchen and bathroom.

School that week seemed an eternity as my teachers droned on about all sorts of nonsense not nearly as important as our duck hunting club. When Mrs. Benz, my algebra teacher, announced a test for Monday, I couldn't believe it. Being stuck in school like a prisoner was unpleasant enough, but having to study all weekend would be cruel and unusual punishment. I needed a weekend furlough and I was going to have it. I made a half-hearted attempt at the books on Thursday night, and figured I'd do okay.

By Friday afternoon, algebra was the furthest thing from my mind as I raced home from school. I had convinced Dad to help me load the trailer the evening before to insure a quick getaway. Our tradition, on the first trip of the season, was to stop at a restaurant called the Granary. Anything to do with good food captured all of my attention. I had been growing about four inches a year, and it seemed to take five meals a day just to prevent my stomach acid from turning to cannibalism.

Stopping at the Granary was a special treat. Their oyster stew was simply superb; sweet cream turned almost yellow with butter and just jammed full of glistening, plump oysters. I tried softshelled crab for the first time that night. After shelling several hundred hard shells the previous summer, I was beginning to doubt if crab meat was worth the effort, but those softies were work-free and possibly even more delicious than their hard shelled brethren.

The sun was beginning to burn through the early morning haze as we drove up the farm lane. A scent of fall lingered from the cool evening, but the day was going to heat up fast as it had every day for the past three weeks. Mr. Roth, looking all crumpled and dirty with uncombed hair and a week-old stubble, was already looking over the site while he nursed his morning coffee. He brayed out a hearty welcome, apparently glad for the reinforcements as well as the company.

A lot of progress had been made since we had last been there. The ceiling had been hung and the walls were in place although we still had to secure the baton strips between the rough hewn planks. The shower and hot water heater were installed and a toilet had recently been set. A large oil burning furnace stood by the bathroom, but it hadn't been hooked up. I could imagine how cozy those rooms would feel after hunting on a blustery, winter's day.

Dad told us that he had a surprise for us. Mr. Roth, my brother Mark, and I exchanged quizzical looks as Dad pulled a long, oval board from the trunk. He flipped it over, and there engraved in gold letters read the words, "Cow Palace". Mr. Roth spewed a mouthful of coffee half way across the room and broke into fits of laughter and coughing. "Well, I'll be damned. It might not be original, but it sure as hell fits," he laughed. With mock solemnity, we attached the sign over the entrance and from that day forward, we never referred to the club house as anything else.

Dad helped Mr. Roth work on the kitchen while Mark and I got assigned duties more closely aligned with our youthful backs. The Cow

Palace had a toilet, but it lacked a septic tank. The plan was to use a 55 gallon drum with the bottom cut out. We needed a hole deep enough to bury the drum, open end down. We would then run a pipe from the john to a smaller hole in the top.

Simple as it may have sounded, the fact was that it hadn't rained in a month and the ground was rock hard. Fortunately, we had both an adze and a pick, because a shovel was pretty near useless. We quickly learned that the hard earth was not our only problem. Stable flies descended on us by the score, alighting on our backs each time we stooped to scoop another bucket of adze-chipped dirt. Their stiletto-like mouthparts, which had evolved to bite through cow hide, easily slipped through our T-shirts in search of blood.

After a while, it became the better part of valor to have one boy work while the other was the designated fly shooer. By dinner, we stood exhausted and filthy, and examined our handiwork. Throughout the years, I never utilized that facility without remembering the sweat and blood that had allowed that moment of comfort.

Sunday was considerably less demanding as Mark and I were assigned to baton strip duty. The one by eights, which were attached vertically, had been green when the wall was constructed. When the wood dried, they shrank leaving gaps between the planks. Our job was to attach one by twos over each crack. There wasn't much to it. One held the strip in place while the other one nailed.

We finished up by mid-afternoon, so we took Duke, our one year-old Labrador retriever, down to the water for retrieving practice. We wanted him to get used to staying in the blind and then taking hand signals for blind retrieves. I fired a .22 blank from inside the blind, while Mark, who was standing on the beach, threw the retrieving dummy out into the bay.

I brought Duke down to the water's edge and used my hand to direct him toward the dummy which he still could not see. We had practiced blind retrieves in the yard, but this was as close to the real thing as he had been. He seemed to understand what I was asking however, and headed straight out into the bay. He lost the line once and I hollered "Over" as I pointed left. He obeyed, instantly spotted the dummy and swam back with it. He shook vigorously and bounded up and down in delight, obviously as pleased as I was and only slightly

My brother, Mark Rohlfs, with his first goose.

wetter.

We made one more weekend trip before everything was ready for the hunting season. The pump had been working overtime, moving water from the bay into our pond which had almost dried up during the drought. Ten days before the opener, it was finally full and the geese had been dropping in every morning. The pond was situated in a large cornfield, so most mornings the geese would land in the pond and then walk into the field whenever hunger moved them.

We dug pit blinds in the dam of the pond and in the cornfield about 200 yards away. The blinds were quite comfortable with a bench, a shelf for shells and calls, and a roof over the bench. The corn stalk covered roof was only about 18 inches above ground level and was almost invisible if you didn't already know it was there.

Three other club members arrived the evening before opening day, so we offered the pond blind to them while we volunteered for the field pit. Most of the guys only hunted three or four times a year, and we were there almost every weekend. We wanted to be certain that they got some shooting.

Rain had fallen all night, pounding a rhythm on the tin roof of the Cow Palace. When I poked my head out the door at 4:30, the rain had stopped and a stiff, moist wind was blowing from the Northeast. The trumpeting of swans and honking of geese floated in from the bay obliterating all sounds save the popping of wind-beaten tarpaper on the old tool shed. The geese should not have flown much during the dark, moonless night, and they would be moving at first light.

Mr. Marsh stood in his long johns cooking breakfast on the gas stove, while the other hunters pulled on their clothes in the chilled, dimly light bedroom. Voices, husky with sleep, began to joke and laugh, and it was obvious that Mark and I weren't the only ones excited about the hunt. Dad made a crack about Mother Marsh slaving away in the kitchen, and he retaliated by flipping a spoonful of scrambled eggs across the table.

We crossed the cornfield in the dark, our rubber boots gathering more mud with each step. The pit blinds had an inch of rainwater on the floor, but the benches were reasonably dry. Dawn crept slowly into the pewter skies, and we shivered in cold and anticipation. A lone goose honked somewhere overhead, and we called out a welcome. He had another destination in mind and winged off into the darkness. Then a thin line of geese appeared, barely clearing the cliff as they flew off the bay. They were headed straight for the pond.

Peering between cornstalks, we hoped the other guys were ready. The big birds didn't even circle, so confident were they in the safety of the pond. As they set their wings to land, all three gunners rose and fired. We saw both lead birds drop an instant before we heard the shots. As the flock tried to gain altitude, one more bird pitched into the pond.

Amazingly, two of the survivors had broken off from the flock and were headed our way. We squatted down and reached for our guns. "Don't let them see your faces," Dad warned. "When I say take 'em, you boys shoot. I'll back you up if you miss." The birds were directly overhead about 30 yards up when we jumped up. Appearing huge at such close range, we could see the white chinstraps vivid against their black heads. I swung in front of the lead bird and he folded, landing with a tremendous thump. Mark had missed the other goose, but Dad dropped him as he tried to escape.

I scrambled out the front of the blind and raced jubilantly across the field to retrieve my goose. He had fallen with his neck propped up by a stalk of corn, looking almost alive. Hesitantly, I grasped his neck as if it were a sacred scroll. The feathers were still warm, the neck all bone and sinew. I lifted him and felt his amazing heft. To me, he was truly awesome.

Mark was disappointed at missing his goose and I'm sure felt some sibling jealousy; an emotion I surely encouraged by endlessly recounting the shot. The day was young, however, and soon geese were in the sky constantly as they headed to favorite feeding grounds. We called an invitation to each flock. Most called back, but didn't change their dining plans.

Finally, a group of twenty flew over and there appeared to be dissension in the ranks. The leader called insistently in an attempt to keep the group together, but five birds ignored him, broke off and began to circle our decoys. Our plan was to let them land, so we could make sure Mark had a good shot. Round and round the blind they flew as we huddled below the front wall of the blind. At last they glided down and landed twenty yards in front of us.

We peeked over the edge and there they were, staring suspiciously at the decoys. Dad whispered, "Mark, stand up and say 'Boo'; and don't shoot until they're flying." The geese stood in utter shock for an instant, then let out a startled honk as they ran and flapped in an attempt to get airborne. Mark waited until their feet were off the ground for two consecutive flaps before deciding that that was sporting enough for him. He fired and "down" fell his first goose. Dad and I each shot one a split second later. Mark must have been the most excited kid on the planet as he literally bounced across the field toward his trophy.

Each weekend at the bay seemed better than the last. My shooting had been abysmal in my first two hunting seasons, but my coordination was finally starting to click. There were plenty of ducks and geese wintering on the bay that year, so we had good shooting nearly every week. When the ducks weren't flying, there were always a few coveys of Bobwhites and dozens of cottontail rabbits to hunt. Many a bluebird day was saved by tromping the edges of the honeysuckle-choked hedgerows and bouncing out a fat rabbit for the pot.

That Autumn was close to being perfect until late in November when it threw me a vicious curve; I received my report card. There it was; insuppressible evidence of long hours of day dreaming, missed homework assignments, and general goofing off: three C's and a D in Algebra. Waves of panic spread through me so violently that I thought my heart would burst. This sort of thing simply wasn't done in my family. Thoughts of running away didn't seem unreasonable at that moment although in my heart, I knew that I needed to face up to it.

For one delirious moment, I entertained the hope that my parents wouldn't find out that report cards had been handed out, but then my brother and sister came prancing into the kitchen showing off their honor roll certificates. I tossed my report card onto the dining room table and made a prudent retreat to my bedroom.

Feeling kinship with death row inmates everywhere, I waited for the dreaded moment to arrive. My throat tightened as I heard my

The Cow Palace, our duck hunting cabin.

father's voice coming through the front door. An eternity, probably about twenty minutes long in reality, passed before I heard my father's footsteps on the stairs. They sounded heavy and purposeful and indescribably ominous. The door swung open. Oh God! This was it! My father, appearing at least nine feet tall, walked in and sat down. That seemed encouraging. I mean if he was going to strangle me, I didn't figure he would sit down to do it.

"I don't guess that I have to tell you that I'm pretty disappointed in this report card. Do I?" he began.

"No."

"Well, what the hell is the problem? I thought that you were the kid who wanted to become a zoologist. Do you honestly think that you are going anywhere with grades like this?"

"No, I mean I do, but that stuff in school is so boring. I've been taking those stupid history and math classes forever. Am I ever going to get a chance to learn something that I'm interested in?" I figured that Dad had already decided what was to become of me, and I didn't have much to lose by offering an explanation.

"Well, I know how you feel," he answered, "but you've got to understand that there is a lot of basic information that you need before you can expect to handle advanced course work."

"That is what everybody always says Dad, but really, what does reading Chaucer or studying the Crusades prepare me for? I know what I want to do in life. Maybe all this stuff is great for kids who don't, but for me it is just a waste of time."

"Some of the classes that you think are pretty useless now, may end up being very important later. There just isn't any way that at 14 years old you can be the judge of what is and what isn't going to be important ten years from now. Besides, just from a practical point of view, you know that you can't become a zoologist without going to college and probably beyond. D's in algebra aren't going to get you through the front door. Now I expect you to bring those grades up. Until the next report period, TV is out. I expect you to be in your room studying every night after dinner."

He paused, and I hoped that was to be the extent of my punishment, but then he continued. "I know how much you love hunting, and I'm not going to take that away from you. But you have to understand that part of growing up is learning that you can't go and play until your responsibilities are taken care of. Going hunting on Saturday is the reward you give yourself for working hard each week. It isn't supposed to be an escape from your responsibilities. Now, you have until next report period to show me that you understand that. If you don't, you won't be hunting with Mark and me for the rest of the season."

Here was a threat that opened my eyes. Not being able to hunt would be unbearable. Besides, Dad was right about one thing; I wasn't going anywhere with grades like those. I just had to start putting some effort into school.

For the first two weeks on my new study regimen, I moped around as if my life had been ruined by an evil tyrant. But then, odd things started to happen. School weeks went by a whole lot faster when I began listening to teachers instead of dreaming all day about next Saturday's hunt. Even stranger, I felt sort of different when I did hunt. It was so hard to figure for a while. Somehow, I seemed to be having more fun than I used to. I had always loved hunting, but there was something desperate in the way I clung, like a dying man, to every sight, sound and smell; each precious memory stored and rationed to sustain me for the duration of the school week. Suddenly, I began doing something I had never done in the field before; I started to laugh.

Chapter Six

CHESAPEAKE SUMMER

My brother Mark and I had been swimming competitively long enough that Dad knew we wouldn't drown, and we had been hunting for several seasons, so he figured we wouldn't shoot ourselves. Perhaps that is why he gave his permission for us to join our friend Bob Payne on a trip to the Chesapeake.

It was the summer of 1968. The war was raging. The schools were filled with S.D.S. radicals. While we all agreed the war had to stop, everything else, from materialism, women's rights, racism, and even patriotism were up for debate. Pot smoking was the favorite pastime on college campuses and in more than a few high schools. In short, it was a time when parents were concerned about their kids. Fortunately for Dad, he didn't have a lot to worry about back in those days. My short hippy stage and Mark's more committed radicalism were still a few years in the future.

Bob, who was the only one of us old enough to drive, picked us up in his black, 1962 Volkswagen. I was only a year away from getting my own license and I envied Bob's independence. Actually being able to date girls without those embarrassing parental lifts would be a relief. Even more enticing was the idea of hunting and fishing when I felt like it, instead of waiting until Dad had a day off. We loaded an assortment of sleeping bags, coolers, fishing rods and .22 rifles into the front end trunk and the behind-the-seat cubby hole; everything we needed to be completely independent of parents or "The Ps" as we had taken to calling them.

We let out whoops as Bob pulled out of the drive, trying to convince ourselves that we were headed for a wild time now that we were free. Despite the theatrics, however, I noticed that Bob barely exceeded the speed limit and was still driving in the right lane. Our good time was more dependent on finding fish than on finding trouble.

Although Bob was two years older than me, we were about the same size. Bob was the saxophone, bandleader sort and I was more into wrestling and swimming. We both knew that if push ever came to shove, I could clobber him. In fact, I never thought about Bob being older than me, until he made an unexpected revelation.

Seems that a girl from school helped Bob to lose his virginity about a month before. I was taken back by the news. I had never know anyone personally who had gone "all the way". I asked the obvious question, "What was it like?" but certain topics simply defy description. As I mulled over this momentous news, an uneasy anticipation crept into my stomach. Silently, I contemplated the changes that I too would be going through in the next few years.

The afternoon heat had just started to subside as we pulled into the rutted farm road. The Cow Palace door swung open unleashing a blast of hot, musty air, redolent of old furniture and feline. A small black cat that had been sleeping on an overstuffed chair, raised her head in alarm. No one had invaded her domain since the end of duck hunting season six months before.

I was glad to see that she was still calling the Cow Palace home. Wayne, the sometime farmer, sometime waterman who owned the property, had lured her into the place with food, and then cut a hole in the wall for her to get in and out. He had gradually reduced her rations until she turned her attentions to, what had once been a prodigious mouse problem.

We tossed our duffels into the bunkroom and claimed beds by flopping down and testing the springs. It felt sort of odd being at the Club when a frigid wind wasn't rattling the windows. Bob dug into his duffel, extracted a pack of Marlboros, and offered us a smoke. Mark jumped at the offer. I might have declined, but then decided that I couldn't have my little brother thinking I was a "goodie-two-shoes". Anyway, if we were old enough to be on our own, we were old enough to smoke.

We strolled along the bay road until we reached the cliff blind. Late winter storms had blown off much of the broom sedge camouflage, but structurally the blind remained sound. We sat on the weathered pine bench where we had spent so many days last fall. Memories of hunts past flooded back, as we gazed out on the gently chopping bay. We reminisced on our triumphs and tribulations; the day I made a triple on widgeon; the day Mark had killed two mallards with one shot; the day I watched a flock of geese for three hours feeding just out of range, and

46

then missed them at 25 yards when they flew over at dusk.

Bob eventually tired of our trip down memory lane, and suggested a swim. We climbed down the, now overgrown, trail to the beach, where we stripped down leaving our clothes in neat piles on top of our shoes. Being less than waist deep out to 100 yards beyond shore, the brackish water had been heated to almost bath water temperatures. Feelings of utter joy and complete freedom engulfed us as we floated in the tea brown bay.

July, being a month without an "R", meant that the oysters weren't fit to eat, but three enterprising lads would have no problem securing a meal in the Chesapeake. We would eat our mothers' cooking one more night, but starting tomorrow we would provide for ourselves.

Wayne kept the duck boat moored on the mouth of the Chester River during the summer. Almost as wide as a lake, with water nearly as brackish as the bay, the river mouth was filled with perch. We followed Wayne's blue pickup along the county roads to where the boat was moored. He grabbed the 10 horse power Johnson motor and the gas can from his pickup bed and handed them to us.

Wayne never for a minute made us feel like kids. He knew we could handle the boat, and he didn't offer any lectures on safety or on being responsible. Wayne was in his late twenties and not nearly as old as our parents, who were pushing the ripe old age of 40. We had hunted together for four years, and he treated me more like a younger brother than a kid. Wayne was the first adult who I had ever considered a friend.

The motor cranked to life on the third pull. The morning air felt almost cool as the square bowed duck boat plowed through the light chop. Redwinged blackbirds screeched their claims to a few square feet of cattails and a bittern flapped heavily down river. During the Fall, a number of guys hunted ducks on this part of the river, usually using a type of blind that we called a booby blind. I suppose it was called that because it would take a real boob of a duck to be fooled by one. Built on pilings placed in the middle of the river and then covered with cedar, they were completely obvious to people, but ducks decoyed in front of them regularly.

The river froze during the winter. When the ice shifted, it pulled up several of the pilings causing the plywood blind to collapse. A number of pilings, some sticking up at odd angles were all that remained of the blind. A pair of ospreys had constructed a nest three feet in diameter and weighing probably 100 pounds on top of one piling. A pair of nearly fledged chicks peeked at us over the edge of the nest. We tied the bow to the piling furthest from the nest and rigged up our spinning rods.

Clams were threaded onto the hooks and just enough lead was attached to cause the bait to drop slowly. The perch must have been starving, because they struck ferociously as the bait drifted down. None of the fish were big; and we tossed a lot back. Any fish longer than nine inches was considered a "keeper". We didn't want to kill more fish than we could eat anyway and we were having too much fun to quit early.

The ospreys put on quite a show for us. For an hour, they circled above screaming indignantly. At last, parental duty overwhelmed their caution. They had hungry chicks to feed. With perch clutched in their talons, the raptors wheeled overhead. They performed a helicopter-like hovering maneuver about ten feet above the nest and then dropped the fish to the waiting chicks. The chicks no longer required being fed bit by bit, but were able to tear into the fish on their own.

We remained on the river until sundown. Blue herons, which roosted in the trees on the banks of the river, began coasting in as the red sun touched the horizon. Black silhouettes, with long bent necks, cupped wings, and extended legs against the brilliant red backdrop were enough to even touch the souls of teen-aged boys.

Two large, cast iron skillets were all we needed to prepare dinner. A half dozen sliced potatoes were carelessly tossed into one pan and an equal number of freshly cleaned perch went into the other. A liberal supply of lemon, butter, salt and pepper were poured over the fish which ended up tender-flaky and almost sweet. It may have been simple, but I can't remember a better meal before or since. Probably the best part of the whole trip was the crabbing. Most folks crab by tying bait into some sort of net ring and then pulling up the net from time to time to collect their crabs. It can be a lot of fun, but the way we crabbed was pure joy. We scrounged up an old inner tube and a bushel basket from the barn, and Wayne provided three dip nets. The nets were about a foot in diameter and were attached to the end of six foot long oak poles.

East Neck Island was a waterfowl refuge a few miles from the club. The water was only thigh deep in the estuary on one end of the island.

Wearing only cut-off blue jeans, we waded out onto the flat. The inner tube was tied to our belt loops, so it could float behind us, and the bushel basket rested in the center of the tube.

The water was clear enough to see crabs scurrying along the bottom. Failure to spot one could result in a seriously pinched toe. The pinch was especially painful as gales of laughter replaced any offers of sympathy. It was one thing to spot a crab under those circumstances and quite another to actually catch him. A stab with the net nearly always came up empty as the crustacean darted away. A slow approach, followed by a lightning quick thrust was better, and we captured several that we deposited in the floating basket.

The best tactic, however, was to team up. The crabs nearly always escaped by swimming backwards and to the side. If one net could move into position behind the crab, while the other nets approached from the front, we could often drive him into the waiting net. A last second adjustment was usually required by the catcher, and even then the plan didn't always succeed, but by day's end our basket was more than half full of blue-clawed crabs.

Our shoulders were sun burned, our skin tasted like salt, and our hair was stiff and tangled from the water and wind. The low sun glittered off the water like a million diamonds and a tangy, salty, muddy, summery smell hung in the air. Puffs of a cool evening breeze picked up cooling our bare backs as we waded the last mile back to the car.

Once the pot was boiling, we tossed in a sack of Crab Boil seasoning. The crabs, as if anticipating their fate, staged a mass break out from the basket. A hole had been snipped through the side of the water-soaked basket, and crabs were now scurrying in all directions across the Cow Palace floor. Recapturing them, with the added danger of pinched fingers, became a sport unto itself. The escapees that climbed under the stove and refrigerator were especially challenging to extract. Amidst hysterical laughter and howls of pain, we eventually rounded up all the strays.

Cracking all those crabs became a major operation, especially as many of them were fairly small. Rather than eating as we worked, we mounded the meat onto a large plate. About two hours later, we had enough for three gigantic crab cocktails which we covered with a ketchup and horseradish sauce. It was a meal fit for a king; however, the entire pile of crab disappeared into our ravenous mouths in about five minutes. I decided that crab tasted a whole lot better when somebody else cleaned them.

On our final night at the Bay, we plotted an attack on the deer that had been decimating Wayne's soybeans. We waited until about 10:00 which was the time Wayne had been seeing them. Armed with flashlights and twenty twos, we sneaked along a big hedgerow which ran along one edge of the bean field. Speaking in whispers, we crept through the dew-laden weeds, our flashlights turned off. At last, we raised up over the fence and shined our lights onto the field. A dozen sets of glowing eyes stared at us in astonishment.

We knew better than to shoot deer out of season, especially as there were a number of does with fawns in the group. Our intention was to scare the life out of them. A helluva racket ensued, as we fired round after round into the air over their heads. The herd bolted out of the field intent on finding safer and quieter dining accommodations. I suppose we would have had quite a time trying to convince the game warden that we weren't trying to kill the deer, but fortunately he never showed up.

We arrived home with a certain smugness; knowing that we had taken care of ourselves, hadn't done anything we were ashamed to admit, and had a damned fine time to boot. I had a feeling that this grown up business was going end up being a lot of fun.

Chapter Seven

GRADUATIONS

The late morning, Sunday sunlight streamed through the windshield as Dad sped down the narrow, sand shouldered road. My stockinged feet propped on the nylon carpet beneath the heater, I sprawled lazily on the gray, upholstered, front seat. A strobe effect of sunlight passing through naked oak limbs overhead, flashed pink and black through my drooping eyelids.

As was our usual practice, we had driven to the Cow Palace on Friday night, hunted ducks and geese on Saturday, and waited until Sunday morning for our return. Normally, I loved those leisurely drives through the Maryland's Eastern Shore. Statuesque homes of clapboard and brick, some dating back to the Revolutionary War, stood like manor houses above a fiefdom of wildlife. Harvested fields of soybeans and corn surrounded by honey suckle and cedar-choked fencerows offered ideal habitat for bobwhite and cottontails. Forested tracts of oak and pine provided sanctuary for the seemingly invisible herds of whitetails that emerged under cover of darkness to feed on the fallen grain.

The season was nearly over with and our trip was being repeated for the twelfth consecutive weekend. The scenery had become familiar – nearly memorized – and I succumbed to my laziness as my head nodded. Dad forestalled my nap, saying, "It seems hard to believe that you will be graduating from high school in a few more months. I've been thinking about what you might like for a graduation present." He commented while never taking his eyes from the road.

Still slouched in the seat, my eyebrows arched and I peered out the corners of my eyes. This had the makings of an interesting conversation! "The best idea that I've come up with is an unusual hunting trip," he continued. "The problem is that I'm not sure what you would like to do most, so I thought I'd just let you design your own trip. How does that sound to you?"

I sat bolt upright, my mouth agape. "Are you serious?" I stammered.

A flicker of a smile crossed Dad's face as he enjoyed my reaction.

"I'm always serious. Why don't you look into the possibilities and we can talk more about it later."

Feeling like a kid set loose in a candy shop, I wrote letters to every outfitter who advertised in *Outdoor Life* magazine.

What would it be? Duck hunting in Mexico or perhaps elk hunting in Wyoming. Moose hunting in Canada might be interesting. The opportunities were endless. Each day, I ran the two blocks from the bus stop to home, anxious to pluck new brochures from the mail. Pamphlets spread across my bed, I poured over every word and picture. How would it feel riding through the Tetons or cruising the shoreline of a northern lake? I scrutinized the smiling faces in the photos in search of clues. Did you have a good time? Was it exciting? Was it beautiful?

I agonized over my delightful dilemma until a brochure arrived from British Columbia. Black and white photos of hunters displaying Stone sheep and mountain goats taken on wind-swept mountain meadows; of canvas wall tents nestled in subalpine spruce; of caribou and grizzly bears ignited my imagination. Since early boyhood, I had savored Jack O'Connor's descriptions of the great northern wilderness, and it suddenly occurred to me that I could see it for myself. The very idea seemed incredible; like jumping into a novel and finding yourself in conversation with the characters. My decision was made.

From my window perch 30,000 feet above the ground, I witnessed the gradual transformation of the earth. My native Pennsylvania appeared as a dense, rolling blanket of verdant, deciduous forest. The emerald foliage of late August obscured all but the largest cities and the meandering, slate-colored rivers.

With every mile traveled west of the Appalachians, the effects of reduced rainfall became apparent. The forest thinned as we crossed Ohio and eventually yielded to a mosaic of green rectangles of corn and bean fields in Indiana and Illinois. Upon reaching Manitoba and Saskatchewan, the landscape was transformed by the golden hues of ripening wheat. Thousands of potholes and lakes scattered throughout the prairie appeared as black polka dots on an endless yellow fabric. Recalling the annual waterfowl reports of the legendary Jimmy Robinson, I tried to imagine the tremendous flocks of ducks just then completing their nesting in those wetlands 30,000 feet below me. Someday, I vowed, I would see that country from the ground.

Gradually descending as we crossed into Eastern Alberta, we distinguished rhythmicaly rocking oil wells toiling amongst the crops. To the east of Edmonton we spotted massive refineries that somehow forced oil through a bewildering complex of pipes and columns to render fuel. The 727 swung north for its final approach, and I caught my first glimpse of the Canadian Rockies. The immense, snow-packed peaks stood as guardians to one of the grandest wildernesses on earth. Man might cling to the edges or to the wide valleys, but those awesome giants would never allow themselves to be dominated. Tomorrow, we would fly deep into the great range toward our final destination.

The journey into British Columbia was an up and down affair as the Canadian Pacific jet stopped at outpost towns of Dawson Creek, Fort St. John, Fort Nelson and finally White Horse, Yukon. Red-cheeked passengers in cowboy hats and denim jackets boarded alongside Indians most of whom had short hair although a few wore long braids. With Western movie depictions of 19th century Indians as my only reference, I considered it incongruous to find Indians on airplanes and even odder that the cowboys and Indians now all dressed the same. I suddenly felt foolish in my ignorance. How little I knew of these people, either white or Indian, from this remote corner of the world. Examining their faces, I tried to envision the tapestry of their lives. Where did they work? What sort of homes did they live in? What did they do for fun? I could only guess.

White Horse was truly a town on the edge of nowhere. The population of 10,000 people represented half the people of the immense Yukon Territory and was the last town of any size before reaching the Arctic Circle. The Alaskan Highway bisected town and nearly every car sported a cracked windshield because of high speed travel on the gravel thoroughfare. Saloons were scattered throughout town, and Indian fur and craft shops served the bus loads of mostly retired tourists who traveled up the Highway during the summer. The hardware store was stocked with equipment for the primary industries of mining, trapping and hunting and sported quite a collection of sheep, goat, moose, bear and caribou heads which sent my mind racing toward what lay ahead.

Heavy rains delayed us in White Horse for several hours and we didn't arrive in Watson Lake until late afternoon. Fletcher, our outfitter, had arranged for a man to meet us at the tiny log airport. Neal was a short, fireplug of a man in his mid-forties with close-cropped hair and work-gnarled hands. He explained that it was too late to get us out on the float plane as the pilot didn't want to return in the dark. Offering us his van for accommodations, he suggested we first get a few drinks and some dinner at the local watering hole.

As we entered the darkened bar room, an unfortunate, stereotypical, drunken Indian sprawled headlong onto the floor overturning a table as he fell at our feet. He struggled to his feet, lost his balance once again and fell backward onto his ass. The bartender suggested in no uncertain terms that he was cut off and had to leave. Despite his inclination to fight, somewhere in his poor muddled brain there must have been a little voice of sanity that told him he could never win and he left peaceably.

Like Dorothy in the Wizard of Oz, I had the feeling I wasn't in Pennsylvania any more. The excitement over, we settled in at a table and Dad actually ordered me a drink; my first in a bar.

Although I slept well on the foam pads in the van, I was up early poking around the dock in the cool, damp morning air. Green-black spruce trees with bottle brush needles encircled the glassy smooth, mist-enshrouded lake. Three brightly painted float planes moored to the dock were the only splash of color in the muted dawn landscape. Peering through the window of the tiny float plane office, I spotted a full body mount of a huge, snarling, jet-black wolf. Incredibly the wolf's back was level with my waist! A small brass plaque described the wolf as having weighed 175 pounds. I had never before appreciated the dimensions of these great beasts; thinking of them as more German Shepherd in size. I couldn't help wondering how many other misconceptions would soon be rectified.

At about 7:00 a.m., a brown pickup pulled into the gravel lot and a thin, blond haired man in his early twenties got out and introduced himself as our pilot. Forming a queue with the pilot in the plane, Dad on the dock and me playing the middleman on the pontoon, We loaded our duffels and rifles into the yellow, two seated Cessna. Dad claimed the available seat and I arranged the duffels into a throne in the rear. The engines sputtered momentarily before bursting to life. Moments later we were racing across the lake, the pontoons bouncing noisily beneath us.

For nearly an hour we cruised over forested mountain valleys, treeless craggy peaks and alpine lakes. Once we spotted a band of sheep feeding on a grassy meadow above timber line, but during the entire flight, not a single building, road or any other sign of civilization passed beneath us as we flew deep into the wilderness.

The float plane started its descent toward a small, oblong lake nestled between boulder strewn mountains. Banking for our final approach, we spotted a camp of four canvas wall tents and about twenty horses among the spruce trees on the south shore. At the bank were three Indian men and two boys waiting for our landing. It had simply never occurred to me that Fletcher was Indian, so I was somewhat surprised although not displeased.

Fletcher was a square jawed man, well over six feet tall, with a moustache, an open smile and dark intelligent eyes. The two boys turned out to be Fletcher's sons, Freddy and Roddy. At 14 and 16 years old, they were still in high school, but during August they helped their father handle the horses. Fletcher's half brother, Elry was in his mid-thirties and served as the wrangler. The final introduction was Tommy, who broke into a toothless grin as he pulled a cigarette from his mouth, stuck out his hand, and uttered, "Howdy Pardner."

Everyone pitched in toting our gear up the hill. "We'll put you fellows in this tent," directed Fletcher. "As soon as you're settled, come over to the cook tent and Doreen will get you some breakfast."

The morning sun bathed the canvas tent in diffuse, yellow light and the sheepherder stove took the chill from the late, summer mountain air. A makeshift table of plywood covered with an oilcloth dominated the tent. Fletcher's wife, Doreen, was a barely plump lady with short hair and glasses. With a welcoming smile, she laid plates heaped with pancakes and eggs in front of us and filled our blue enamel cups with coffee.

Fletcher poured a cup for himself and joined us at the table. "Since you and I are about the same age Walt, why don't I guide you and Tommy can guide Mitch. We'll let these young bucks charge up and down the mountains and we can just try to out think 'em. We had a big fire in this country last month and I'm afraid most of the sheep have moved out of the area. We still might be able to find a few rams, but I can't make any guarantees. We've got some really beautiful goats in this country though and the caribou ought to be moving through on Level Mountain. Who knows, we might even pick up a moose over there. I'd suggest we spend a couple of days trying to locate some sheep, but if we don't find them, we can go after the goats and caribou. Of course if you fellows have your hearts set on a sheep, I'll do my best to get you one."

"How do you feel about it, Mitch?" asked Dad. "This is your hunt."

"Dad, a sheep would be nice, but I've never shot a goat or caribou either and I'd be real happy with that. I think we should follow Fletcher's better judgment. After all he's the expert."

The best goat area was a day's ride away, so Fletcher and family began the arduous task of breaking the large camp. Doreen dismantled the kitchen; wrapping each plate, glass, pot and pan in newspaper and placing them in the green wooden panniers. The men busied themselves packing duffels, collapsing tents and packing horses. With hands in pockets, I watched impotently not knowing how to help, before finally realizing my help was neither needed nor expected. Much work remained to be done, so Dad and I ambled off in search of a safe place to test fire the rifles in order to be certain the scopes hadn't been knocked off center during the trip.

A black horse with a white blaze on his face, named Spade was to be my mount and Dad would ride a roan gelding named Twilight. Fletcher, Doreen, Dad and I departed first leaving the rest of the party to follow with the pack horses about an hour later. My previous riding experience had been limited to a few weekend rides at local hack stables and I had yet to get over the thrill of sitting astride such a powerful animal with the wonderful rich odor of horse and leather filling my nose. Totally free now, I was no longer constrained by the need for roads. On horseback, the wilderness was mine to explore.

Less than a mile down the trail, the halter rope slipped from the saddle horn and swung free at Spade's feet. I attempted to dismount to retrieve it, but my wide hunting boot hung up in the stirrup as I stepped off. Losing my balance, I flopped onto my back with my foot still stuck. A jolt of panic shot through me as I envisioned myself being dragged down the trail a la the gunned down, bad guy in the Western movies. Spade jumped sideways further tightening my foot in the stirrup, but fortunately he didn't bolt. Being careful not to inadvertently kick him in the ribs, I gingerly eased my foot loose. My heart still pounding, I moaned a great sigh of relief. My trip was nearly over before it started.

Each mountain pass revealed another spectacular view of spruce covered valleys and looming peaks. A cow moose and her gangly calf fed on streamside willows. A herd of snow white nanny goats grazed on a high meadow as five kids romped at their sides. Despite the beauty around us, the adage "that the mind can only appreciate what the butt can endure" was proving true once more as I began to develop a colossal case of saddle sores. While Spade walked, the discomfort was tolerable, but when he trotted, my riding inexperience caused me to bounce painfully in the saddle. Sure that my pelvis was soon to tear holes through my skin, I devised the very un-macho solution of tying the reins behind the saddle horn, placing one hand on the horn and the other on the pommels. Whenever Spade felt compelled to trot, my pride yielded to the need for survival and I raised up on my hands thereby lifting my aching posterior.

While embarrassed by my discomfort, I didn't want to humiliate myself by complaining. Grimly I stared stonily into the distance hopeful that camp would lie around the next bend. About 5:00 that afternoon, Fletcher at long last led us into a copse of firs and announced that we had arrived. A simple log corral and a rocked-in fire ring testified that this was one of Fletcher's established camps. Relieved of their panniers and top packs, the horses seemed as glad as I to be at journey's end (although in truth no one could have been that thrilled) as they rolled happily in the dirt.

Freddy, Roddy and I strolled to the swift brook that flowed by camp for a drink and to wash our sweaty faces. Kneeling in the sand, we saw before us a huge, platter-sized track with deep claw prints. Despite never having seen such a track before, I knew instantly that only a grizzly could leave such an impression. I shuddered in both dread and anxious anticipation at the prospect of meeting up with the creature who left such fearsome tracks. One thing for certain, our fishing tackle would include a rifle from now on.

I was hesitant to climb into the saddle the following morning, but fortunately my soreness got no worse and even seemed to lessen as the morning progressed. We made a steep ascent through the timber eventually reaching the timberline in about an hour. After three days of travel, it was good to be actually hunting at last. At each rise, we dismounted and spent long periods stretched on our bellies glassing the surrounding mountains. Initially, I cursorily scanned the slopes with my binoculars and determined that they were devoid of wildlife. Fletcher and Tommy on the other hand meticulously scrutinized every rock pile and shadow. Their patience paid off time after time as they pointed out game that I had overlooked, and I soon was trying to mimic their skill.

Just before lunch, Tommy noticed the tracks of a ram in dried mud. Fletcher explained that the tracks were only about a day old and the sheep might still be nearby. We redoubled our glassing efforts, and while we failed to locate the sheep, it wasn't long before Fletcher pointed out a goat on a cliff nearly a mile away. "I think that might be a billy," he conjectured. "Let's work our way over there for a better look."

My adrenalin began to pump. I had been dreaming of this moment for almost a year. We dropped below a ridge to screen our progress from the keen-eyed goat. Leaving Elry to hold the horses, Dad, Fletcher, Tommy and I crawled to the rise for a better view. We had closed to 1000 yards; too far to shoot, but close enough to size him up. There he stood, perched on a sheer cliff. His thick white fur quivered in the breeze as he gazed intently for danger from below. I could barely wait to begin the stalk, but Fletcher announced, "He isn't very big. I'm sure we can find a better one." My heart sank, but I didn't say a word. We stood exposing ourselves to the goat for the first time. Immediately he bolted; not across the cliff as I expected but straight up the escarpment. His hooves somehow grasped hold on the narrowest of ledges and his powerful shoulders effortlessly drew him upward; a surprising feat at any speed but simply amazing at a dead run.

Our afternoon was cut short by a mountain storm which poured a flood of fog into the valleys. As we made the long ride back to camp, visions of the billy we had passed up preyed on my mind. My ruminations were disrupted upon arrival at the happy camp. Freddy and Roddy had spent the day catching small trout from the stream and had nearly 80 of the six to eight inch rainbows stretched on a tarp. I rolled up my sleeves and joined them on the downed tree where they had already begun cleaning their catch.

The days in the outdoors were doing wonders for my appetite and

I awoke ravenous. A plate of hash from the previous night's leftovers, four pancakes, three trout and four cups of coffee disappeared before I pushed away from the table. Like most mornings in August, the weather was crisp and clear. The sun, which had been up since 4:00 A.M., sparkled through the firs spreading dappled light across the forest floor.

Tommy strode toward me leading our horses. With his cigarette clenched in the corner of his mouth, he grinned his semi-maniacal smile and said, "Pardner, today is THE day!" "I'm ready, Pardner," I responded enthusiastically. We mounted up and rode to where we had been forced back by the fog. "We're about to enter goat heaven", announced Fletcher as we rode through the pass into a narrow canyon rimmed by limestone cliffs.

Dad and I had been following our guides for less than an hour when Fletcher glanced behind us, did a double-take and yanked his binoculars out of his saddle bag. Instantly, I spotted what had drawn his attention; a lone billy on the ridge. "He looks like a good one from here. Tommy, you take Mitch up through that saddle in the mountain. Look him over again before you shoot to be certain he's what you want. Walt and I are going to try and find our own."

Tommy and I gave our horses a kick and galloped up the hill. "I think we have him cornered," I said as we dismounted. "Timber grows on the north slope of this mountain, and he is between us and the trees. Goats don't spend much time in timber, do they?"

"Pardner, I think you're right. If we slip along quietly we might walk right up on him. Be ready though, 'cause it might happen in a hurry." I chambered a 150 grain bullet into the Model 70 Winchester .30-06. With each step, my tension level grew as I expected the billy to step into view. My nerves weren't being settled any by Tommy's frequent question, "Are you ready?" Closer and closer we came to the timber and finally we were there. But where was the billy?

"Do you think he went into the timber after all?"

"Could be, but I doubt it. Let's see if we can find some tracks." Sure enough, there were tracks in the loose gravel running down the east side of the mountain. "That bastard must have started running as soon as we spotted him. OK, there he is way down in that side canyon. You see 'em?"

"Yup. It looks like he's working his way up those cliffs on the far side. There isn't any way we can climb down there."

"Our only chance will be to beat feet down this side and shoot him across the canyon before he gets over the top. Hand me your rifle, I'll carry it for you."

We ducked out of sight and madly charged down the mountain. Unused to the rough terrain, I repeatedly stumbled on the loose rocks, causing me to crash to the ground. Determined, I bounced up and raced on. Fortunately, Tommy was more surefooted than I, so my rifle was in safe hands. Gasping for breath, we peeked over the ridge. "He's still there, but he's almost to the top. We've got to keep going. You okay?"

"I'll make it, but I'll need a few minutes to catch my breath when we get there. I can't shoot puffing like this."

"We can worry about that later. Follow me."

Our frantic scramble continued as we drew closer to shooting range. Twice more Tommy peeked over the ridge only to drop down and resume running. The altitude was taking its toll on me and I started to fall behind. Tommy chanced one last peek and dropped to the ground. I crawled toward him as much in exhaustion as stealth. I repossessed my rifle and then plopped down right on Tommy's foot. "Get the hell off me," he hissed. "You'll blow my ear drums out at this range." Despite the tense moment, I couldn't help but chuckle at his apparent horror.

At that moment, the billy stared directly at us from a mere 150 yards away. I forgot all exhaustion and quickly centered the cross hairs behind his shoulder. Unconscious of pulling the trigger, the rifle suddenly fired. The goat instantly collapsed from the lung shot. As I accepted Tommy's congratulations, the billy shuddered and leapt to his feet. Recovering from surprise, I swung through and shot barely over him. The third shot took him through the shoulder and dropped him for good. Over and over he rolled all the way to the canyon floor.

We climbed down to the billy and Tommy once again congratulated me. I gazed at the goat unbelievingly. Here was the culmination of a dream. With a tinge of sadness, I stroked his thick white fur and his jet black horns. What a magnificent beast. His hooves were designed with hard edges but pads that were soft almost like a dog's – an adaptation for gripping rocks on the sheer cliffs where being surefooted was a life and death talent. I was amazed at the thickness of his body. No taller than a deer, this animal had to weigh 300 pounds. Upon examining the massive musculature of his front quarters, I now understood how these big animals could pull themselves directly up a cliff.

Tommy pulled a tape measure from his jacket and' stretched it over the horns. "Ten inches long and 6 inch bases!" he exclaimed. "You did good Pardner. Now let's take some pictures and get this old boy caped and skinned."

After accepting congratulations from Doreen and the boys, I stretched out on the ground in front of the fire to while away the afternoon and to wait for Dad and Fletcher.

Completely content, I was warmed as much by the day's events as the crackling fire. Just before dark, whoops echoed through the camp. It was Dad and Fletcher.

"Wait 'til you see what the old men got!" shouted Fletcher as they rode into camp. He dismounted and grabbed the reins of the packhorse. Tossing aside the tarp, he yanked out the head of a magnificent billy. "Eleven and a half inches!" he crowed. "What you are looking at could be a new world record!"

Dad then spotted my goat on the tarp by the fire. "You got that billy! Fantastic!" he said grasping my hand. "This is a night for a celebration," he said and then slipped into the tent and returned seconds later clutching a bottle of Scotch. "This is the only bottle I brought," he said, "but there ought to be a glass for everyone. I want to make a toast."

Doreen scurried to the cook tent and returned with glasses and Dad poured. "To the goats! They lead us a good chase," offered Dad. "And to Fletcher and Tommy," I added. "And to you fellas for shooting straight," laughed Fletcher.

My saddle soreness fading to a memory, I was now more comfortable on horseback. Leaning back in the saddle and cocking my ankles with toes up and heels down prevented me from bouncing about every time Spade trotted. Still on a cloud from the previous day's success, I was unconcerned about finding a ram although that was our day's objective; to be alive in this wilderness was enough. A small band of ewes and lambs trotted up a brushy slope across the canyon from us.

Rock ptarmigan, seemingly unconcerned by our presence, sauntered boldly through a rocky basin nearly devoid of vegetation. A young golden eagle, his wings and tail still showing the white bands of youth, soared into the valley below.

The scarcity of sheep forced us to once again break camp. It would be a three day ride to Level Mountain where the caribou should be. The turbulent weather systems drifting in from the Pacific brought intermittent showers throughout our journey and we quickly learned to keep our rain gear tied behind bur saddles for easy access. The first day of travel was particularly grueling. At 9:00 p.m., as dusk began to settle around us, I sat hunkered down in my saddle numbly suffering through yet another squall. Fletcher was leading Dad, Doreen and I through a pass far above timberline. Suddenly, Fletcher whirled his horse around. Lying flat on the horse's back, he quickly rode back toward us.

"There's a ram in the basin just ahead," he hissed.

This news came as quite a shock as I had already dispensed with any hope of taking a Stone sheep on this hunt. Nonetheless, it appeared that I would now get just that chance. We crept forward and peered over the pass.

"Do you see him?" asked Fletcher.

"No," we replied in unison.

"He is right there in the middle of the basin about 1,000 yards away." Fletcher's spectacular eyesight as well as his ability to immediately spot the slightest aberration in any scene left me amazed. For long moments he tried valiantly to point out the ram to us and we tried equally hard to see it. Our ineptitude bordered on the ridiculous, and we soon found ourselves struggling to control our laughter. Our shoulders began to convulse uncontrollably, as we rolled on our backs in restrained hysteria.

"OK, let's pull ourselves together here," urged Fletcher. "I can't be sure if he is a legal ram. His horns are real dark and I just can't be sure from here."

"All right, I see him. My God! He is so black and these wet rocks are exactly the same color. How did you ever spot him?" The basin he was in was bisected by a small valley perhaps 200 yards across. The ram slowly descended into the valley, disappearing from sight.

"Quick! Let's hurry to the edge. We need to close ground on him while he can't see us. Now remember, he may not be legal, so don't shoot unless I tell you to." In a half crouch, we trotted toward where the ram had just disappeared. "Shoot! Shoot! He's a big one!" yelled Fletcher.

My eyes searched frantically for the ram. Where the hell was he! There! Thirty yards away! My rifle flew to my shoulder. For an instant, he was in my scope, but just as I began to squeeze the trigger he trotted behind a boulder. Only the top of his head and those great horns were visible.

"OK, he's going to come up the other side. Be ready." I settled into a sitting position just as he emerged running hard straight up the far side of the valley. His back was my only available target. I fired wildly at first and missed. I partially regained my composure and held the cross hairs on his nose. The shot passed right beneath his horn shattering rock immediately below his face and causing him to rear up slightly. My third shot was slightly in front of him. Then the ram unexpectedly stopped and turned broadside about 300 yards away. I was totally flustered by now and missed badly causing him to take off. My fifth and final shot was to no avail. Dad realizing that I was out of ammo, fired several shots at the ram that was now nearly 400 yards distant, but he failed to connect.

Oh, the desolation! I had a gift chance at a full curl Stone sheep and I had blown it. Desperately, I replayed the sequence in my mind somehow hoping that the outcome could be altered. Of course, the result remained the same and I knew that I would have to live with that failure for a long, long time. Would such a chance ever come again? The rain began to fall once more and darkness was fast approaching. For the next three hours we rode through the inky blackness with the rain driving down and I felt the kind of lonely that only a 17-year-old boy who has failed can ever know.

My heart still heavy, I emerged from our sleeping tent to face a sunny, crisp morning. The camp, which had been obscured by darkness when we arrived, was nestled among lodge pole pines at the shore of a tiny lake. The beauty of this pristine site was almost enough to cheer me up.

The weather was improved and we were only forced to don our rain gear twice during the afternoon. We dropped below timberline into more rolling, forested country leaving behind the mountains and any hope of seeing more sheep. My attentions therefore turned to spotting a moose that Fletcher assured us lived in this country. We did find tracks but failed to locate any of the gigantic deer.

As we wearily rode into our new campsite on the shores of a large lake, equipment and trash were scattered everywhere. "Damn it!" lamented Fletcher, "that bear has been into my cache again. That little bastard has already cost me $500 in ruined equipment, and now this." We dismounted and began to gather up the far-flung debris. An opened lard can provided conclusive evidence of the perpetrator's identity. The bear had crammed his face as far into the can as he was able, leaving a clear face print. He wasn't a particularly large specimen and Fletcher suggested that he was a three year-old black bear in his first season away from Mama.

"Men, I'm sorry but we are going to have to spend an extra day here putting this mess back together. We can hunt moose from this camp while the boys and Doreen get us reorganized."

Our day of moose hunting was uneventful and was the only day of our trip thus far that we had failed to see a single big game animal. We returned at about 8:00 to find camp clean and neat. Their tasks completed, Roddy and Freddy had retired to the lakeside where they were attempting to catch a few fish for dinner. I watched while they cast heavy Dare Devil lures to the hungry, unsophisticated rainbows. The fish they landed were considerably larger than the little trout from the goat camp going 14 to 18 inches.

In mid-retrieve, Roddy abruptly froze, allowing the spoon to sink to the bottom. "Look! A bear!" standing on the grassy edge of the lake a mere 75 yards away stood a young black bear. I made no attempt to retrieve my rifle until I heard Fletcher bellow, "Somebody shoot that little bastard, before he wrecks anything else." I raced back to the tent to retrieve the .30-06. The bear remained in place when I returned, somewhat winded from my sprint: Despite my sitting position, the rifle rose and dropped with each breath as I struggled unsuccessfully to hold steady. Because of the steady pressure from my knees, the cross hairs were lined up from left to right, but one second they were too high and the next too low. Anxious that the bear would disappear back into the forest at any moment, I decided to pull the trigger the next time the cross hairs dropped.

At the bark of the rifle, the bear whirled with cat-like quickness and in a single leap disappeared into the trees. I raced around the lake with Tommy, who had retrieved his lever action .30-.30. The bear had only covered a few yards when we arrived and had already slowed to a staggering walk. Tommy, being first on the scene, finished him with a shot in the lungs. My shot had broken his shoulder low and passed into the chest barely above the brisket. I doubt that he would have gone far in that condition even had we not put the finishing shot into him.

One more day of travel lay ahead before we would reach Level Mountain and hopefully caribou. Slowly climbing throughout the day, we gradually emerged from the timber into rolling country of gravelly soils overgrown with head-high brush. Topping out on a small knoll, we spotted our first bull moose of the trip. He had an odd looking rack with his left antler large and well dished, but his right antler was tiny in comparison. No sooner had we passed him up, than I spotted a second bull on the far side of the knoll. This bull was considerably better with a rack which looked to go about 50 inches in spread, but the antlers were somewhat narrow.

"Do you want him?" asked Dad.

"I don't know. What do you think, Fletcher?"

"He's not bad, but I think we might be able to do better."

"Why don't you take him Dad. That twisted knee is starting to wear on you and you might *not* have another chance."

Dad answered my suggestion by sliding his Remington .30-06 pump from the scabbard. The moose was standing broadside at about 200 yards distance, stared at us stupidly. Dad fired but the moose neither flinched nor ran. "Did I hit him?"

"I couldn't tell. Shoot again," ordered Fletcher. The destination of the second shot was equally mysterious. We saw brush shatter below the bull on the third shot and we quickly conveyed the news.

"I'm not sure where this thing is shooting. Hand me the Winchester." In five shots from the .30-06, we detected only a single miss yet the bull stood unmoving and seemingly unhurt. The moose at last lumbered forward about 10 yards and lay down as if he were bedding. We climbed down the knoll and found him quite dead. Six perfectly expanded bullets rested beneath the hide on the far side of his lower chest in an area the size of a paper plate. As Fletcher commented, "Moose don't give up the ghost easy."

The days of travel had taken their toll and we all slept in until 10:00 the next morning. After another huge breakfast – this time of bear meat and flap jacks, we mounted up to explore Level Mountain. The terrain on top was as its name implied, a vast plateau with a completely tundra-like flora of mosses, lichens and low herbaceous plants. The region didn't remotely resemble any of the country we had thus far seen. In the afternoon, we spotted a herd of caribou at least three miles away, but it was too late in the day to pursue them, so we returned to camp.

Leaving camp much earlier, we rode the identical route as the previous day, but this time we were in a different world. We found ourselves in the midst of a new wave of migrating caribou. In the first hour, we had stalked within shooting range of twenty caribou. Never having seen such beasts, I quickly prepared to shoot, but Fletcher stopped me. The cows (which also sport antlers) and the young bulls that I was so anxious to slay seemed gigantic compared to the white tailed deer in Pennsylvania, but were in fact very small caribou. Skirting herd after herd, we were unable to locate any large bulls although I remained willing to shoot any of them.

A tiny stream had eroded through the soft, gravelly tundra creating a gorge 200 feet deep. Peering into the gorge, I was thrilled to see a mature grizzly. Deep brown with silver tipped pelage, his immense head, humped back and massive forelegs appeared the essence of raw power. Here stood a huge primeval force. We needed to drop into the gorge and cross the stream in order to continue our hunt, so we shouted and whistled in hopes of scaring the beast off. Nothing doing. We simply had aroused the curiosity of a creature who had never conceived of fear. He charged up our side of the gorge, arriving at the top less than 100 yards from us. Lifting his great head he tested the wind for the scent of these strange interlopers into his kingdom.

"Everybody dismount," ordered Fletcher. "Get out your rifles, but do not shoot unless I tell you." We stared each other down for some minutes, but the big grizzly was in no mood to back off. At last Fletcher suggested that we continue on. As we rode into the gorge and up the far side, the bear paralleled us, seemingly contemplating our demise. Across the 200 yards that separated us, I could sense his great intelligence and his supreme confidence. We were nothing more than bugs with the temerity to tread through his domain. For the next half hour, the great bear loped along watching us. When we finally stopped to glass yet another herd of caribou, he continued running out of sight although he will remain forever seared in my memory.

With so many caribou milling about, the inevitable finally happened. We spotted a mature herd bull grazing a short distance from a band of cows. Now I could see why we had waited. His arching, heavy beamed antlers dwarfed the bulls that we had previously seen. The rut was still a few weeks away, and he was more interested in protecting his velvet covered antlers than in cavorting with the cows. His white shaggy neck contrasted beautifully with his ashen gray body.

We stalked to about 250 yards using a conveniently placed rise as cover. I underestimated the range, and my initial shot passed slightly below his chest. Not sure where the shot had originated, the bull raised his head in confusion but did not run. Quickly, I worked the bolt while forcing myself to remain calm. I wanted no repeat of my frantic misses on the ram. Lying prone with the rifle resting on a lichen covered boulder, I held the cross hairs on his spine and squeezed off my second shot; this time hitting him squarely in the lungs. He staggered, blood pouring from his mouth. Just as I prepared to fire a third time to finish him, he collapsed. While he posed no threat to the record books, I couldn't have cared less. He was a fine, mature caribou bull that I had crossed a continent and some of the most beautiful country on earth to find and I was simply thrilled.

Dad also scored later that same day on a double shoveled bull slightly smaller than mine. Dad had now taken all the game available to him and his sore knee had carried him about as far as it was able, so for the next two days he relaxed in camp while I tried to fill my moose tag. My luck had apparently run out, however, and after two days of searching it was time to break camp one final time.

Pack train in tow, we rode toward our rendezvous with the bush plane. A melancholy feeling swept over me as we made this final leg of our journey together. Now that I had experienced this pristine wilderness, oh, how I would miss it! Certainly Dad wouldn't be picking up the tab for any more such trips; I would soon be a man and would be expected to pay my own way through life. Would I ever return?

Yes, somehow I would have to. After all, I had some unfinished business with a full curl ram.

The author with his Rocky Mountain Goat shot on his high school graduation trip in August of 1971.

Chapter Eight

RUDE AWAKENINGS

The excitement I felt about starting what I hoped would be an improved era in my education, had suddenly evaporated. "Going off to college" had been little more than an abstraction until the moment that I drove up the elm lined road leading onto campus. The reality, which crashed down, was that I was moving away from home to live with complete strangers. I didn't have any notion of what would be expected of me or even whether I would cut the mustard. My days as a kid were over.

My assigned dormitory was an ancient, four story, stone edifice with a slate roof. The barracks-like stairwell smelled of recently applied detergents and cleansers, which I suspected provided temporary disguise for the normal odors of smoke, beer, sweat and mildew. Several doors into the hallway remained open as the early arriving freshman hauled in clothes, stereos, lamps, bicycles and books.

Eventually, I located my room and discovered that my roommate, who was of course a total stranger, had already moved in. Jack seemed a nice enough fellow. We both planned to major in biology, and we vowed to help each other if we could. I didn't anticipate any problems sharing a room with Jack, which was at least one concern off my mind.

Two other rooms on the hall were occupied; the remainder apparently to be claimed by upper classmen when they arrived in two days. Across the hall were Tom and Bob. Tom was a little fireplug of a guy who hoped to go into medicine and Bob was an Asian-American who looked like he lived in the weight room. He had been a serious javelin thrower in high school and planned to continue the sport in college. They were in the process of papering their walls with every Playboy pinup from the last ten years.

At the end of the hall was an absolute wild man named Pete. While I wasn't sure if we would ever be friends, I suspected he would be good for a few laughs. All in all, my dorm mates seemed like a pretty good bunch, and despite the fact that I would miss my girl friend, Claudia, back home, I began to think that college might be fun after all.

On Tuesday morning, we gathered at the Dining Hall to register for classes. Most of us, thoroughly confused, spent half the morning standing in the wrong lines. I was disappointed to discover that, as a freshman, I would be taking only required courses like calculus, physics, chemistry and English composition. Apparently finishing high school didn't mean I was finished paying dues. Still, I would be denied studying anything that truly interested me. That afternoon, I learned how high those dues were going to be.

All freshmen majoring in biology and chemistry were summoned to the chapel where we would be addressed by the Dean. The chapel, situated at the center of campus, was a beautiful structure constructed of massive stone blocks with arched entries and a huge bell tower. We filled in, hushed by the church-like atmosphere. Banisters of dark, tropical woods and white painted rails enclosed a balcony that surrounded three sides of the auditorium. The lower level, filled with straight-backed, oak pews, faced a mahogany podium.

The Dean, a dark haired man of about 60 with a face like a cigar store Indian, made his entrance and strode to the podium. His face looked like it would shatter should he ever attempt a smile, but I suspected there was no danger of that happening anytime soon. He welcomed us to college in a voice seeming more threatening than cordial, and in an onerous tone described for us what lay ahead.

Two thirds of us were apparently predestined to flunk out of our major. Most of us would be able to remain in school, he warned, only by getting out of the sciences altogether. He exhorted us to study as we had never done before and then abruptly dismissed us. I sat in complete shock. What had I gotten into? Was this the truth?

The upper classmen began arriving that evening and the quiet dorm scene of the day before was but a memory from another world. The halls echoed with screams as old friends welcomed each other back. Freshmen were studiously ignored for a few hours in the general melee, but later that evening some of our new neighbors stopped by our room to introduce themselves. When they asked Jack and I about our majors, some laughed and others just wished us good luck. All of their kidding wasn't helping my anxiety level a bit.

I had to be alone. I started walking and as luck would have it, ran into an old friend who I had wrestled against in high school. He had graduated a year ahead of me, and I hadn't known we were attending the same college. He was a chemistry major who had survived his first year and was confident that he would make it through. Here was a man that I needed to talk to. He confirmed what the Dean had said and added that nearly all those who flunked out did so in the first two years. The only way to avoid being one of those unfortunates, he suggested, was four to six hours of study per day. That, he assured me, was the only way it could be done and even then there were no guarantees.

In high school, I had rarely studied four hours a week. Was I capable of that sort of discipline, and even if I were, did I really want a biology degree that badly? For the remainder of the evening, I fought the desire to jump in the car and drive home. I could get a job. Perhaps I could even persuade my parents to give me the money they had saved for my education, so I could set up a little sporting goods store or something. But what a fool I would appear running for home like a scared eight-year-old. I was completely paralyzed; afraid to try and afraid not to.

The first two days of classes did little to alleviate my fears. Each professor, logically enough, began the course by listing the subjects to be covered. There was so much to learn! It all seemed insurmountable. I was sinking deep and fast. I absolutely had to put some space between myself and school.

Saturday afternoon found me with shotgun on shoulder looking across a freshly cut cornfield. My tattered camo shirt was already stuck to my back and a trickle of sweat crept down my temple. The late summer haze seemed harmless for the moment but might portend a thunderstorm before dark. I had hunted this farm a few weeks earlier and had found some local doves feeding. In my absence, a new wave of migrants had moved in, and even now, were lazily making the commute from the woods to the corn field.

I waited for about a half hour, trying to learn their flight pattern. From the roosting area in the wood lot, the doves cut across a fallow field, usually passing over a lone locust tree before descending into the cornfield. I tucked myself into the weeds at the base of the tree, convinced that I would soon have shooting.

My wait was short; three birds winged directly overhead. I swung through the lead bird and dropped him in a puff of feathers. Too often, I had lost a downed dove by shooting at a second bird that I invariably missed anyway, so I went directly to him, never taking my eye off the spot where he landed. The afternoon flight had not yet begun in earnest and the shooting was sporadic for the next few hours, although I did manage to scratch down three more.

About 4:00, the doves started leaving the woods in droves, heading for food. The gunning, if not the shooting, was spectacular. I hit doves, I missed doves, fortunately didn't lose any doves, and had the time of my life. I dropped my 12th and final bird an hour later and headed back to the car for a much needed Coke.

For the first time of the day, thoughts of the past week resurfaced, but I was tired of being scared. Graduate with honors or flunk out in a semester, life would always be good with days like this to look forward to. Sitting on the running board of my little Volkswagon, I did some serious thinking.

I wasn't willing to give up everything in my life during the next four years in order to earn a degree, but I wasn't going belly up without a fight either. I made a deal with myself. I would attend every class, I would study at least four hours a day, and I wouldn't give up even if things looked bad; but Saturdays were for hunting and Sundays were for Claudia. If that wasn't good enough ----- Well, it would have to be!

Chapter Nine

HUM 'ER RIGHT IN THERE

Reflections of headlights glistened on the damp blacktop as we drove our white Volkswagon down an empty Main Street. Like so many small Pennsylvania villages, this former coal town was a shadow of what it had once been. Business was scarcely adequate to maintain the hardware, drug, and auto supply stores whose lights shined through illuminated plate glass onto the cracked sidewalks. Old homes stood enshrouded in the drippy shadows of overgrown firs and red oaks.

Claudia used a hand-written map to navigate us to our destination; one block north of the railroad tracks, east for one-half mile. We parked on the gravel pull-off by the mailbox in front of a two story, green-shake house. Deciding' that this was indeed the correct address, we climbed the concrete steps to the wide wooden porch and rang the cracked plastic bell. Through the window on the heavy oak door, we could see Dave trotting down the hall to greet us.

He was dressed in blue jeans and an old green cardigan sweater with holes at the elbows. Dave's bright eyes smiled at us through rimless glasses. A nearly completed fight with a serious case of teen-aged acne caused him to look even younger than his 19 years. Dave and I had met in college while struggling through an organic chemistry course from which we were mercifully on a Christmas furlough. While not a brilliant student, Dave managed to fair pretty well in his classes due principally to prodigious study.

Up until this time, most of our relationship had centered on mutual academic survival. Late at night in the library when we could no longer bear staring at our books, we would quiz each other in preparation for exams. When one of us had to miss a class, we could count on one another to take good notes. It wasn't until mid-semester that we discovered our shared interest in hunting and in beagles.

The dimly lit living room was furnished with overstuffed chairs, a couch covered with a tan afghan, and an old upright piano. Dave's father flipped off the television and his mom laid her sewing on the coffee table as they rose to meet us. Mrs. Wolfgang had wavy blond hair pulled back into a small bun. She wore glasses and Dave clearly favored her. A pink sweater complimented a simple flower print dress gathered with a thin belt.

"How was your trip," she inquired.

"Oh fine, it only took us about two hours and we didn't have any problem finding the place. Dave drew us a good map."

"Well, we sure are glad that you could come up for a few days. Dave has told us a lot about you."

"Uh oh!" I uttered.

"No, no," she laughed. "It was all good."

"He *is* a terrible liar," I replied.

"Claudia, we are so glad you could come."

Mr. Wolfgang was a wiry, little man with close-cropped hair combed back into a flat top. He had been painting the porch behind the kitchen and his khaki pants were stained with white smears of paint. His forearms were dotted with tiny drops from the paint roller.

"I understand from Dave that you are quite the hunter," he opened.

"Well, I don't know about that. Let's just say that I like to go as often as I can."

"Did you bring your dog?"

"Oh yeah. She is out in the car."

"Is she house broken?"

"Yeah, she lives in the house all the time," I replied.

"Great, why don't you bring her in, we will introduce her to Peanut."

Peanut was a little crossbreed dog with coloring like a beagle and a body like a stretched out Chihuahua. She was a cute little critter who would stand on her hind legs and bark if you told her to beg.

"This isn't your hunting dog is it?" I asked.

"No, no. They are in the pen out back. Peanut here is useless, but she is part of the family," said Dave.

"Excuse me, I'll go get Peaches out of the car."

"Peaches huh! Is that really her name?" Mr. Wolfgang chuckled.

"Yeah, but believe me it sort of fits her."

Peaches who had once spent three months living undetected in my brother's college dormitory, easily adjusted to new situations.

She trotted calmly up the steps and into the strange house. Peaches wasn't the prettiest beagle that ever lived. She was awfully white across the back. Her ears were small for a beagle and her body was barrel-shaped, making her look fat even though she really wasn't. There was something about her though that everybody seemed to like. She was always friendly without being effusive or pushy and her household manners were impeccable. A hand signal could stop her at an open door while another would allow her to enter. She lay down and stayed when told and she knew enough to get out of the dining room during meals.

"By golly! She is a big beagle," opined Dave.

"You're right," I answered, "She weighs over 30 pounds. Her sire was built just like she is but she is colored just like her dam. The sire was named Buck and he was really a good rabbit hound. Her dam might have been a good rabbit dog but she was hopelessly gun shy."

Claudia was to expropriate Dave's room while Dave and I were to bunk with his younger brother Jimmy. Awake long before the alarm rang, I lay listening to the heavy breathing of my slumbering companions. In the pre-dawn light, I could make out the shadowy images of an archery bow, a school pennant, and a coat rack draped with shirts hanging from the walls. The rumbling of a freight train in the distance grew louder, finally creating a vibrating roar as it passed immediately behind the house. Neither of my roommates stirred as a result of the din, and I contemplated what it must have been like growing up and going to school in this small town; what life in this friendly little family was like, and how differently I might view the world had I been raised here.

In hushed tones, Dave and I chatted as we consumed a huge breakfast of sausage, eggs, toast and coffee while the rest of the family slept. Stuffing shells in hunting jackets, we grabbed our shotguns and slipped quietly out the back door with Peaches trailing close behind. A chilly-damp, gray morning greeted us as we strode toward the kennel. Emerging from two straw-filled, plywood boxes came two yawning beagle faces. Upon seeing the guns under our arms, the pair rapidly extricated themselves and bawled excitedly. The two dogs trotted on stiff legs to investigate their considerably larger canine visitor.

"The whiter hound is named Susie and the darker one is Janie," Dave commented. "Susie is seven or eight and Janie *is* about three."

My beagle, Peaches, rabbit dog extraordinaire.

"We may as well hunt directly from the house," suggested Dave. "I often find a few rabbits in the honeysuckle that grows along the railroad tracks."

Dew dislodged from the honeysuckle and grass, beaded up on my freshly Sno-sealed boots and my pant cuffs were quickly drenched. Russian thistle scrapped loudly against my duck cloth jacket as I weaved my way through the cover. Not knowing each other very well, our dogs hunted separately, with Susie and Janie on one side of the tracks and Peaches investigating the brush on the other side. Suddenly, Janie let out a bawl from deep within a thicket and Susie chimed in right behind her. The chase was on, but it turned out to be a short one. The cottontail made the fatal mistake of charging over the tracks as it escaped the dogs. Dave rolled it over.

Despite our early success, rabbits proved hard to find that morning, so we left the tracks and hunted a grassy hillside covered with small pines. Dave finally jumped another cottontail which he missed as it darted through the trees. Unfortunately, the rascal ran straight for a hole, eliminating the chance for a chase.

"It is getting close to lunch time. What do you say we head back?" asked Dave.

"Sounds like a good idea. It is starting to turn nicer. Maybe the bunnies will want to come out this afternoon and enjoy the sunshine after all this wet weather."

Our ranks swelled by two that afternoon, as Claudia and Jimmy decided to join us. We headed to a rolling hillside covered with young oaks and maples with a few hemlocks in the bottoms. All of my previous rabbit hunting had been in farm country, but Jimmy assured me that there were quite a few rabbits in this part of the forest. We tromped through the fallen leaves, enjoying the now bright winter sun. Once again Janie was the first to open up. Susie and Janie trailed the bunny into a little opening in the forest with a light ground cover of green briar. Peaches wanted nothing to do with the trail, apparently not comfortable enough with the strange hounds to hunt side by side with them. Susie and Janie worked back and forth through the thicket constantly giving tongue, but it gradually became obvious that the rabbit had long since departed. I wondered why they didn't cast out and try to pick up the trail where the rabbit left the thicket. Apparently Peaches was wondering the same thing because she wandered downhill about fifty yards and let out a yip.

"There we go! Peaches has got 'em," I shouted. "I'm not sure where this rabbit really started, so I'm going to stay close to Peaches. Jimmy, why don't you and Dave find some open areas and stay put. Maybe Peaches will push the rabbit past you."

Peaches took off at a dead run, yipping maniacally, and I knew she wasn't far behind the bunny. The sounds of her yips rang through the forest, further and further away until they could barely be heard in the distance. I couldn't possibly stay with her so I waited about half way between her and the other guys. Suddenly her barking stopped. Perhaps the rabbit had holed up, but it was more likely that he had pulled one of his tricks and Peaches had overrun the trail. She had to go back and find out where she made her mistake or simply make a wide circle and pick up the trail once again. Several minutes passed.

Finally I heard a yip, followed a few moments later by a second; then a third, fourth and fifth bark in rapid succession. Louder and louder her barks became as the rabbit headed back toward us and home. My eyes scanned the forest floor knowing that the rabbit would come streaking past soon. There he was; a brown blur racing through the trees about thirty yards distant. I had no chance for a shot. He was past me. All I could hope for was that Jimmy or Dave would get a shot. A few moments later Peaches came barreling along the trail still in hot pursuit. I kept waiting to hear a shot, but none ever came. The rabbit holed just before he reached Dave or Jimmy. We had all enjoyed the fine chase so none of us were too disappointed.

We continued hunting along the hillside for another two hours without starting another rabbit. At four o'clock we reached a place where the hillside dropped precipitously.

"I don't think we want to go down there. It is getting pretty late in the day and if we head that way, we won't get back until after dark," warned Dave.

"That's fine with me," I said. "I'm sorry we didn't get a few more bunnies, but I've had a great day."

"Boy, Peaches made a heck of a chase on that one, didn't she," commented Jimmy.

No sooner were the words out of his mouth, than Peaches jumped a cottontail that had been sitting just over the break in the hill, not 10 yards from us. It bolted off with Peaches in high gear behind it, leaving us all in shock.

"It isn't over yet boys," said Claudia.

"Well, we darn sure know where *this* one jumped. Let's spread out and wait," I said.

In a replay of the first chase, Peaches chased the rabbit nearly out of hearing range, lost it for a few minutes, and picked up the trail once more. Her yips grew louder and we knew the rabbit was heading back. Closer and closer Peaches came until she sounded as if she were on top of us. Where was the rabbit? There! Running through the little pines at the edge of the drop-off. I swung through and shot, but I missed. Then I heard a shot from Jimmy's position, followed by a shout, "I missed him."

I was crestfallen. I didn't care that much about not getting the rabbit for myself, but I felt that I had really let old Peachy down. I almost cringed when she came along the trail past me.

"I'm sorry Peachy," I murmured contritely. The shadows were beginning to grow long, but Peaches was no quitter. Ignoring our incompetence, she pushed on, intent on the quarry before her. This time the cottontail ran even farther than the first circle leading Peaches completely out of hearing range for a full ten minutes. I called over to Dave, "I'll bet she's lost it..."

"Wait a minute, I think I hear her. She's bringing him back!" said Dave.

"God! Let's not miss him this time," I answered.

Once again, Peaches' yips told the story. Closer and closer she came, and suddenly there was the rabbit running straight at me. I raised the gun and shot just as the rabbit darted to the right, causing me to miss. Anxious at the thought of blowing my chance once more, my finger tightened imperceptibly on the trigger, causing the gun to go off at the instant the next shell was pumped into the chamber.

Despite the unexpected discharge, I had hit the rabbit with a few pellets. He continued to run, but was off kilter and was running crazily, out of control. I pumped the gun again to push my final shell into the magazine. But click! I had failed to reload after my shot on the first circle! I was kicking myself for my stupidity but then realized that the rabbit was continuing to run directly at me, apparently not seeing me. I lowered myself into a catcher's crouch and extended my hands as if readying myself for a fastball. Ten feet away! Five feet!

Was he really going to run right into my hands? Three feet! Suddenly he realized that something was wrong! He tried frantically to cut to the right. I lunged at him, extending my leg to a near split and pinned his hind foot beneath my heel. I dispatched the hard-running cottontail and left him lying there. He belonged to Peaches.

Dave and Jimmy joined Claudia and me and we told them of the amazing events of the rabbit's capture. Meanwhile Peaches was still yipping her way through the nearly dark forest, unwilling to leave the trail. Finally, she came into view and followed the scent right to the dead rabbit. She pounced upon it and grabbed it by the neck. Fiercely, she swung the rabbit back and forth. We all laughed, as we patted her on the back and told her what a fine dog she was.

As we walked along the old logging road on our way home, the rabbit dangling from my hand, and Peaches trotting contentedly by my side, Dave paid me the ultimate compliment. "Are you planning on breeding that dog?"

My good friend, Mark Frye, taken in September of 1971, while backpacking near Slate Run, Pennsylvania.

Chapter Ten

NEW HORIZONS

March in all of its wretchedness had at last released the earth from its tempestuous grip. Daffodils glowed like dozens of miniature suns on the green carpet of grass. Dogwoods of pink and white joined purple azaleas in decorating the lawn of my mother's suburban home. I sat in the rocker on the flagstone porch enjoying the warmth of the afternoon sun, grateful for the week break from my freshman year classes. Through the screen door, I heard the telephone ring in the foyer.

"Hello," I answered.

"Mitch, you're back. How are you doin'?"

"Fine Mark! What have you been up to? I haven't heard from you since hunting season."

"Not a helluva lot. Say, do you have any plans for the next few days?" he asked.

"Not really, what do you have in mind?"

"Well, my Dad, Henry, and I were going up to Potter County to camp out and do some trout fishing. Want to come along?"

"Hell yeah! It sounds fun. I don't know very much about trout fishing, but I'd love to check it out," I answered.

"Great, we're planning to leave about 10:00 in the morning. Bring your sleeping bag, rod and clothes. We have all the camping gear. See you then."

The Country Squire station wagon was crammed with equipment as we sped up the turnpike on our escape from the city. Driving beyond the suburbs, we passed through fertile farmlands of winter wheat and newly planted corn. Woodlands, initially appearing as isolated patches, gradually expanded into vast forests as we wound our way into the rolling Allegheny Mountains. Only a few leaves were visible on the hardwoods at this elevation, making it seem that our journey had carried us back several weeks in time.

The car slipped between a pair of ancient hemlocks guarding the entrance of a State Forest campground. A soothing melody enveloped the camp, created by the rush and flow of Kettle Creek enveloped the camp. We reached for jackets to ward off the late afternoon chill. "We may get a little frost tonight," said Mr. Frye, as he pulled the venerable, tan canvas tent from the car. Mr. Frye supervised the erection of the tent while Mark established a kitchen on a massive pine picnic table.

"You boys, head over to that brush pile and get some firewood before it gets dark," commanded Mr. Frye. "I'll see if I can get some dinner started."

"OK Dad. What are we having?" asked Henry.

"Camp beans and steak," answered Mr. Frye. Little did I realize that camp beans were a Frye family tradition requiring several hours of preparation. Mr. Frye started by frying a half pound of bacon until it was nearly cooked. He drained off most of the grease and then added two chopped onions which were sauteed until browned. Two cans of Campbell's baked beans, ketchup, mustard, a dash of chili powder and several tablespoons of brown sugar were added to the mixture and the entire concoction was simmered almost into a paste.

The fire had to be tended carefully, before the steaks could go on the grill. Mr. Frye insisted on a two inch thick bed of coals with no remaining flame. I couldn't figure out if the extensive preparations were required to develop the proper flavor, if it was an excuse for Mr. Frye to savor a few bourbons, or if he simply delighted in the anticipation of three ravenous teenagers. Whatever the reason, dinner was extraordinary. The thick T-bones had been seared to perfection; sealing in the juices of the succulent pink meat. The camp beans were like nothing I had ever tasted; sweet, tangy and rich.

As we moaned out our compliments, we were treated to a spectacle on the eastern horizon. The midnight blue sky began to lighten with a pale glow; gradually intensifying into a brilliant white. A colossal full moon of pure silver peaked over the ridge silhouetting the leafless trees at the summit. Inching upward, the immense sphere poured out its light until the entire valley was illuminated.

Up at dawn, a quick breakfast, and into the car; we drove a few miles downstream to start fishing. Mr. Frye, being a dedicated fly fisherman, assembled his split bamboo rod and tied on a nymph. Mark, Henry, and I screwed on our spinning reels and ran hooks through a few night crawlers. While I had minimal experience with trout, I had caught a lot of sunfish when I was a kid, so I decided to use the same tactics. I located an undercut bank that looked promising and I tossed my worm in the dark, swirling water. Almost immediately, I felt a tap on the line and tried to set the hook. Failing to make the connection, I tried once more. This time the trout wasted no time. He slammed the worm as it drifted beneath the bank and hooked himself. Afraid that he would wrap the line around a submerged root, I yanked him quickly out of the water. I dropped to my knees to seize my prize as he flopped about on the mossy earth. He was a beautiful olive black with orange and purple spots.

"That a boy, Mitch!," called Mr. Frye. "That's a nice little brookie you have there."

I was fooled into thinking that the fishing would be easy. Perhaps if I had known how to read the currents it would have been, but all of my previous experience had been in slow creeks, and I was woefully ignorant of mountain streams. After a few hours of fruitless fishing, I tied on a spinner and cast repeatedly as I waded up stream. The gold blade whirred about the shaft as I retrieved the spinner through a shallow riffle at the head of a pool. A sudden flash of silver was followed by a powerful strike. The trout used the swift current as its ally in a bid for escape, but I "horsed" the twelve incher into the gravel bank. This was a different sort of fish than the first and I couldn't identify him. I hooked my finger behind a gill and set off in search of Mr. Frye.

"Mr. Frye, look at this," I called excitedly. "What kind of trout is it?"

Placing his rod beneath his arm Mr. Frye stepped carefully from the water. "That's a brown trout. See those large brown spots on him. His sides are more silver colored than the brookies which are the only other trout in this stream," he explained.

I excitedly told Mr. Frye about catching him, and then I asked, "How are you doing?"

"I suppose I've caught about 15, but I just kept these," he responded as he opened his wicker creel. Resting on a bed of ferns were four deep bodied, dark olive colored brook trout, all about 14 inches long.

"Wow, they're beautiful," I enthused. "And you caught them all on flies?"

"Once you learn how to use flies, you'll find out that it is one of the most effective ways to fish," he explained. "After all, insects make up a trout's primary diet".

I was convinced that he was right but I wasn't convinced that I could ever master such a complicated art. For the moment, I was proud that I had caught a pair of trout on my first day out and that I had done as well as Mark and Henry.

After a scrumptious dinner of fried trout, salad and home fried potatoes, Mark suggested a drive to look for deer. Dirt roads transected the entire state forest and Mr. Frye seemed to know all of them. Up and down the hollows we drove. Dozens of white tailed deer, in small groups of twos and three, trotted across the roads in front of us, often freezing in the glare of the headlights and giving us an extra close view. Regardless of how far we drove into the forest, we continued to come upon small houses.

"Do people really live way up here?" I questioned. "Maybe a few of these places are occupied year round," answered Mr. Frye, "but most of them are deer hunting cabins. The state owns the land, but they give these clubs 99 year leases. Memberships are passed down for generations."

"There are lights on in a few of them," I commented.

"Those are probably some of the guys up for the week-end to go trout fishing."

"Hey Dad, on the way home, let's drive out through Slate Run," suggested Mark. "I want to show Mitch where Chris and I went backpacking last summer."

"Sure, then he will get to see one of the finest trout streams in the state where you two guys almost starved to death because you couldn't catch any fish," teased Mr. Frye. "It is a fly fishing only stream," rebutted Mark.

"That's no excuse," said Mr. Frye, "I've been after you to put down that spinning rod and start learning to fly fish. Maybe you should have broken down and accepted a few lessons."

From the high bluff overlooking the watershed, not a single sign of civilization could be detected. Thousands of acres of uninterrupted hardwood forests blanketed steep slopes and rounded mountaintops. Deep runs carved ravines through the ancient hills on their journey to join Slate Run. Far below us, the creek appeared as a black and white ribbon formed by the dark pools and frothy riffles.

"Mitch, why don't you and I come up here this summer and backpack the entire watershed," suggested Mark. "I've learned my lesson though. We'll bring plenty of food this time."

"That sounds like fun, but I'll have to get a back pack first."
"I'll help you pick one out when we get home," he offered.

School and summer jobs prevented our return until just after Labor Day. Trout season had just ended and hunting season hadn't begun so the valley was deserted. We pitched our blue nylon fly tent on a flat slab of slate located a short distance from the road. We fell asleep quickly in our warm sleeping bags, but we became increasingly restless as our hips became sore from sleeping on the hard rock. We were unaware of the availability of foam sleeping pads, but at least the weather was warm enough that we didn't freeze as a result of our ignorance.

The morning dawned clear, and we anxiously repacked our gear and headed up the trail. The path switched back regularly as we climbed the ridge. The weight of a pack was unexpected, but my young legs soon became accustomed to the new load. We were prevented from glimpsing a view of the valley, until reaching a gap in the forest canopy created by miniature burned patch. We shed our burdens, and sank wearily to earth. From our aerie, we could view an endless blanket of lush, summer green veiled in humid haze. The mid-morning sun had climbed above the distant ridge, adding warmth to the vibrant wilderness. Relieved to have the climb behind us, we hiked the rolling ridge spine at a leisurely pace. Happily alone and totally self sufficient with our camp and food packed neatly on our backs, we reveled in our total freedom from responsibilities or commitments.

By mid-afternoon, we reached the top of Red Run where the trail headed back toward Slate Run. Hot spots on my heels and toes were aggravated into full-blown blisters by the descent on the steep, rock-strewn path. A leafy, flat site surrounded by several huge boulders resting in shadows of broad-leafed oaks provided an ideal camp at the mouth of Red Run. Our tent pitched, I suggested a stroll down to the stream. Clear water rushed over the rocks in a picturesque waterfall and dropped into a pool about four foot deep. We moaned in ecstasy as our hot feet slipped into the icy water.

Mark leaned forward on his, rock perch, squinted his eyes, and exclaimed, "Man!, Look at all of those trout".

"Oh, I hadn't even seen them. There must be twenty of them," I responded excitedly.

"Yeah, and there are some nice fish too. It is hard believe that the fishing season has just ended and there still so many trout. All of the streams around home are put and take. There aren't any fish in those streams by mid-June, not to mention mid-September."

"The fly fishing only regulations must really make a difference though," I said, "because there aren't this many fish left in *Kettle* Creek by this time of year. Are there?"

"Definitely not," answered Mark.

"Mark, you and I ought to start learning to fly fish. I want to give this stream a try next year."

Classes resumed two days after our return. I had a new roommate during my sophomore year, and as luck would have it he was a fly tier. Don was quite generous with his equipment and gave me free access to his tying bench as well as lessons on technique. My first lesson was a brown bivisible because it was such a simple fly; lacking a body or divided wings. The bivisible, nonetheless, demonstrated the concept of curling a rooster feather around a hook shank to produce hackle. We advanced to March Brown nymphs to learn bodies and ribbing. From there, we progressed onto wet Gordons as an introduction to wings: Eventually we tackled the Adams dry fly to work on divided, upright wings.

My initial efforts were laughable, completely out of proportion with wings and tails too long, bodies too fat, or the head obliterating the eye of the hook. Persistence paid off, however, and by spring I was creating flies that at least resembled the ones pictured in the tying manuals. I anxiously awaited the upcoming trout season and wondered if my creations would fool the well-educated denizens of Slate Run.

The late April afternoon was unseasonably warm as I hustled away from my Friday afternoon Biology lab. The tent, sleeping bag, and fishing gear were already tucked under the hood of my little Volkswagon, and I raced off to pick up Mark. Our journey continued until midnight when we finally reached the dirt road above Slate Run. Exhausted, we tossed our sleeping bags and pads on a leafy bench of the steep hill and slept beneath the stars.

A year had elapsed since the mayflies had hatched from eggs. The nymph's flattened bodies allowed them to cling to rocks, in the quick currents of the stream. They had thrived in the oxygen-rich water and had grown robust on their streambed diet of algae and detritus. The first warm flush of Sping was the signal that they had awaited to begin their ephemeral adulthood. Detached from the safety of the rocks, they were tossed in the currents as they struggled to the surface. The nymphs split their exoskeletons at the thorax, and wriggled free as winged adults. Trout, their own metabolisms accelerated by the warming water, hungrily attacked the emerging mayflies.

The mayflies' strategy was to escape the water in mass. The trout could not possibly consume them all. The survivors flew to streamside vegetation and rested. In late afternoon, immense swarms of the lacey winged adults formed above the water in a frenzied orgy. The mated females once more risked their lives by returning to the pools. Thousands were consumed by splashing, leaping trout as the mayflies hovered above the water or landed on the surface. As before, the insects' survival lay in their synchronous mass assault. Each female that survived long enough to lower her ovipositor into the water deposited hundreds of eggs that tumbled to the streambed below. The survival of the future generation was assured.

Born with only vestigal mouthparts, the adults were unable to feed. Their mission complete, they fluttered dying back to the stream. Even in death they performed one final role by satiating the ravenous trout and thereby providing cover for their sisters who had yet to run the picscene gauntlet.

Such a spectacle was the stuff of fly fisherman's dreams. Each pool was alive with splashing, feeding trout. Unfortunately, my casting skills were rudimentary at best. Even in the forgiving, high water conditions, I repeatedly frightened the trout. Fish stopped feeding for several minutes each time my line slapped down on the water. All too often, I snagged my fly on an overhanging branch, and the trout would dart for their rocky refuges as I trudged through the pool to untangle myself. Mark was faring no better and our frustration mounted as the fishless day wore on.

By evening, I had fished upstream for several miles and found myself at the same pool where Mark and I had discovered the trout last fall. The activity in the pool was absolutely frenzied. The mayflies were returning in droves to lay their eggs and the trout were taking full advantage of it. By this time, I was able to lay my line out well enough to avoid spooking the trout, and on my third cast I got a splashing strike. I jerked up on the rod, but I missed him. Encouraged, I cast again. A strike! But the same result. Again and again I enticed the trout into striking, but I remained entirely inept at hooking them.

Mark had resigned in frustration, and he now sat on the bank chortling in his amusement at each missed fish. I refused to admit defeat, and I continued flailing and failing. I hadn't noticed the stranger who had fished upstream behind me and now stood quietly observing my tribulations.

"Hello," Mark chimed out.

I turned my head to see a long-haired chap four or five years older than myself.

"Howdy," he replied. "How are you fellows doing this evening?"

"Not too good," I blurted out. "I just started fly fishing and I can get the rascals to strike, but I'll be darned if I can catch them."

After a long pause, the stranger quietly asked, "Would you like me to give you a few pointers?"

"Absolutely. I need all the help I can get."

He slipped into the water at the tail of the pool and told me to stand to his left. "OK," he began, "the first thing that we want to do is figure out where the fish are."

"They're all over the place," I said.

"Not exactly, each fish is in his own feeding position in the current.

He doesn't go roaming around looking for food; he finds a good spot where the food will come to him. See that trout there? Now keep watching that spot. OK there! He just took another mayfly. There are at least eight trout actively feeding in this pool right now. I am going to cast to the closest one first. That way I won't lay my line on top of a feeding fish and drive him down."

My new friend stripped line of his reel and began to gracefully false cast until the fly was passing directly over the targeted fish. "I don't want to put the fly at exactly the place where we have seen him rise," he explained. "When a trout sees an insect floating above him, he will drift downstream with it for a few feet before striking. Then he will return to his feeding station. So, what I want to do is place my fly about six to ten feet in front of where I see his splashes."

The line released from his hand as his rod came forward. The line rolled out on the water, barely creating a ripple. The fly floated down last, delicately, lighting on the water just like a live insect. "The fly will float back toward us in the current," he continued. "I must strip in line with my left hand to prevent getting slack in the line. You weren't doing this and that was part of your problem in hooking fish."

"Aha! Well that makes sense," I exclaimed.

"Another thing. It is very important that the fly have a natural float. Watch this. The line is about to move into the quicker current but the fly is still in quiet water." The fly began to skate across the surface. "A trout will almost never hit a fly when it does that, and it can spook them. The best thing to do then is pick up and cast again."

Once again, my friend laid a perfect cast on the water. The Light Cahill floated buoyantly on the pool. Splash! It was gone. The rod bowed and we had a hook up. He allowed the fish to run, and then gradually worked him in. Again the fish ran and my friend allowed him to go; enjoying the fight. The fish tired rapidly and the 10 inch brook trout drifted into the open hand of my companion.

"I'm going to release this fish, so I don't want to touch him with a dry hand," he instructed. "If you disrupt the slime layer on a trout, he can lose his protection against bacteria. He might look fine when he swims away, but he could easily die a few days later."

He grasped his tiny fly between his fingers, reached into his vest, and retrieved a tiny jar. He then daubed the fly in some sticky looking jelly.

"What is that for?" I inquired.

"Once a fly has caught a trout, it will have his slime all over it and it won't float very well," he explained. "This is a silicone fly dressing that will keep the fly afloat. I do this after every fish."

He scanned the pool looking for his next target. "That looks like a bigger fish feeding over there. I don't want to cast to him from here though because I would have to cast over the quick current going past that boulder. I wouldn't be able to get a realistic float. Being in the right position is real important."

We stepped quietly toward the far bank and found the proper position. On the third cast, the trout exploded beneath the fly and my friend hooked him. While he was playing the hard fighting brown, he asked, "Did you see how I hooked that fish? I didn't yank the rod up or I would have snatched the fly out of his mouth. Instead, I pulled down with my line hand and then simply raised the rod."

"Are you ready to give it a try?" he asked.

"I sure am," I responded eagerly. "For the first time I at least know what I'm trying to do."

"Would you like to try my rod?" he offered.

"If you don't mind." I took the delicate four weight rod in my hand. It felt like a feather compared to my big combination fly/spinning rod. Several minutes of experimentation were required before I developed a rhythm to my casts. A trout rose about 30 feet in front of me and I attempted to lay the fly in front of him. My accuracy left a lot to be desired though and my fly landed at least 10 feet to the left. I tried again and got a little closer. On the third try, the fly landed perfectly and I was rewarded with a splashing strike. I missed him.

"That's okay," my friend reassured me: "You still had a little too much slack in the line, but you're getting the idea. Just try to strip in a little faster."

During the next fifteen minutes, I managed to entice two more fish to strike, but I was a little slow and did not hook either. The fish were starting to be spooked by my errant casts, so I passed the rod back to my coach. "I don't want to take up any more of your fishing time," I said. "I can't tell you how much I appreciate the lesson." We shook hands and he wished me good luck before he departed.

Mark and I rested the pool for a few minutes, and before long the trout resumed feeding. Once more I waded in, hoping to catch one fish before dark. The line formed long loops as I back cast. I lay my fly on the water just where I wanted it. There was a splash. In my excitement, I yanked the rod skyward, and a little six-inch brook trout came hurtling out of the water and flew over my right shoulder. He flopped on the rocks behind me. I scrambled out of the pool to pounce on my first fly-caught trout. I slipped on an algae-covered rock and fell, knocking my reel completely off the rod. By this time, it didn't matter because the trout had thrown the hook and was flopping back toward the water. Amidst howls of laughter from Mark, I threw the rod down and dived to the ground attempting to pin him. At long last, I got my hands on the poor creature.

Mark was nearly apoplectic by this time.

"Now that's what I call playing a fish," I laughed.

We climbed up to the dirt road and began the walk back to camp in the dark. My thoughts were of the people who had opened my eyes to this wonderful place and this fascinating sport: Mr. Frye, Mark, Don, and my friend. Damn! I hadn't asked his name.

Again, my good friend, Mark Frye.

Chapter Eleven

BUDDIES

Blisters, mosquitoes, wet sleeping bags, freezing sleepless nights, no-see-ums, hunger, wrenched knees, frostbitten fingers, exhaustion, leaky tents, hooked ears, deer flies, thirst, three-day downpours, frozen boots, poison ivy, sun burn, twisted ankles, and yellow jackets are just part of the cost of the outdoor life. Surviving these travails can be remarkably easy or miserably difficult depending on one's companion.

The same friends who make perfectly wonderful dinner guests or tennis partners, may metamorphosize into grumbling whiners when caught in a early spring snow storm. The true horror of such dilemmas comes with the realization that the companion cannot be escaped. Every moment for the remainder of the trip will be spent listening to a litany of woes from the unhappy camper. Friends are best enjoyed within the confines of civilization and preferably in small doses. What is needed when clamoring up a mountain in 90 degree temperatures with a fifty pound pack is not a friend but a buddy. Let me tell you what a buddy is......

After an intense, touch-and-go battle, the cantankerous, single-burner, gasoline stove was finally lit. Hungrily, we unwrapped the big T-bone steak and flopped it into the fry pan. Tomorrow was opening day of deer, archery season and we had arrived at camp in total darkness. Quick nourishment was all we required before crashing into a short night's sleep.

Unfortunately however, our stove problems were not rectified, and the entire apparatus burst into flames. Mark chortled a curse as he deftly rescued the steaks and booted the stove. End over end, the stove bounced through camp in a ball of fire before eventually extinguishing itself in a cloud of dust.

Mark carefully inspected the meat and declared, "I think it is done enough."

"Mark!" I admonished, "that steak isn't even browned."

"Well so what, let's just eat it anyway. I'm hungry."

"At least it is dark and we won't have to look at it," I laughed. "What the hell, I'll eat it if you will."

With trepidation, we sliced the raw flesh. Forks poised, we stared each other in the eye, daring the other to go first. Breaking the impasse, Mark let out a blood-curdling roar and plunged a slice into his mouth. I broke into laughter and followed his example.

During the Spring of my junior year in college, Mark and I regularly drove my diminutive Fiat to upstate Pennsylvania for weekends of trout fishing. I kept most of our essentials for camping stowed under the trunk hood, so when I picked up Mark all that he needed to do was throw together his personal gear and we were off. Nonetheless, Mark was blatantly cavalier about packing; usually spending less than five minutes on the chore. He simply defied something as trivial as forgotten equipment to ruin his good time. In fact, I suspected that he intentionally overlooked items just to challenge himself. I therefore took no pity on him and would break into laughter at the familiar words, "Uh, oh, I forgot something."

One cool evening in early May, Mark and I and my beagle Peaches sped west on Interstate 80. "Uh,oh I forgot something."

"No kidding," I responded.

"No, no. This is something that you're never supposed to forget on a camping trip."

Now he had my interest piqued. "What is it, your fishing rod?"

"No."

"Your waders?"

"No, much worse than that."

"Well what then," I asked just dying to hear the punch line. "My sleeping bag," he muttered abjectly.

I nearly drove off the road in my hysteria. Now this was rich. We were three hours from home; it was 10:00 at night and all the stores were closed, supposing we even had any money. I questioned whether even Mark could maintain his good nature under circumstances this dire.

"Do you want to go home? We can go fishing next weekend."

"Nah, I'll think of something."

We finally arrived at Slate Run and made our way slowly up the dirt road to our streamside camping spot. I laid out my foam pad and sleeping bag preparing for a restful night beneath the stars. "Well, what have you come up with?" I asked.

"Can I borrow some clothes?" Mark pulled on enough of my extra pants, shirts, and sweaters until he resembled an overstuffed sofa. Gingerly, he lowered himself into the reclined, front seat of the car. "Take the rest of the clothes and sort of dump them out on me. Would you?"

For a moment, he lay in silence, then let out a plaintive call "Here, Peaches. Come here, Peachey." The little hound trotted to the open car door and cocked her head at the spectacle in the front seat. "Come here, Peachey," pleaded Mark as he patted his chest. Peaches, being an obliging beast, climbed on top of him, turned around three times, curled up and went to sleep. Watching this scene, I couldn't help laughing. Mark neither laughed with me nor begrudged me my good time. He simply and quietly said, "Please shut the door. Good night."

A few months later, Mark and I were backpacking. For two days, the ridges of the Allegheny Mountains had successfully stalled every passing cloud causing them to dump buckets of rain. Everything – backpacks, tents, foam pads and sleeping bags – were wringing wet. Mark stood grinning with rain dripping off the brim of his baseball cap. "I'd say this camp is getting a little soggy. Wouldn't you? We're out here to hike so by God let's go hiking. We can't get any wetter and I'm tired of trying to wait this thing out."

I crammed the clammy nylon tent and sleeping bag into my pack, and we headed down the Black Forest Trail. Great drops splattered audibly on the broad lush leaves of summer. Our steps were cushioned by soft mud and spongy moss. Overhead, warblers flitted through the tree canopy in pursuit of insects or in search of a drier perch. A porcupine crossed the trail before us and we charged after it. The plump little creature waddled at top speed but we quickly overtook him. Slipping on wet grass, I nearly fell on top of the prickly, little beast. Mark gasped at my impending ventilation, then sighed in relief as the porky offered a reprieve by not swatting me with his multi-quilled tail. With heaving sides, the porcupine escaped our attentions by climbing a sapling for refuge, so we continued our hike through the verdant, sopping forest.

Through the cloudy, afternoon gloom, a cabin appeared in a grove of hemlocks. "Do you *see* what I see?" I asked.

"All right!" Mark yelled. "A porch!"

The cabin was a simple log structure built as a deer hunting camp. Typical of most such cabins, it was unused for most of the year. A wide porch with a tongue and grooved floor offered a perfect refuge. We trudged up the steps and propped our packs against the railing.

"I'm getting a little cold. I'll make some hot chocolate," I volunteered.

"Good. I'm going to rig some clothes lines to see if we can dry out some of this stuff."

"We aren't ever going to warm up in these wet clothes," I said. "These fiberfill sleeping bags are supposed to be pretty warm even when wet. Maybe if we strip down and get into them we would be warmer, and our body heat might even dry the bags out."

We stretched the wet bags out on the floor and arranged our stove and food between them so we could cook in "bed". Mark and I stood naked on the porch shivering, hesitating to make the plunge into the soaked bags. "Ahhhh God! Is this thing clammy," I cried as I laid the bag open.

"May as well get it over with," said Mark. "Let's do it at the same time." We sat on the cold, wooden floor and simultaneously scooted in. Our screams penetrated the silence of the forest.

Times change and things change. Mark eventually moved to Laramie, Wyoming, to attend the University, and I went on to graduate school in Auburn, Alabama. We occasionally saw one another when we returned home at Christmas, but we missed getting out together. When Mark called early one spring and suggested that I come out to join him and his Dad on a mule deer hunt the following fall, I accepted in an instant. I applied for my license and anxiously checked the mail each day. Fortunately, I did draw the license. Unfortunately, I received it in the hospital two days after a complete knee reconstruction.

I shared the good news with my surgeon wondering what his response would be. As I suspected, he cautioned that my knee would not be strong enough by October. I vowed that he was wrong and that I damn sure would be ready.

Six weeks in a full leg cast and ten total weeks on crutches left my leg a pathetic, spindly thing by mid-July. Every afternoon on the way home from work, I stopped at the weight room and sweated through my rehabilitation exercises. Withered muscles slowly gained strength and although my repaired, taut ligaments prevented me from entirely straightening my leg, I felt strong enough to chance the trip west. Stepping off the plane, I immediately spotted Mark and Hank leaning against a newspaper machine in the terminal. Mark had adopted the standard Wyoming attire of a white Stetson, blue jeans and a red and black mackinaw, but otherwise looked unchanged. Hank was considerably grayer around the temples than I remembered, but otherwise looked good. We shook hands heartily, elated to be together once more.

"Looks like you have some blood on your hands Hank. What have you been up to?" I asked.

"We just came in. Mark and I both shot nice antelope this morning."

I peered through the grimy tailgate window of Mark's decrepit, Plymouth station wagon to view the morning's game. They were indeed nice antelope, both with horns slightly more than 13 inches. As we butchered the antelope in Mark's garage, Hank related their hunt.

"Mark had spotted several bands of antelope about 20 miles outside of town. We wanted to get to them first thing in the morning, so we carried bedrolls out into the sage brush last night. The wind blew a little but we had a good night sleeping under the stars and listening to the coyotes. At dawn, we woke up and started walking. There were antelope everywhere, and we passed up a half dozen bucks before I shot this one. Mark picked his buck from a herd of about 30 animals."

We repacked the station wagon, stopped off for groceries and headed out for our mule deer hunt. The area Mark had selected for us was a rolling stretch of sagebrush interrupted with patches of brilliant yellow aspens. In fading light, we pitched our blue nylon tent beneath a large juniper, organized our gear, and set up our kitchen. Finally, with bourbon in hand, we stretched our legs in front of the camp fire and watched the antelope steaks sizzle.

Long into the night we talked of family and hunting and dogs; of our lives since we'd last been together.

"I'm going to take Dad into the canyon at first light. Will you be okay on your own? I mean will your knee hold up?"

"I think so. I'll take it easy for a while and see how it feels. You two go ahead. I'll hunt over to the west for a few hours. Maybe we can meet back here at 10:30 or 11:00 to eat a late breakfast."

Clear and cool, but not freezing weather made for a perfect morning's hunt. While I didn't see any bucks, I caught sight of a coyote and a half dozen does. The does seemed gigantic compared to the white tails back in Alabama. Repeatedly, I reached for my binoculars to identify song birds which were new to me. Clark's nutcracker, pinyon jays and red breasted nuthatches became new additions to my life list of birds. Most importantly, my knee felt surprisingly strong and with each step, I grew more confident that my hunt would be unhampered.

The still dawn gave way to a brisk wind, so I made my way back to camp. Hank and Mark had a pot of coffee ready and sausage in the skillet when I returned. When Hank crawled into the tent to retrieve some gear, Mark whispered to me, "Boy, Dad is really in bad shape. We weren't hunting that hard and he was gasping for breath out there. Too damned many cigarettes! I hope he doesn't have a heart attack or something."

"Hmmm, that's bad. My knee is going to be fine so you don't have to worry about me. Just stay with your Dad and take it easy. Maybe you can find a good place where you can glass a lot."

We continued to spot does in the area for the next two days, but had only seen one buck. At lunch on the third day, Mark commented, "I think I might have made a poor choice on this spot. I'll bet the bucks are still up high in the mountains. I think we should move up toward the Continental Divide tomorrow."

"Sounds good to me," I answered. "But what should we do this afternoon?"

"I've got an idea," said Hank. "Let's put on a little drive. Why don't I slip up to the head of that draw down there and you fellows work your way up from the bottom. Maybe we can catch a buck sneaking out."

Mark and I remained in camp nursing an extra cup of coffee in order to give Hank time to get into position. "How is your Dad doing?" I asked.

"A little better, but not great. You know this seems strange to be worrying about the old man. All my life he has been watching out for me and now all of a sudden, the shoe is on the other foot."

"He'll be all right. We just have to be certain that he doesn't over do it. Maybe we can get him a deer this afternoon and he can take it easy for the rest of the trip."

Beaver dams were profusely scattered every 100 yards or so along the draw as Mark and I stalked through the magnificently hued aspen thickets. Deer sign was plentiful and we both hoped to hear the roar of Hank's .300 mag. The draw turned out to be steeper and much longer than we anticipated, but we pressed on for more than a mile. Finally, we reached the head where the aspen gave way to sagebrush. To our surprise, Hank was nowhere to be seen.

"This is strange," said Mark in a worried tone. "I wonder where he could be." Mark raised his rifle and fired. We waited listening intently for an answering shot but none came.

"I bet he figured that he was in the wrong draw because it took us so long to get here. He probably went back to camp."

"Maybe. Let's get back there and make sure."

We hustled toward camp firing shots every ten minutes. At dusk we trotted into an empty camp. "Oh, man!" lamented Mark. "I have a real bad feeling about this."

Until this point, I suspected that Mark was worrying about nothing, but upon finding the empty camp, I too became concerned. "Let's leave a note on the windshield in case he returns while we are looking for him. We'll tell him to shoot a few rounds."

"Good idea," responded Mark. "We better try to retrace his route. Look sharp for him. I hate to say it but he could be down somewhere."

"We'll find him," I answered sounding more certain than I felt at the moment.

In the fading light, we scrambled up the hill in search. My leg was exhausted from the long day's hike but I barely thought of it. I kept wondering what could I say to my best friend if we found his father dead. Dusk gave way to darkness and our search became more frantic. We zigzagged through the sage brush convinced by now that we were looking for a fallen man. We shouted his name in vain.

Suddenly, Mark stopped me. "Listen! Listen!" In the distance we could make out the faint honking of a car horn. "Thank God! He's Okay," sighed Mark. I wrapped my arm over his shoulder. "I'm glad it turned out this way Buddy, but if it hadn't I sure would have wanted to be the one who was with you."

Epilogue: As it turned out the bucks were at higher elevation and we all took bucks two days later. Hank may not have been in very good shape, but he was still the most skillful hunter among us. He ended up shooting the largest buck of the trip – a big three pointer.

The author with an Alabama white-tailed buck shot in 1977.

Chapter Twelve

ALABAMA WHITETAILS

Stereotypes, many of them contradictory, represented the sum total of my knowledge of the South. Southerners were still fighting the Civil War; hated Yankees; called black people "niggers"; and considered Country music stars to be gods. On the other hand, Southerners were genteel, friendly, possessed impeccable manners and were outstanding sportsmen.

Those stereotypes got loaded into the U-Haul truck right along with the furniture and clothing as we prepared to move to Alabama in September of 1976. Attending graduate school at Auburn University presented a real opportunity to jumpstart my career, and we looked forward to escaping the endless Philadelphia suburbs. We nonetheless viewed the Deep South as kin to a foreign country.

In the sweltering July heat, I made my first trip to Alabama in search of living quarters. I looked up a friend of a friend of a friend. These virtual strangers invited me into their home for two days, fed me and helped me locate a house to live in. This ultimate gesture of southern hospitality confirmed one stereotype, and my host's assurance that the house I was looking at "Never had a nigger in it" confirmed another.

The old farmhouse, eleven miles outside of Auburn, was unlike any home I'd ever been in. The tin roofed structure had been constructed in 1908, prior to the advent of air conditioning. It was designed to be as cool as possible in the torrid Alabama summers. Situated in a grove of pecan trees on the crest of a hill, the house caught every stray breeze. Air even flowed beneath the house that rested on a dozen stone pilings. Twelve foot tall ceilings allowed heat to rise. An extensive porch guarded the 6 foot tall windows on the east and north faces. To prevent direct afternoon sun, only three windows faced west and none at all were on the south side.

A relatively modern kitchen and a bathroom had been added to the house which otherwise remained rather primitive. The interior walls, floors and ceilings were built of rough-hewn planks. Heat was supplied by two fireplaces, a wood heater and propane space heaters. There was no insulation and the window screens were simply tacked into place.

The landlord, a retired military man, had sponsored a family of Vietnamese after the war and they had been living in the house for two years. They were rural people unused to living in western style homes and through ignorance had mistreated the place badly. Unfamiliar with the use of the fireplaces or the wood heater, they had built fires on pieces of tin on the floors and vented the smoke out the windows. Smoke had stained the walls a grimy black and left a dank, pungent odor throughout. Trash had been left in every crook and nanny.

However, at $125 per month, the price was right and the landlord assured me that the place would be in tiptop shape before we arrived. He promised to paint, insulate the walls and ceiling and install storm windows. I unwisely had passed on his assurances to my wife.

Interstate highways possess a certain sanitized look. The landscape changes with the miles, but the truck stops and tourist traps seem immutable from one side of America to the other. We had driven all night, finally arriving at the Auburn exit off 1-85 at dawn. Only then, did it dawn on us that we had actually arrived in the South. Auburn was an attractive little village of neatly kept homes dominated by the towering, brick university buildings and an even larger football stadium.

Bevies of co-eds, all in dresses and high heels, their hair permed and curled and impeccably made up, strolled between buildings. Not realizing that we were witnessing Sorority rush, my wife panicked. "Is that the way these women go to class?" she sputtered in horror. "I don't have those sorts of clothes. I can't dress that way. I wouldn't even if I could."

Our second episode of culture shock occurred on our drive into the country. An unpainted shack with a tin roof and walls so flimsy that light shown through, was tucked into pinewoods along the road to our house. Laundry was draped over every available bush to dry. Shoeless, black children in raggedy clothes played in the bare dirt yard. The scene could have been from Civil War days. Claudia rolled her eyes and stared in gape-mouthed wonder. We sure as hell weren't in the

Philadelphia suburbs anymore.

Oddly enough, the next house, scarcely a quarter mile up the road, was a perfectly modern brick structure with a well kept lawn and two new cars in the drive way. Like contradictory stereotypes, the juxtaposition of wealth and abject poverty was simply a fact of life throughout rural Alabama.

Our rental house remained exactly as I had seen it six weeks before. That is, it had not been repainted, insulated or had storm windows installed. A look of barely concealed panic spread across Claudia's face as she walked through the filthy, isolated house. At times like those, quality tells, and not a word of recrimination was forthcoming.

The landlord, a six-foot seven-inch retired Air Force major, who I thus far had met only via telephone, drove up to give us the keys. He apologized for the condition of the house, which really didn't help solve our problem. We didn't begin unpacking until he agreed to forgo rent for two months while I painted and cleaned. Alabama winters were as yet a mystery to us, so we had no idea how cold the place would be without insulation.

Our rental house in Waverly, Alabama.

For three days, we unpacked, scoured and cleaned, bought paint and caulk, whacked thigh-high weeds from the front lawn and in general tried to make the place livable. The Major, being a good hearted if less than reliable chap, dropped by on Saturday morning to admire the efforts of his Yankee tenants. He invited us to the Auburn football game followed by dinner at his home. Glad for a respite, we accepted.

There is perhaps nothing as astonishing to a northerner as seeing the spectacle of a college football game in the Deep South. Professional football captures most of the attention in the northeast with scant attention paid most college games. Not so in Alabama. The stadium was packed with 65,000 fans despite the fact the town of Auburn was only home to 20,000 people. Attire at northern games was purely functional – blue jeans and sweaters being the norm. The Alabama crowd, especially the women, were dressed to kill in sun dresses and high heels. The quality of football was unlike anything I had seen up North. In that one game, I saw three future All Pro running backs: James Brooks, Joe Cribbs and William Andrews.

By December, the house was painted and neat although we were beginning to freeze at night. The winter of '76 was fierce with the temperature dipping to 0 degrees one night and no amount of firewood could heat the cavernous house. The fish bowl had two inches of permanent ice, sealing the death warrant for our pathetic little gold fish. The plumbing froze and for two weeks we gathered water from a spring and sponge bathed with water heated on the stove.

We had noticed that the bedroom, bathroom and kitchen had standard eight foot ceilings while the remainder of the house had twelve-foot ceilings. We didn't think much about it until the neighbors rescued us by explaining that the low ceiling rooms were supposed to be winter quarters. By hanging rugs or blankets over the doorways and just heating the winter quarters, it was possible to remain tolerably comfortable. They also suggested we bury the plumbing and be certain to leave the faucets dripping at night to prevent freeze up.

We remained too poor to afford all night heat however and each night we slept beneath a mountain of blankets. First one up raced to the space heater, lit it with a kitchen match and bounded back to the bed where we cuddled until the heat spread. Despite the hardships, we were indescribably happy.

We felt undeniably tied to the land. The weather was more than a topic of conversation. It was part of our lives. When it froze, we hauled more wood. When the rain knocked pecans from the trees we feasted on pecan pie. Hunting now took on meaning beyond recreation. Meat was beyond our meager budget, so each animal slain was protein for our bodies.

The Alabama deer season was legendary, being 60 days long and having an unbelievable limit of a buck per day. Additionally, the state allowed hunters to use hounds to hunt deer, a practice strictly prohibited in the North. A neighbor gave me permission to hunt his 1,100 acres and I was able to hunt the 80 acres where I lived as well. Slipping out the door at dawn with my rifle on my shoulder, I often spotted the tracks of nocturnal deer in the lawn beneath the pecans.

In the uplands, the Alabama woods were similar to Pennsylvania's although there were more Loblolly pines and fewer hardwoods. The bottomlands however were swampier and much denser, filled with green briar and honeysuckle. A diminutive bamboo locally referred to as switch cane (because of the use of the canes to switch naughty children) grew in dense stands along the streams.

I used most of that first hunting season exploring the local woods and locating the bedding and feeding areas as well as the escape cover. Deer were numerous but not easy to come by. It took nearly every weekend and many weekday afternoons of that first season to take two bucks and a doe. The three deer kept us in meat until early summer, but by the following fall, we were getting tired of brown rice and garden-grown squash.

I was hoping to shoot at least four deer in my second season. I had identified five locations for tree stands that looked promising. Two sites were along escape routes that the deer often used when being chased by dogs or other hunters. One site overlooked a small wheat field where the deer fed. Two additional sites were in the swampy woods behind my house that the deer used as a daytime refuge.

On summer weekends, I strapped lumber, a hammer, a saw and some nails onto a pack frame and trekked into the woods. I selected close-growing trees situated in areas open enough to allow good visibility and clear shooting lanes. Steps were nailed onto the trunks up to a height of about ten feet. Two by fours between the trunks served as supports for the platform. Determined to build stands that were comfortable enough to remain in for long hours, I added seats to each stand.

Preparations and high hopes don't necessarily create success, and I had no way of knowing that the hunting season of 1977 was to become my most frustrating. Things began to go sour before they even started. A thief broke into my house and stole my Model 70 Winchester .30-06. As a poverty stricken student, I barely had money for groceries and tuition much less a new rifle. I considered using my shotgun with slugs, but the thief had also made off with the slug barrel for my shotgun. My experience in forcing a slug through a modified choke had been woefully unsatisfactory in terms of accuracy.

Emergencies of this magnitude, were tailor made for caring parents. Dad had an old Remington Model 742 pump action rifle in .30-06 that he had not used in years. He gave me the rifle just before the season started. The rapidfire capability of the pump could prove handy in the thick Southern woods, but the trigger creep was simply miserable. From the point at which pressure was applied, to actual firing was a full half inch. Nonetheless, I was lucky to have any rifle at all.

When the season opened on November 20th, the weather was still warm. Deer weren't moving much and I saw only a few does during the first three days of hunting. On Thanksgiving morning, I hiked through the dark to one of my escape route stands. Hunters, building appetites for the afternoon feast, might push a deer past me. Dawn broke sunny and clear and the temperature surged toward 70. Squirrels hopped lazily through the oak leaves for an hour or so and then retired to their dens for a nap.

Hours ticked by without catching a glimpse of a deer and I became bored. I climbed from my tree and began hiking across the pasture toward the car. Without warning, three does and a fork horn buck erupted from a wooded fence line. Nearly running over me, they charged across the open pasture. I threw the gun to my shoulder, but the buck was so close that I could not locate him in my four power scope. Frantically I waved the rifle around and finally found him.

By this time he was running dead away from me offering only a shot at his fanny. All composure gone, I blazed away missing each time. In retrospect, I'm certain that all my shots were high. I found one single drop of blood but despite a half hour search on hands and knees, I saw no more. I suspect that I punched a hole through his ear and did no lasting harm.

The scope I decided was more hindrance than help, and I removed it that afternoon. The next dozen days of hunting produced not a single glimpse of a buck although I saw does nearly every trip afield. The weather turned cold and the leaves fell from the trees. Before classes, after classes, Saturdays and Sundays, I returned to the woods grimly determined to provide meat for the freezer. I began to wonder if buck deer existed at all or were figments of my imagination. My miss loomed ever larger and I castigated myself unmercifully.

At last just before Christmas, my chance came. Heavy frost glowed like silver on the limbs and brush as dawn broke. I had abandoned my stands and was sitting at the edge of the forest overlooking an overgrown pasture. As the sun peaked over the horizon, a herd of eight does daintily picked their way through a series of briar patches about 125 yards distant. I strained my eyes hoping to spot antlers where none existed. No sooner had the does disappeared than I heard a strange grunting noise. A few seconds later, the sound came again and then again. A six point buck drifted into view and I realized that I was hearing the tending grunt of a buck following does. I had read about deer vocalizations but had never actually heard it before.

I raised the rifle, now cursing myself for removing the scope. The buck was completely unaware of my presence. I aimed carefully, felt the trigger creep and the rifle fire. The buck raced away and I fired two more shots. I had missed again! A wave of despair rose from my heart to my throat. How could it have happened? All those days waiting for just this moment, only to blow my opportunity. I felt sick to my stomach as I walked home. I had no confidence left that I could ever again kill a deer.

I reinstalled the scope the following day. Christmas came and went and I hunted on day after day, but the gods of good fortune had forsaken me. The rut was in full swing and I wandered the woods searching for scrapes where the bucks announced their presence to the does. I located several scrapes and waited by them for days on end with no luck. The weather worsened and I came down with the flu, but still I hunted, determined to break this string of bad luck and restore my confidence.

One week of the season was all that remained. After class, I mechanically gathered up my rifle and headed toward one of my swamp tree stands. A chill overcast had settled over the countryside, offering not a hint of breeze. The woods were eerily quiet. Even the sparrows and chickadees seemed determined to travel in silence so as not to disturb a slumbering world.

Dusk crept up slowly in the already dreary afternoon. Hope hung by a slender thread, but was instantaneously renewed when a doe appeared slipping beneath the pines. Out of nowhere an eight point buck raced into view, pranced around the doe for a few seconds and raced out of sight as quickly as he had appeared. The doe, which was surely in estrus, continued walking toward me. Again the highly agitated buck appeared and disappeared. The doe continued on and was at last standing less than twenty yards from my tree. With the gun to my shoulder I waited. My breathing became ragged and my stomach felt as if it were being tied in knots. The buck ran into sight and stood directly behind the doe. My nervous system was about to overload. I had to shoot, but thoughts of missing flooded into my brain. I struggled to place my shot carefully, but I knew I was about to choke. The trigger crept and crept and at last the rifle roared.

With blinding speed, the buck raced away before I could fire again. I climbed from the tree literally shivering all over. I was close to vomiting. I found the place he had been standing when I shot. Halleluiah! Blood! Just a splash, but definitely blood. I followed for a few hundred yards, but no deer. By now it was nearly dark. I had no choice but to return home and wait until morning. I desperately hoped it would not rain and wipe out the trail. I NEEDED to find this deer.

My case of nerves never completely departed throughout the night and I slept fitfully. Awake before dawn, I ate a big breakfast and was back at the stand by daybreak. Fortunately no rain fell and I quickly picked up the trail. The buck had run beneath a power line and had circled back into the swamp. There was an ample amount of blood but not a copious amount and I was still unsure of where he was hit. I had hopes that he had run a short way and had laid down and stiffened up.

Less than 250 yards from where the trail began, I found where the buck had bedded. Blood was fresh and wet. He obviously had survived the night and was once again on the move. The blood on the bushes was no higher than two feet off the ground and I suspected that he was hit high in the front leg. The buck was now aware that he was being tracked and had started to run. The blood trail became fainter as the morning wore on and I was forced to crawl from one drop to the next. At 11:00 the blood trail ran out and no amount of searching could relocate it.

Morosely, I returned to the house. As I sat eating my sandwich, a thought came to me. I had a young beagle by the name of Briar. She was an excellent rabbit dog that had the bad habit of occasionally running deer. Although I normally punished her for chasing deer, I decided that now would be a good time to make an exception. Unless I missed my guess, that buck was hurting enough that he probably had bedded down again once he realized that he wasn't being pursued. In all likelihood he had bedded somewhere in the swamp.

Slowly Briar and I zigzagged through the swamp. After about an hour's search, Briar gave tongue on a trail. She ran straight away, baying for all she was worth, and I was certain that she had jumped a deer and not a rabbit. The question remained however; was it my buck or a different deer. Briar was not one to chase a deer far, as she knew that she wasn't supposed to chase them at all. In a few moments time she came trotting back, looking both happy and guilty at the same time.

My heart jumped when I saw her, as I instantly knew that she had chased my buck. Blood from the brush along the trail and rubbed off on Briar, leaving her flanks a crimson red. A telephone line ran through the forest and I was certain that Briar had run the deer beneath that line. I picked up the trail where it had crossed. The blood flow was heavier now and hope came surging back. I was going to find this buck if it took three days. It was a matter of time and determination.

The buck had crossed onto old Mr. Davids' place. Mr. Davids was a notorious drunk, known to shoot first and ask questions later. He didn't allow any hunting, but nothing was going to stop me from finding this buck. In all probability, the buck would cross out of Davids' property before I caught up with him anyway.

The trail was steady and I had no trouble staying with it. As the trail lead me across a pasture, I found a pool of thick gelatinous blood, and my spirits soared. Surely the deer was weakening. I had to admire his stamina and courage, and I felt more than a twinge of guilt about the pain I had caused him. Then 200 yards ahead, there he was; running on three legs, his front left flopping uselessly at his side. I raised the rifle, somehow calm now and determined to right what I had made wrong. The rifle roared and he collapsed.

Mr. Davids came charging out waving his pistol. Even though we had met a dozen times, he rarely remembered who I was, much less that we were neighbors. I explained who I was and why I had come onto his land. Thankfully, he was sober and did in fact remember me. He was actually quite nice and even loaded the buck into his truck and drove me home.

At home, Claudia and I shared a jubilant toast. The long drought was over. The five day doe season opened the next day and I shot two does on consecutive mornings. I had managed to stock the freezer and downed the first eight-point deer of my life. I had truly been a hunting season to remember.

Chapter Thirteen

WOODCOCK MORNINGS

Rain pelted the windows of my East Alabama home as the wind sent pine limbs whipping. The ditches along the road ran red with rainwater. A thoroughly miserable evening, but conditions could have been worse. On the TV, two northern football rivals were battling in the first major blizzard of the season. Players, nearly obscured by driving snow, stood huddled by the heaters on the bench, and fans bounced in place, slapping arms to their chests in vain attempts to get warm. While I had to sympathize with their plight, I could not help being enthusiastic about the arrival of winter.

In the Deep South, winter was the finest time of year to be outdoors. Clear nights frequently caused temperatures to dip into the twenties or even teens, but days that followed were usually crystal blue and perfect. A long john top, flannel shirt and hunting vest were plenty to ward off the chill, but still allow a man to walk all day without breaking a sweat. Leaves had fallen from the trees, and the once formidable tangle of vines and brush had been battered down by a dozen or more killing frosts.

Winging through the winter night skies flew the ideal reason to get out and enjoy the delightful season. Woodcock driven the final leg of their migration by snow and ice, arrived on the wintering grounds of Dixie. The 'cock began their trek several months earlier, leaving the nesting areas in the northern U.S. and Canada. During their journey, the birds dropped into favorite coverts to spend a few days or weeks before frozen ground or restlessness drove them on once more. Usually they stopped in thick, damp, forest bottoms with partially open floors. Here the 'cock would probe the soft earth with their long, sensitive bills that allowed them to feel and then grasp earth worms and other invertebrates.

Along the migration route, hunters who knew of these havens anxiously awaited the arrival of the woodcock and the exciting sport they provided. My turn came at the end of the woodcock's journey.

The next night, while returning from work, the radio weatherman predicted an end to the rain and the arrival of a high pressure front. Deep frosts would grip the state overnight, but would gradually yield to bright sun the following day. Work would have to wait a day while I used some vacation time to investigate "my" coverts.

I awakened to a dawn as perfect as promised. A leisurely breakfast of eggs, sausage, grits and coffee tasted delicious as the wood heater came back to life, spreading warmth through the cold kitchen. I felt no hurry to start hunting, as woodcock often spent the night feeding in nearby pastures, and returned to their forest haunts at daybreak. Hunting would be easier after the birds had settled into the woods and left some ground scent for the dog.

Sandy, my English setter bitch, pranced excitedly by the gate, then bounded into the pickup truck as soon as I released the latch. We headed for a small swamp in Tuskeegee National Forest that had produced well for us in the past. Beavers had dammed a stream a few hundred yards above the confluence with a larger creek, providing excellent woodcock habitat. Redbud, poplar, maple and oak saplings, privet and green briar choked the places where sunlight found openings in the longleaf pines. Where standing water had killed the pines, saplings and blackberries proliferated into a nearly impenetrable thicket.

My breath formed clouds before me as I loaded a pair of 7½s into my skeet-choked SKB over and under. Skim ice on the puddles cracked beneath my feet as I drifted off the road and into the forest. Within a few steps, I was certain that the woodcock had indeed arrived. Splashes of watery, white and brown dropping dotted the creek bottom, and in the muddy open areas were unmistakable traces of the probings of long, narrow bills. Sandy, who usually kept up a rapid pace, sneaked along with out-stretched neck, eyes darting about as if pursued by an unseen presence. Woodcock scent must have permeated the entire covert.

With Sandy acting so birdy, I followed directly behind her to prevent bumping birds into flight before she located them. Sandy's nose dropped as if suddenly weighted, her tail whipping furiously. She paced confidently to her left and locked onto a gorgeous point with front legs flexed, head cocked left, tail high and hind legs stiff. The intensity in her eyes left no doubt that she was nearly on top of the bird. I enjoyed her point for a moment, as there was no hurry. Once pointed, woodcock generally sit tighter than any other game bird. This particular 'cock was in sparse cover, so I guessed the get away would be low and straight away. Sure enough, she flushed just like a quail, and I dropped her in a puff of feathers.

Accepting the woodcock from Sandy, I admired the unusual yet beautiful animal. The breast feathers were orange and the back and wings a collage of brown, black and white. Her head was disproportionately large and the great, night-adapted eyes were closer to the back than the front of the head, which allowed the woodcock to see danger from above while the nearly three inch long bill plunged into the ground. The relatively large body size and the width of the three outer primary feathers (which were greater than one-half inch) identified this bird as a female.

Sandy did not share my interest in the downed bird, for she knew there were more tucked into this swamp. Despite her cautious gate, she bumped two birds to her right. In thick cover, the un-pointed birds made for difficult shots; which is to say, I missed. I didn't blame Sandy for her transgression. The thick blanket of woodcock scent must have been bewildering. With luck, the escaping 'cock would remain in the covert to be relocated.

Sandy disappeared into a thicket and never emerged. Her bell fell silent, so I called her name. Still no bell. I searched and eventually found her pointing patiently beneath some ten foot tall privet. Discovering an opening to reach the point, I flushed the bird. The large hen fluttered straight up in an attempt to clear the midstory and attain some flying room. I shot while she was rising and missed. The top barrel caught her at the apex of her rise, and the day's second bird was in the bag.

The woodcock that had escaped had flown across a logging road into the densest part of the swamp. They had been down long enough to leave some scent, so I whistled for Sandy and plunged in. I struggled through the myriad saplings and ankle deep water as the blackberry thorns clung tenaciously to my sleeves and hat. Realizing that I had been foolish to enter such a thicket, I was about to beat a prudent retreat, when Sandy's bell fell silent. Now there was no choice but to forge ahead.

After several minutes of intense profanity, I found Sandy on point. I attempted to flush the bird, but nothing happened. This was just the sort of cover that woodcock occasionally ran in; usually going just far enough to put an obstacle between themselves and the hunter or to find an opening through which to fly. Suddenly, the cock took off behind three tall saplings. I only had time for one rushed shot that succeeded in damaging a tree beyond repair, but not in pulling a single feather.

I shook my head knowing that I had been beaten fairly, and then realized that Sandy was on point once again not 30 feet away. My shooting prowess was doubly impressive on this occasion; I missed with both barrels. The thicket was simply impossible to shoot in, so I called Sandy and headed out. Finally reaching the edge, I discovered that Sandy was no longer with me. Not wanting to accept the inevitable, I called to her. A faint bell tinkled in the depths of the swamp and then fell silent.

Braving those thorns for the privilege of missing another woodcock didn't seem worth it, so I attempted to call Sandy off point. She wouldn't budge. My only alternative was to crash back in, flush the bird and drag my dog out of this woodcock heaven. Miraculously, as I fought the last few yards to the point, this bird flew through the only shooting alley available and I connected. As the bird fell, I thundered out, "There, By God!" Oh, sweet revenge.

Though I could legally shoot two more birds, I was ready to head home. Sandy seemed satisfied as well, trotting by my side as we headed for the truck. To my surprise, a small male flushed from the open pine-needle-covered forest floor in front of us. Hurrying, I missed the first shot, but regained my composure and connected cleanly on the second. He was undoubtedly one of the birds we had moved earlier, and I plain lucked into him.

The birds spread on the tailgate; I sat alongside them, slid out of my wet boots and into dry sneakers. The mid-day sun was almost warm now, but the air still felt fresh and cool in my nostrils. A cold beer and a sandwich never tasted better. With the help of perfect weather, a good dog, and a fine game bird, on this day I had truly lived.

Chapter *Fourteen*

BLACK BELT BOBS

Mr. Stone chatted amiably as the tires on his four wheel drive spun through the rain-slickened gumbo. "My property line runs along the creek to that ol' shack down yonder. I've been seeing a right smart number of coveys along the edge of that field," he drawled, pointing to a 40 acre bean field at the base of a wooded hillside. "There is about 600 acres for you boys to hunt, so that ought to be enough to keep you busy."

"Wow, this looks fantastic," I enthused. "We sure do appreciate it."

We returned to the house to pick up my dog and truck. Upon receiving the last of our instructions from Mr. Stone, Mrs. Stone stepped out on the porch where we were introduced. A short woman solidly built, with a man's haircut and dressed in blue jeans and cowboy boots, she said in a husky voice. "Now we'll see you boys back here at noon."

"Maam?" I questioned.

"For supper," she replied as if the reason was obvious.

"Uh.., we brought along sandwiches," I stuttered somewhat in shock.

"No, no," she said sternly. "You all come back and eat with us."

"Yes maam. Thank you," answered Will, my hunting partner.

While I had anticipated good quail hunting in Alabama's Black Belt, I was flabbergasted by the gracious hospitality shown to virtual strangers.

"I can't believe that invitation," I muttered to Will as we pulled down the driveway.

"It is an old tradition down here, but I'll admit it doesn't happen often anymore."

"Funny, she doesn't exactly look like the southern belle type."

"Hospitality, like gold, is where you find it my man," he responded with a broad smile.

A misty fog lingered after the all-night rain, shrouding the field in a silent cloak. The cedars on the adjoining hill appeared nearly black in the subdued light. Sandy, my orange and white setter, dashed through the soaked broom sedge, excited to be free after the two hour drive. Evidently, Sandy was no more prepared for what happened next than we were. A covey of about 20 birds erupted in front of her and sailed directly over our unloaded guns.

The singles twisted between the trees and quickly disappeared as Sandy dropped her head in embarrassment.

"I'll bet those birds were feeding on beans at the field edge and ran back into the woods when we pulled up," remarked Will.

"Well, there is one sure way to test that idea," I responded cryptically.

"Okay, I'll bite. How?"

"Let's shoot a few and look into some of their crops."

"A few birds went up into that draw but most of the singles flew straight ahead. Let's follow those," suggested Will.

Sandy, sober now from her humiliation but anxious to atone, quartered through the oaks and cedars. A streak of white combing the forest floor, she passed in and out of view, but her bell allowed us to monitor her movements easily. The steady tinkling was suddenly interrupted by silence.

"We've got a point up here!" called Will. "She is locked up pretty as a picture in a honeysuckle tangle along the fence. Why don't you cross over and I'll cover this side."

With guns at port arms we stepped tentatively forward, all systems on alert for the single that was sure to explode into flight. One more step, and the sound of rushing wings surrounded us. Nervous systems approaching overload, we simultaneously realized that Sandy had pointed a whole new covey. Rattled by the unexpected appearance of at least a dozen brown and white speedsters, we both missed on our first shots. Will, at least, recovered to drop a cock on his second barrel, but I was not so fortunate.

"Can you believe this?" I asked in astonishment. "We haven't walked half way around the first bean field yet and we've already moved two coveys."

"We might be able to find them all right, but we sure aren't doing much on shooting them," Will chuckled. "There are enough singles spread out in here to keep us busy for the next hour or two. They're all in the trees so the shooting won't be easy, but I can't think of a better way to spend a Saturday morning. Can you?"

"No Sir! Sure can't," I answered emphatically.

The creek on the west side of the bean field gradually curled toward the hillside on the east causing the beans to yield to a narrow, grassy flood plain dotted with thigh-high clumps of sharp-thorned Cherokee rose and scattered saplings. Sandy picked her way around the rose patches, not anxious to be impaled by the treacherous spikes, and finally locked onto point next to a particularly impressive thicket. We approached from either side and this time the expected lone bird flushed on my side. I swung through the buff-chinned hen as she streaked toward the creek and the charge of 7½s dropped her cleanly in a shower of feathers. At the report, a pair flushed just in front of us and we each managed to knock down one of the wild flushing duo.

The rose patches which offered an ideal refuge from hawks and foxes were less than perfect for evading humans who could easily shoot over the cover. We picked up three more Bobs before doubling back through the hillside forest. The shooting was far more difficult there as the lightning-quick quail rocketed between the trees. After missing four consecutive, pointed birds, Will finally downed a cock as it erupted from a green briar thicket.

"That makes seven birds from those two coveys," I said. "Let's leave them alone and try to find another bunch. I'd like these birds to be around all season."

"Good idea", agreed Will. "And if the covey gets down to six birds, we shouldn't shoot at them at all for the rest of the year. They need that many in the roosting circle to prevent freezing to death on cold nights."

"Let's follow the creek back toward the truck. We sure don't want to be late for supper now, do we?"

Bobwhite hunting such as this had seemed but a distant dream. Images painted by Ruark, Babcock and Buckingham were seared into my memory, but the scenes they depicted were far from my boyhood, Pennsylvania home. Life however is filled with unexpected turns, and a graduate school opening at Auburn University sent me into the heart of Dixie.

The South was a changed place from the one those immortals

My English setter, Sandy, with bobwhite quail taken near Selma, Alabama, in 1982.

had known in the first half of the century. Social changes had largely eliminated the small, sharecropper's farms of small fields and brushy fence rows, and soil depletion had caused the ruin of many of the larger plantations. In their place, pine forests had proliferated, reducing quail carrying capacity but creating ideal habitat for white-tailed deer and turkeys which became the mainstay of the local sportsman.

Fortunately, the Black Belt, named for the black clay soil which rested in a "belt" across the center of the state, remained largely agricultural, primarily growing soybeans and cotton along with a little corn and sorghum. The region did not lend itself to ultra-clean farming practices. Low spots which remained too wet to plow on many farms were allowed to grow up in oaks and blackberries, providing both nesting and escape cover for the quail.

Mr. Stone, a short, stocky man with dark thinning hair, met us at the kitchen door with a warm smile. "You fellows do any good this morning? I thought I heard a few shots."

"Yessir, we found two coveys along the hill and another down by the creek."

116

"Good! Now y'all come in."

We pulled off our muddy boots and followed him into the living room of the modest, two-story brick house. The furniture consisted of inexpensive upholstered sofas and chairs that were still relatively new. My attention was immediately drawn to the framed collections of quartz arrow heads on the wall. "These are beautiful," I commented. "Did you find them on this farm?"

"Everyone of them," he answered proudly. "They're all over the property. I'm pretty sure the Creek Indians roamed this country. There are so many points that the Indians must have kept a camp around here. I'm sure that if you fellows keep your eyes open, you will find one or two today."

"I didn't find any this morning, but I did find a nautilus fossil," I said as I pulled the two-pound stone from my jacket pocket.

"I've seen those around here for years, but I didn't know what they were. What is it exactly?"

"A nautilus is a sea creature with a spiral shaped shell. Inside the shell there are a series of chambers. The animal can fill the chambers with water or pump water out to move up or down in the ocean. Obviously, this farm was under the sea at one time."

"Well, I'll be. Let me take a closer look at that rascal," he said, seeming genuinely pleased to have learned something new about the land he knew so well.

Being a Yankee used to eating sandwiches for lunch, I was pleasantly surprised to learn what a "down-home supper" was all about. Mrs. Stone emerged from the kitchen with a pale blue platter heaped with fried chicken. Long accustomed to the greasy abomination served in fast food chains, I marveled at the crisp, light, almost oil-less breading. A serving bowl filled with butter beans reminded me of the lima beans we ate up North, but they were tan rather than green and had a more delicate taste. I especially enjoyed the thick, moist, squares of sweet cornbread which I smeared with butter and washed down with lightly, sweetened iced tea. The collards were rather bitter to my tastes, but were heartily enjoyed by my dining companions.

Pleasantly stuffed, our minds turned once again to the birds. "You fellows ought to park out by the barn and walk down to those bean fields that I showed you this morning. You haven't gotten to the best bird country yet."

"Sounds hard to believe, but I'll gladly take your word for it," I said.

The sun had burned off the morning mist, allowing us to strip down to T-shirts and hunting vests. Black clay that remained both sticky and slippery on the farm road clung tenaciously in ever-growing clods to our boots. Golden-yellow hickory and brown-red oak leaves fluttered in the gentle afternoon breeze as we strolled down the wooded hill. Sandy, replenished by her siesta and my unneeded sandwich, raced ahead of us. Appearing through the trees, we caught sight of 400 acres of recently harvested, river bottom soybeans intersected by cedar-lined gullies and surrounded by wooded hills.

We were so impressed by our newly discovered Bobwhite heaven that we almost failed to notice Sandy pointing intently at the edge of the woods. We nearly reached her when the covey of about 10 birds flushed. One foolhardy bird flew along the field edge and I dropped him just as he prepared to cut back into the trees. The remainder headed directly into the forest, offering only the slightest opportunity.

"Let's forget about those singles," suggested Will. "Why don't we just hunt coveys for a while so that we can get around the farm before dark. It is getting pretty warm, so the birds are probably resting in the edges of the woods about now."

"How about all of these gullies out in the middle of the fields?" I asked. "We could get clearer shots if we walked on either side of those."

"I think it would be better to save those for last. The birds will probably use the draws to travel out to feed on beans late this afternoon."

"Okay, that makes sense. Why don't I go into the woods about 15 or twenty yards and you stay out on the edge?"

Will's tactic worked to perfection. While I ended up flushing all three of the coveys we found, mine were mostly snap shots through tangled brush. Will saw far fewer quail as he waited for the odd bird to fly along the field edge, but his shots were unobstructed. Despite the discrepancy in ammunition expended, three birds hung from each of our bird straps when we reached the abandoned sharecropper's shack at the far end of Mr. Stone's property.

Increasingly fatigued by our long hike in mud-caked boots, we set out in dwindling light along the fence rows and gullies toward the truck. Sandy, who had surely logged 40 miles, looked somewhat worse for wear. Her belly and flanks were caked in dried mud which hung in crusty clods of fur, and her ears and tail were a hopeless snarl of cockleburs. But at four years of age and in the prime of her life, she continued hunting, searching the down-wind sides of the gullies with her alert nose.

Her persistence and Will's astute prediction of the bird's behavior paid off. Wherever the gullies approached the woods, Sandy invariably located a covey, which had emerged to consume a final meal of beans before going to roost. We hunted away from the woods toward the open fields in an attempt to direct the singles further out into the fields where we could get some clear shots. Our tactic was only partially successful. Most of the quail, realizing that true security rested in the woods, curled back directly over us and winged for the trees. None-the-less, a sizable minority flew down the edges and pitched back into the gully about 100 yards away. Pursuing those singles, we eventually re-flushed and had shots at a number of them.

"What do we have? About eighteen birds between us?" asked Will. "Why don't we call it a day?"

"I agree. A couple more birds couldn't make this day any nicer than its already been. What do you say, we clean these birds by the creek and give the whole bunch of 'em to the Stones? They sure have been kind to us."

The yellow porch light shone as we drove toward the house. Both the Stones met us at the door as we wearily trudged up the steps.

"You fellows sure gave it your all, you look like you've had the course," chuckled Mr. Stone.

"We've had a super day. Thank you so much," said Will.

"We wanted you to have these birds," I offered.

"We don't want to take *your* birds. You worked too hard for 'em," protested Mrs. Stone.

"No, no, we want you to have them."

"OK then, thank you," they said together.

Mr. Stone then uttered the words that made my heart leap: "Ya'all come back. Anytime."

Chapter Fifteen

SWAMPERS

The first time I saw a swamp rabbit, I didn't know there was such a thing. He came charging through a patch of switch cane looking, for all the world like a cottontail with a glandular condition. In slack-jawed astonishment, I forgot to raise the gun to shoot. The critter had to weigh six pounds! He was proportioned like a regular rabbit and didn't have that leggy look of a jack. The pelage across his back was more blackish than the reddish coloration of the cottontail, but other than that he was just a magnum rabbit.

My beagle, Peaches, raced up the trail yipping excitedly. Our eyes met as she ran by and I saw a look of bewilderment as if she were asking, "This is a rabbit I'm chasing; isn't it, Boss?" I hoped that she would bring him around in a circle, but she got confused where the track went through a stream.

I had moved to Auburn, Alabama, three months before to attend graduate school in the Zoology-Entomology Department. On Monday morning, I paid a visit to Dr. Julian Dusi who was the curator of the Department's museum. Smiling in gentle amusement at my incredulous description, the Doctor led me into the musty bowels of the museum. He began opening the long shallow drawers of a massive pine cabinet. Each drawer was crammed with specimens of the state's birds and mammals.

He extracted a rabbit skin stuffed with cotton, which looked like it had been mounted by a taxidermy student who had flunked. I immediately identified it as the mysterious rabbit. He explained that I had seen a swamp rabbit whose scientific name was _Svlvaginus aquaticas._ It was in the same genus as the cottontail, but as the name denoted, was a water loving species. Apparently, they were quite common in bottomlands throughout Alabama.

Peaches and I hunted a lot of rabbits that first year in Alabama. The country was all new to us and we explored every chance we had. Mostly, we hunted in upland areas more hospitable to the cottontails. The first swamper that I ever shot came in February during the last week of the hunting season. I wasn't even hunting at the time. Claudia and I were walking with some friends around the overgrown farm we had rented. Peaches and a new beagle puppy named Briar were tagging along.

Peaches started a chase in the swamp on the north end of the property. We listened to the hound for a time and then continued our stroll. Peaches knew her way home. An hour later we could still hear excited yips coming from the woods, and I was feeling guilty. The little dog was putting on the chase of her life and I was loafing on the porch with my friends. At last, I could stand it no longer. I went to the kitchen, grabbed the old Ithaca pump, and hiked through the lengthening shadows into the swamp.

A narrow stream, which meandered through the middle of the swamp, periodically overflowed its banks leaving a muddy flat about 20 yards wide. A few sprigs of switch cane protruded from the mud, but it was one of the few places in the swamp where there was a chance of getting a clear view of a running rabbit. The flat was close to where Peaches had originally jumped the swamper, and I knew that if she could stay on his trail long enough, he was bound to head back to the area. It seemed like my best bet for an ambush.

The swamper was running wider and longer than any cottontail I had ever run into. Several times, Peaches barks melted into the distant woods only to drift back within earshot ten minutes later. Dusk was descending swiftly as I stood silently in the swamp. Just as I thought that we would lose shooting light, I heard Peaches turn toward me. Her barks became frantic as the rabbit had quit playing tricks and was now running straight for home.

There, crossing the flat, crept a soaked and muddy swamper. He was running at about half speed and I easily shot him. I left him where he was. He didn't belong to me yet, and he wouldn't until Peaches gave him to me. This was her rabbit. At the sound of the shot, her excited barks elevated to another plane of intensity as she bore down to claim her reward. What a joyous sound it was, and what a sight when the drenched, mud-coated hound broke through the gloom and seized the swamp rabbit by the head, savagely whipping him back and forth in triumph.

That chase hooked me on hunting swamp rabbits. These big rabbits didn't hole and they ran big. Problem was that I didn't have permission to hunt anyplace where I could find many of them. They were more of a bonus during a day of cottontail hunting.

Midway through my third year in Alabama, I became friends with Allan Andress, who was working as a technician for one of the professors of wildlife at the university. Allan was a coon hunter who kept several fine coon dogs. He loved hunting with hounds even more than I did. Over coffee one morning, he mentioned that he had heard that I had a good pair of beagles. He suggested a swap. He would take me coon hunting, if I would take him swamp rabbit hunting.

It was a ridiculously easy sell. Allan had hunted coons in several swamps in the Tuskeegee National Forest where he claimed to have seen plenty of swamp bucks, as he called them. We arranged to meet on Saturday morning. It had poured rain all day Friday and throughout the night, but the initial puffs of a cooler, drier air were starting to stir when Allan and I released the hounds.

By this time, Briar was no longer a puppy, but had developed into an exceptionally large beagle, weighing almost 35 pounds. She was the closest thing to a wild animal I had ever owned. For the first year of her life, she would go berserk if I tried to put two hands on her at the same time. I literally had to tame her even though she had been a housedog since she was six weeks old. Over the years, many people had told me stories of fabulous puppies who could do it all at nine months of age. Up until the time I got Briar, I had never believed any of those tales. Under the tutelage of Peaches, Briar was bringing rabbits in circles at eight months. She had that combination of outstanding nose, independence, cooperation and savvy that most hounds didn't develop until they were two or three.

Dead, brown needles from the longleaf pines were plastered down into the moist, sandy soil. Drops of water showered from the leaves of the water oaks each time the breeze picked up. The hounds spread out and disappeared into thickets of greenbriar, searching for a trail. Allan stuck a chew of tobacco into his cheek and offered me the pouch. I declined. We had almost reached the creek, when Briar's deep throated bawl echoed through the woods. Peaches quickly joined in. Her high pitched yips told us she too was on the job.

Allan and I split up, each seeking an opening to intercept the rabbit. The chase didn't last long, as I heard Allan's 12 gauge boom. He had guessed right and tumbled the swamper as he raced through the switch cane. The dogs performed their ritual of possession, each giving the rabbit a thorough shaking, before disappearing back into the woods in search of another swamp buck.

The next swamper made a dash for Tuskeegee Creek as soon as the dogs started him. The creek was about 50 feet wide and flowed briskly after the previous day's rain. Apparently the rabbit had swum across the creek, because the dogs never slowed down when they arrived at the steep bank. Briar plunged in first with Peaches right behind her; both hounds bawling as the current carried them downstream.

There wasn't much that Allan and I could do but enjoy the sounds of the chase, and hope that the rabbit would swim back to our side of the creek. The chase continued for about twenty minutes, and then the dogs fell silent. We waited anxiously as the hounds tried to decipher the swamper's trick. I was about to call them, when reliable, old Peaches pierced the woods with a victorious yip.

The swamper was nearly out of tricks. He was headed back to the Creek at top speed. By the time we determined where he would cross, he had already done so. Again the beagles plunged in, without the slightest hesitation. Once across, it only took a moment for the dogs to race up and down the bank and find the place where the swamper emerged.

We scrambled into open positions near where the rabbit originally jumped, in hopes of getting a shot. Allan was truly a hound man, so he understood that rewarding the dogs for a wonderful chase was far more important than a rabbit for the table. The tone of the chase suddenly changed. The barks became elongated and frustrated, and the chase seemed to have stopped.

We arrived to find the beagles with their noses stuck right up the trunk of a hollow, but still standing, tree.

"Darn it. He got away," I lamented.

"Wait a minute; not so fast," answered Allan. "Let's try something."

I waited curiously as Allan unsheathed his knife and cut a finger-thick sapling. After trimming the branches, he stuck the sapling into the hollow bole, and began poking around. He retracted the stick and examined it closely.

"Look here," he instructed. "See the hair. We can get this swamp buck." Pushing the sapling back into the tree bole, he rapidly twisted the stick in a circular motion until it wrapped around the rabbit's hind leg. The dogs, still bawling from time to time, had been watching our actions with great interest. At the moment the swamper was dragged from his refuge, Briar thrust her head into the hole, nearly removing several of Allan's fingers in the process. The beagles exacted their revenge in a matter of seconds, and after a few victorious shakes, dropped the huge buck at our feet.

More rabbits were surely hiding in the swamp, but neither of us cared to hunt any more. We each had a big swamp rabbit to take home, and we knew that we wouldn't experience another chase like that. As I loaded Peaches and Briar into the truck, Allan made a simple comment that, coming from a serious houndsman, filled me with pride. "Well, Yankee," he said, spitting an amber stream of tobacco juice, "Those are some damned fine hounds."

Chapter Sixteen

GO WEST YOUNG MAN

The phone sat on the table, silent and uncaring. The decision was now out of my control and I could only await the outcome. The interview felt good to me though and in fact had almost been fun. I had attempted to twist each answer to allow myself to talk about my experience and I was hoping the tactic had succeeded. All my interviewers had been bright, likable people and it was easy to imagine working with them. The critical question however, was did they feel the same about me. I cautioned myself not to get my hopes up, but I couldn't deny my optimism.

It seemed incredible that a person who hated school as much as I, had continued studying until his 30th birthday. High school and even college had left me feeling like a starving man staring through the window of a banquet room. Devoid of aroma or taste, the subjects were tantalizing but unsatisfying. Weakened by lack of sustenance almost to the point of despair, my hunger to know persisted, so I remained, nose to the window, waiting.

In graduate school, the door to the banquet swung open at last and I found myself in the midst of a feast of knowledge. Information I had long sought, and much that I was entirely ignorant of, swirled around me. I plunged into the subjects of population ecology, predator-prey interactions, evolution, genetics, entomology, herpetology, ornithology, and wildlife management. Sitting in class, which had been an ordeal during my entire education, suddenly was fascinating, as professors unveiled the reasons for phenomena of nature, which I had long observed but had failed to understand. Each course was like a road leading me deeper into a cosmos of comprehension.

While all the courses were interesting, some, like insect morphology were simply amazing. Under magnification, the multitudinous forms, each evolving from the same basic plan, were awesome. The variation in the structure of mouthparts alone, from long sucking tubes to multi-toothed jaws to sickle shaped mandibles, was incredible. Electric colors on the bodies and wings exploded through the lens of the microscope.

Even more elucidating than the class work were the opportunities to conduct research projects under the tutelage of experienced scientists. Initially, research work was tedious as I struggled to define a project.

Long afternoons spent poring through scientific literature was critical to learn what had previously been discovered, but it left me restless. I often found myself staring out the third floor library windows much as I had done as a schoolboy; anxious to get outdoors and see for myself.

I eventually managed to clear that hurdle and begin the actual business of conducting experiments. To my delight, it was extremely similar to hunting. Just as I had slipped off after class to hunt, I now slipped off to the forests or fields to unravel the lives of predaceous beetles or parasitic wasps. The same combination of reasoning and trial and error which allowed me to figure where the quail were late on a mid-January day, helped me to perfect the methods for my experiments. Methods that failed were like patches of empty cover explored. I at least knew what didn't work and that often led to new ideas. Far from being failures, they were pieces of a puzzle.

By the time my methodology was perfected, I usually had a notion of what the results would be. Only by completing the experiments however could I learn if my hypothesis was correct. Like finding fresh deer tracks in the snow; one could be reasonably certain that a deer was nearby, but only by following them could one be certain. Most of the time, the results confirmed my suspicions, but when they didn't, it cracked the foundation of my theories; forcing me to rebuild a scheme which would incorporate those unexpected results. It was a grand game.

My studies were now completed however; my final diploma in hand. It was time to leave academia behind. Besides, poverty was becoming tiresome and my wife and two babies at home needed Daddy to get a real job. The opportunity to make a good living while doing research on the biological control of insects promised to be a fascinating job.

I walked toward the ringing phone telling myself this wasn't the call, but my racing pulse told me it probably was. I answered and then nodded emphatically to my wife signaling that this was the one! Claudia paced across the living room floor, a look of hope and fear written on her face. Phil wasted no time. After apologizing for taking so long to get back to me, he offered me the job. My beaming face told the story. Claudia clapped her hands twice and clenched her fists as she stepped out onto the porch to contemplate the end of speculation about our future and the beginning of real plans.

The only down side was that the job was in California. I had grown to love the rural life in Alabama, and I hated to say good-by. I would miss the camaraderie of graduate students struggling together for an exam or sweltering in the fields to complete our research during an Alabama summer. I would miss several professors who had become friends as well as fellow softball players. I'd miss the friends with whom we survived new parenthood. Most of all however, I would miss the oak-swamp, tree stand where I shot my first eight point buck; the overgrown clear-cut where my beagles and I had chased both cottontail and swamp rabbits; the creek bottom where my setter, Sandy, excelled on the wintering woodcock; and the black belt soybean fields where I discovered the magic of bobwhite quail hunting.

In late September, I drove the rental car from the Sacramento airport in search of a place to live. Driving first north toward Yuba City and then west toward Vacaville, I scanned the countryside. Years of Southern living left me unprepared for the heavy traffic on the eight lane highways. I struggled to recall the urban driving skills of my youth as cars jumped between the lanes around me. Housing lots, of postage stamp dimensions, were apparently standard in the area, but seemed a considerable step down from my acre and a half back home.

The agriculture was equally foreign. Yellow fields of rice (a crop I had never before *seen*) were being harvested by mammoth combines moving methodically through the waist-high grain. Huge wire teeth directed the stalks toward the chattering blades which cut off the heads. In the interior of the massive, grumbling machinery, the rice was stripped and emerged as a golden stream exiting the arching spout into the hopper.

Orchards of pears and peaches were familiar, but the almonds, olives and kiwis were entirely new to me. While the abundance of the agriculture was impressive, something seemed strange. I then realized what it was. Every square foot was under intensive production. There were no wood lots or even tree lines or hedgerows. Where could wildlife survive in such a place? A tightness gripped my chest. Had my luck been too good? Did providing for my family require such an agonizing sacrifice? If I couldn't hunt, I would shrivel and die. Of that I was certain. Maybe though I could survive on occasional trips far from here.

I warned myself that I was probably panicking. Perhaps it was not as bad as it seemed: maybe if I kept driving.... Turning east, I headed toward the Sierra Nevada Mountains. I breathed a sigh of relief as the agricultural fields of the valley floor gave way to rolling hills of brown grass, blue oaks and digger pines of the foothills around Auburn, California. The knots in my stomach eased slightly. It wasn't perfect.

There were still too damned many people, but perhaps this would be a place to call home. I pulled off the interstate in the late afternoon dusk and pulled into the parking lot of the first hotel I spotted. Tomorrow, I'd do some exploring and maybe call some Realtors to show me around.

The scampi at dinner had too much lemon, but the large prawns were delicious nonetheless. The cheesecake with cherries was a true New York, cheesy, cheesecake that I've always loved. The only real complaint about the meal was that I ate it alone. Chatting with the waitress as I paid the tab, I heard laughter coming from the bar. On the spur of the moment, I decided to stop in for an after dinner drink.

The crowd was distinctly middle aged with only a few under forty types scattered about. A piano bar stood in the corner, but mercifully it was unmanned. A thick haze of cigarette smoke wafted through the room. On one end of the bar was a short, bear of a guy with a massive torso and almost no legs. His smokes lying on the bar beside him, he leaned forward, talking with a plump woman about 40, with protruding teeth and short curly hair. Apparently, "the bear" had said something funny because her piercing laugh momentarily silenced the crowd.

On the far end of the bar, a trim man in his early fifties with receding, tight curly, gray hair, slouched comfortably over his brandy. I guessed that he was a regular by the quiet conversation he was having with the bartender who was washing glasses at the sink. I slid onto a stool two seats away and ordered a bourbon and water. The bartender, in his early forties with a conservative nineteen fifties style haircut, blended perfectly with the denizens of the bar.

"I haven't seen you in here before," said the gray haired man. "You from out of town?"

"Not for long," I replied. "I'm thinking about moving here in the next few weeks."

"Well, is that right? What brings you up here?" he inquired enthusiastically.

"I've been living in Alabama but I just took a job here in California. I'll be working out of my house and then traveling occasionally, so the company doesn't care where I live so long as it is within an hour's drive of the Sacramento airport. I love to hunt and fish and this area looks a lot more inviting than the valley."

"It is," he answered doubtfully. "I get a deer every year up in the National Forest, but it used to be that you could hunt deer and quail right around here. Now everybody owns their 20 acre ranchettes and the hunting is pretty well finished." He spat out the word 'ranchette' leaving no question of his feelings about the recent development of the foothills area. "What did you hunt down in Alabama?" he asked, obviously wanting to change to a happier subject.

"Well, I deer hunted a lot. You know, in Alabama the limit is one buck a day and the season lasts two months. Most years, I took four or five."

"Really! That is unbelievable. Here we can only shoot one a year."

"My true love when it comes to hunting is bobwhite quail and woodcock hunting over pointing dogs."

"A bird hunter, huh?" he exclaimed excitedly. "What is your name? Mine's Gene."

"Don," Gene called to the bartender who was filling an order for the dining room waitress, "Come here, there is someone I want you to meet." Turning to me, Gene confided, "Don is probably the best bird hunter in this whole county."

Don offered up a perfunctory smile as we shook hands. I could tell he had met a lot of self-appointed experts on bird hunting while pouring drinks, and he was withholding judgment on me. "What kind of dogs do you work?" he asked slicing instantly to the question most likely to establish my credibility.

"English setters," I responded and I could see his look soften. Had I not kept dogs, he surely would have dismissed me as another 'wanna-be'. "One is seven years old and the other is about nine months. How about you?"

"I've got German shorthairs. Do you have any chukars back there?"

"I think some shooting preserves release them, but they don't live in the wild back East. I've never even seen a picture of one. What do they look like?"

"They are about twice the size of a quail and are mostly brown with black stripes on their faces and flanks. Chukars are the main birds I hunt. Sometimes, I do a little bit of pheasant hunting down in the rice fields but mostly I like to hunt chukars. They live on the desert side of the mountains and if you're willing to drive over there, you usually have the place to yourself. That is the part I like best about 'em."

"The reason you have the place to yourself is that those SOBs live in the nastiest canyons on God's green Earth and they'll run a man to death," interjected Gene good-naturedly.

Noticing the minor league, beer belly on Don, I was surprised that he found such rugged hunting of interest, but he certainly seemed to be speaking from experience.'

"Are they a covey bird?" I asked.

"Yeah, sometimes big coveys too. Forty birds is not unheard of."

In the way of hunters everywhere, differences in our age and background were ignored in our mutual love of the hunt. I sipped my way through four more drinks as we animatedly traded notes on Western versus Eastern bird hunting. Just before I turned in for the night, Don said to me, "When you get moved in, come on down to the bar and I'll arrange for you to join me on a chukar hunt sometime."

What luck! Maybe California wouldn't be so bad after all.

My breath clouded about me, in the predawn November darkness. The parking lot was empty save Don's and my trucks. The old setter pawed the crate door anxiously wanting to get out. I had not wanted to inflict a half-trained pup on Don, so I only brought Sandy along. The gear and then Sandy were loaded into Don's big Chevy 4x4. The heater blasting away underfoot felt good as we pulled onto the Interstate, headed toward the still darkened east. Within a few miles, snow began to appear on the sides of the road. By the time we reached the summit, the light from the headlights reflected off drifts of snow, which rose like dunes between the silhouetted conifers.

A rosy glow at last appeared in the sky as we descended from the mountains into Reno. Don pulled off the highway into a huge casino. The pores of my skin were open from sitting in the warm truck, and the 15 degree air hit me like a jump in a pool. "Ready for some breakfast?" asked Don. "Cheapest food in the country is right here in these casinos."

Despite the hour, a few sallow-faced gamblers grimly hung on in the shadowy, smoke-filled rooms. Slumped over the machines like automatons, they fed coins into the ever-hungry slots. The gaming rooms were strangely devoid of human voices. Ringing bells, which signified a winner, were greeted with stoic silence by the exhausted players who promptly re-deposited the winnings in the machines. I felt out of place in my hunting clothes as we strode toward the coffee shop, but no one seemed to notice or care. Other than Don and I, the waitress appeared to be the only person in the shop who had slept last night. Despite the rather depressing surroundings, the food was plentiful and inexpensive. Don had French toast and bacon and I had eggs and sausage, for a total of four bucks.

My friend and chukar hunting guru, Don Wescott, taken on a Nevada chukar hunt.

Heading north towards Susanville, the morning light revealed an alien world. High, treeless mountains covered with blue-green sagebrush loomed around us. Occasional outcroppings of jagged, lunaresque rock jutted through the thin stratum of vegetation. The rare trickle-sized streams flowing out of the hills were easily identified by groves of naked-limbed cottonwoods, which grew in clusters along the banks. The terrain was unlike anything I had ever hunted. Where did one begin to find chukars in this vast country. There were no crop fields or brushy hedgerows or abandoned orchards, which cried out to be searched, simply mile after mile of the most rugged landscape that I had ever laid eyes upon.

I locked in the hubs of Don's four wheel drive before we turned up a little-used two track which wound through the sage brush. Don crept the truck along in low, first gear as he picked his way through the boulder-strewn, dry, stream bed. The road eventually petered out at the base of the mountain and we parked.

"Which way, Kimosabe," I asked teasingly.

"Well, Tonto," he jabbed back, "it is still early so the birds are probably just coming off the roost up high in those rock piles or in the tops of the draws. This creek bed will lead us quite a ways up the mountain so we don't need to charge straight up."

In the first half mile of our hike, I stumbled or fell a half dozen times as loose rocks rolled beneath my feet. Sure-footed Don shook his head and smiled at his new, clumsy partner. By watching Don, I realized what I was doing wrong. Don walked with his head down carefully placing his feet in secure positions. Occasionally, he'd glance up to survey his surroundings or locate the dogs but his attention quickly returned to the challenge of remaining upright. Born and raised a farmland hunter, I was used to scanning the area in front of me and watching the dog as I hunted. Clearly, that was a dangerous strategy in this terrain.

My heart rate quickened and my lungs greedily sucked oxygen as we plodded up the mountain; my body stubbornly resisting the demands of the climb. Searching for bobwhites in soybean fields had never felt like this. Chukar hunting seemed a blend of hunting, mountain climbing and cross country racing, and I began to question the sanity of the sport. Any questions that I had about Don's fitness were quickly erased as it was I who struggled to keep up. By concentrating on pacing myself, I eventually stabilized my breathing and steadied my racing pulse.

"Come over here," called Don. "There is something I want to show you." Pointing to the ground he said, "See those brown and white turds. Those are chukar droppings. When they're brown like that it means that they are at least a day old. They'll be green and white when they are fresh."

"At least we know there are birds around, now we just need to find them," I commented hopefully.

We reached the elevation where Don had thought the birds should be but for two hours we searched fruitlessly. "Let's take a break down by the water hole so the dogs can get a drink," suggested Don. "I don't know where those sorry rascals are today." The dogs greedily lapped water from the trickle. Once satiated, they flopped down in a small pool with tongues lolling.

I began to say something when Don pointed a finger skyward and said, "Shh, Shh! Do you hear that?" An odd cackling, chuckling sound rang through the mountains. "Those are chukars," he explained in a conspiratorial tone. "Can you tell where the sound is coming from?" We strained our ears trying to pinpoint the birds and simultaneously pointed to the hillside above us. I grabbed my shotgun and started up the hill. "Whoa boy, whoa!" ordered Don. "If we come at them from below, they'll run clear to the top faster than the dogs can follow them and then probably fly before we can get into range. We need to circle around and get above them. If we can come down on them, they'll probably stay put."

My heart again began to pound as we gained elevation, but the prospect of getting a shot at the chukars overshadowed my exertion. "I think we're up high enough now," said Don. "Let's side hill our way over to the slope where we heard them talking. When we get over there, we will want to zigzag our way down. If they give us the slip and get above us, then we'll be out of luck. Oh, and don't talk when we get close. Sometimes, the birds will flush at the sound of a voice."

I began to worry that the birds had climbed above us, after five zigs and zags failed to produce any action. Suddenly, Don's shorthair, Shotsy, went on point above a rocky outcropping which stood about twenty feet over the sagebrush.

"Get ready," whispered Don. "I'll go on this side of the rocks, you take the other."

A whir of wings and a "pitoooo" chirp startled me as the chukars flushed from the top of the rocks. I caught only a glimpse of the streaking partridges as they attempted to escape toward Don. Two shots rang out, but I couldn't see if he connected. Sighing in dismay at not having a shot, I was startled once again when a lay bird erupted at my feet and pitched down the mountain. I recovered in time to fire twice but I missed cleanly.

"Damn it!" I cursed. "Did you get any?"

"Yeah, I got a pair down over here. Fetch, Shotsy."

I climbed over the rock pile in time to see Don accepting the second bird from Shotsy.

"Can I take a look?" I asked.

Don handed me the plump, limp partridge still slightly wet from Shotsy's mouth. The dominant grayish brown back and wings blended perfectly with the surroundings, but the barred flanks and striped face were prominent after I turned the warm body over. The legs and bill were an unusually brilliant red, which I had never seen on a game bird before. I held the bird under Sandy's nose. "This is what we're looking for girl," I told her.

"My God, those things fly fast! I had a good shot bird going straight away, but somehow I missed him," I lamented. "I can't figure it out, I felt like I was right on him."

"Was he going down hill?"

A good string of chukars.

"Yeah, he was."

"I'll bet you held right on his butt like you would on a rising pheasant, right?"

"Yeah," I responded, feeling the answer was obvious.

"That down hill shot is real tricky. You've got to lead way below them or your shot will go high. Chukars are about the only bird that offer that shot and you have to hunt 'em for awhile before you get the hang of it. Don't worry about it. You'll get another chance. Most of the covey headed toward that draw over there. Let's see if we can find 'em again."

"Did the birds on your side fly down also?" I asked.

"Yeah, but usually even if chukars take off going down, they'll eventually curl back up the hill. I usually relocate birds at about the same elevation where they initially flushed."

With renewed determination, we set out toward the draw. This time it was Sandy's turn to find birds. I looked up to see her pointing into a clump of tall sage. We hurried to close the distance to the birds. Sandy broke point, moving to her left. The instant she moved, the entire covey exploded from the brush fifteen yards in front of her and just barely out of shotgun range.

"I'm sorry about that Don," I apologized. "I think she was trying to circle around and point from the other side. That's what she used to do when we hunted quail."

"Oh. That's okay. She just hasn't figured these chukars out yet. These birds won't let a dog get closer than 10 or 15 yards from them especially when they're still bunched up. Sometimes when they're alone, a dog can get closer. She'll learn not to push her luck with chukars."

"As a matter of fact," I said, "I expected that to be a single. Any chance that was a different covey?"

"No, I don't think so. When chukars flush together, they usually will stay together all the way to the ground. If you happen to locate a covey that has been feeding and is scattered out, they'll often flush in waves of five or six at time. When that happens, you not only get some great covey shooting but the birds land as singles so you get more chances. The other way to get the singles to scatter is to flush the same covey two or three times."

"I don't think that's an option with this bunch. They flew all the way across the canyon."

"It's about two o'clock anyway. Why don't we hunt back down toward the water. I'll bet a covey or two has headed that way for an afternoon drink. As warm as it is getting, they may even take a siesta in those willows along the stream."

Don's hunch had been a good one. As soon as we reached the stream, I began noticing chukar droppings, but this time they were bright green and white. I began to report my discovery when I saw Shotsy and Sandy go "birdy". Sandy's long plumed, white tail and Shotsy's brown stub whipped furiously. Shotsy was first to lock up on a short ledge above the creek. Sandy caught wind of the chukars an

135

instant later and pointed to Shotsy's left.

"Don," I hissed. "We've got a point." I growled a "whoa" at Sandy, not wanting a repeat of her previous performance.

A dozen birds erupted beneath the ledge. This was more like it. Birds flying down might befuddle me, but a rising bird was something I knew how to handle. I swung on the lead bird and folded it in a puff of feathers. I swung on a second chukar but Don's second shot knocked it down an instant before I squeezed the trigger. Don didn't stop there however, and completed a triple as the covey reached the edge of shotgun range. I was thrilled with killing my first chukar and simply amazed at the shooting display I had just witnessed.

I walked toward my downed bird and stumbled into another group of five chukars that had remained hidden in the cheat grass. I took my time, knowing Don's gun was empty, and dropped my second chukar. At the shot, one last bird flushed from the creek to my left and I added him to the bag. I heard Don scream in mock agony as he frantically jammed shells into his autoloader, too late.

"We've got eight birds between us and we're still about an hour from the truck," said Don. "What do you say we head back. My legs have about had the course. Who knows, we might find another covey on the way."

"I'm satisfied," I replied, stroking the three hefty partridges which hung from my bird strap.

We sat on the tailgate sipping a well-earned beer, our legs still tingling from exertion. The dogs burrowed deep into the straw of their boxes and groaned as they laid down. I wiped my brow and felt a gritty sensation. Examining my fingertips with my eyes and then my tongue, I realized that I was covered with salt from my dried sweat. "Well, what do you think of chukar hunting?" asked Don.

"You know, if bobwhite hunting is a gentleman's version of wing shooting, I think that I'd have to call chukar hunting the athlete's version. Hunting these birds is a tremendous physical challenge. I still mourn the loss of my bobwhite quail hunting, but it's going to be fun living in a place where I can get to know these chukars. Thanks for the introduction."

Chapter Seventeen

ALASKA

In the mid 70s, my brother Mark moved to Alaska for a short time. He paid the bills by working in a butcher shop in Seward but primarily was there for the adventure. Without a wife or family to care for, and not being tied to any career track job at the time, he wanted to be part of the boom town atmosphere created by the construction of the oil pipeline. During our infrequent phone conversations, he described running from grizzlies at the town dump, catching dozens of fat salmon during the runs, brawling in the bars at night and seeing glaciers calve into an icy green sea.

I had chosen a more traditional lifestyle ... married, in graduate school, getting ahead and all that. I didn't regret my choices but I couldn't help being a little envious. I dreamed that some day I would see Alaska for myself. There are dreams and there are fantasies however, and I feared that visiting Alaska was quickly becoming the latter. My brother had been back from Alaska for ten years and I was no closer to going than when the dream began. By the time graduate school ended, I had two daughters and a wife to provide for. I had been fortunate to find a job I enjoyed on the West Coast. We had bought a new home that we loved, but the payments were a bit of a strain. Alaska, it seemed, would remain forever suspended between dreams and fantasy ... a place I would go someday maybe.

I was surprised to hear the phone ring in my Arizona hotel room. I had just left my co-workers in the meeting room downstairs and only my wife knew where I was staying. I picked up to hear the familiar voice of my brother-in-law and good friend Tom Wilson.

"What are you going to be doing in June?" he asked. "I'm going to be in Anchorage for a medical convention and I was thinking that maybe we could get together for some salmon fishing. I've got it all checked out. We take a bush plane out of Anchorage and get dropped off on the Deshka River. The outfitter supplies a raft and everything else we need. After a four or five day float down the river, the outfitter picks us up and flies us back to Anchorage. You can get away for a few days can't you."

"God, it sounds like a great trip," I said. Oh, how I wanted to jump at the chance, but as always there were reasons that I couldn't.

Despondently I answered, "I could probably get the time off Tom, but I'm just not in the financial shape to afford it right now."

"Damn it. I want you to come. I'll tell you what. If you can pay your way to Anchorage, I'll take care of the outfitter."

I wasn't sure if I should accept. A grown man was supposed to pay his own way in the world. But if I said no, when would the next chance to see Alaska come along?

Tom sensed my hesitance and said, "Come on, man. We haven't fished together for years. We'll have a great time. Believe me, I'm glad to do it."

A slightly guilty smile spread across my face as I answered, "Then I guess we're going salmon fishing, son."

I'd had a tantalizing glimpse of tremendous snow-blanketed mountains towering over the coniferous coastal plain as I peered through the windows of the Alaskan Airlines jet. Anchorage, however, was just another American town complete with fast food chains and hotels. The only proof that we were in Alaska was the length of the day. When we went to bed at 11:00, dusk was just beginning to fall.

Nighttime must have been short lived, because at 7:00 a.m. when we arrived at the lake where the float planes were moored, the sun was well above the horizon. The outfitter was about 30 years old, with sandy red hair that looked blow dried. He hardly fit my image of an Alaskan guide. He wore deck shoes without socks, blue shorts, a sleeveless T-shirt with some sort of logo on it and sun glasses. He looked as if he had just moved from Los Angeles.

I didn't relish the thought of being dumped in the wilderness by a guy who didn't know a salmon from a blue gill. There was not much I could do about it at that point, but I did make a careful inspection of the equipment he was providing. The tent, sleeping bags and foam pads were all there. The lantern and propane stove worked fine. The oars and foot pump were with the raft, which I had to assume held air. When my search revealed a rubber patching kit, I began to feel a little more secure. The outfitter must have at least a modicum of experience to include that easily overlooked detail.

We loaded the equipment along with our rods and duffels into the sparsely painted aluminum, twin engine, Otter float plane. The raft was cumbersome and heavy so Tom and I helped hoist it into the plane. Two other fisherman, both doctors attending the same conference as Tom, were to join us for the flight in but would be dropped at a fishing lodge many miles down river from where our float would begin. The interior of the plane was entirely stripped. Nothing which failed to serve the purpose of hauling cargo was included except for the seats and those were merely nylon straps on tubular metal frames.

Tom, who was an experienced private pilot himself, hopped into the cockpit with the bush pilot, and in moments we were airborne. My nose was glued to the window, anxious to absorb every moment of the trip. I was amazed at how quickly we left civilization behind. Within five minutes, we looked down on a virtual wilderness. The terrain outside Anchorage was a vast coastal plain with patches of green forest appearing as islands amidst a brown sea of boggy, brushy meadows. It looked like ideal moose habitat. Snow covered peaks were clearly visible in the distance, but we wouldn't be going that far. Our raft trip would carry us through the forested plain.

A thirty minute flight took us to the mouth of the river. The plane banked for an approach, revealing nearly 100 boats anchored in the river. At first, I wondered where we would find space to land, but the pilot swung down river to open water and landed safely. The fisherman beside us groaned as they saw the number of people on the river. "Not what I thought Alaskan fishing would be like," grumbled one. I couldn't have agreed more and I was mighty glad that Tom and I wouldn't be departing along with them. Those guys might catch salmon, but I was interested in doing more than sitting in a parking lot and hauling in fish.

We unloaded the fishermen and wished them luck before taking off once more. The pilot turned and said, "The run of kings is just getting started. That's why there are so many boats here. There will already be some fish up where I'm taking you guys, but more should be coming up every day. I'll be taking you about 35 miles upriver. I'll pick you up on Friday at the river mouth where we dropped the other fisherman. You'll have time to stop and fish but don't dally too long or you won't be here in time to meet me. I'll fly directly up the river so you guys can get a look at the water you'll be fishing." The river, which meandered through a spruce forest, was only about 25 yards wide with occasional mild rapids, although the tea brown river was primarily smooth water.

A lake of about 20 acres, which nearly merged with the river, was to be our drop off, and the pilot glided the Otter smoothly onto the glassy water. We pulled on our hip boots and began unloading the gear. All went well until it came time to transport the raft. Minus the help of the outfitter, the cumbersome, rolled-up raft was almost more than Tom and I could manage. With a plop, it fell off the pontoon and into the shallow water near the bank. Grasping hold of the ropes which held the bundle in place, we dug our feet into the muddy ooze, and eventually skidded the raft onto dry land.

In the few short minutes required to complete the unloading, the mosquitoes had detected our carbon dioxide stream and had descended upon us. Emitting a high-pitched whine, they attacked as if they were starving. Swatting them proved futile, as reinforcements arrived immediately. Being an entomologist, I was not totally surprised by the onslaught. I rummaged through my duffel and retrieved a plastic bottle of 95 percent DEET which we applied to all of our exposed skin as well as our long sleeved shirts.

The repellent successfully prevented us from being bitten on the skin, but soon the voracious bloodsuckers began to bite right through our hair. Although I had brought a head net along, I hated wearing the thing. It blurred my vision and I felt like my head was in a shopping bag. The solution was obvious but rather repugnant. I poured a pool of repellent onto my palms and then hesitated like a swimmer about to plunge into icy water. I let out a roar and rubbed the putrid oil through my hair. "Just call me Repellent Man!" I screamed. I knew that DEET would be absorbed through the skin into the body and that within hours even my urine would be laced with the stuff, but compared to the alternative of exsanguination, it seemed worth the risk.

We were faced with a short portage of about 100 yards to the river. Moving the coolers and waterproof duffels proved to be no problem, but the raft was another story. The muscles in our shoulders strained as we tried to lift, but the bundle barely budged. "Now I know why that pilot was in such a bloody hurry to get out of here," I griped. "He didn't want to get stuck helping us with this chore." We contemplated the alternatives and decided that rolling the raft might work. Like pushing a gigantic, lopsided snowball, we grunted each time we turned the raft over.

Stopping to mop sweat from my forehead, I said, "I'm afraid that we are going to put a hole in the raft doing it this way. I think if we just hold our mouths right, we can lift this S.O.B." Grasping the ropes from opposite sides, we twisted our faces into our most determined expressions and lifted with all our might. Sure enough, we got it off the ground and began to stagger unsteadily toward the river. A half dozen rests later, we dropped the raft for the final time at the water's edge.

"Are you ready to get this thing blown up?" asked Tom.

"Whoa, Hoss!" I answered sitting down next to the gear. I reached into the cooler and extracted two of the local Chinook beers. "As of now, we're on vacation. Sit down and have a beer."

Tom popped the lid and sat down heavily beside me. With a smile he raised his bottle and said, "Welcome to Alaska, my friend."

The raft was designed with four air compartments so that a leak in one area would not cause the craft to sink. We attached the foot pump to the nozzle on each compartment and soon had our raft inflated. A foam pad was perfectly cut to fit into the floor of the raft to protect it from punctures. We snapped together the aluminum frame which held the oar locks, and set it in the center. The larger cooler containing our food was set in the middle of the frame and served as a seat from which to row. The smaller cooler containing the lantern, stove and fuel was placed in the stern and served as the other seat.

Tom rigged his spinning rod with an orange Spin and Glo which was a round, marble-sized piece of plastic with spiral shaped blades which caused it to spin in the water. He threaded the 20 pound test monofilament through the Spin and Glo and tied on a hook to which he fastened a knot of orange yarn. The man at the tackle shop had described the set up and explained that we should simulate the look of salmon eggs. He told us that adult salmon did not really eat anything while they were in fresh water, but they had an instinct to pick up eggs dislodged from the gravel and carry them about in their mouths. Trout were supposed to actively eat the eggs.

I decided to try my fly rod, which was a nine foot, nine weight graphite with a floating line, and 200 yards of backing. I selected one of the larger, orange, yarn-egg flies that I had tied before leaving home and attached it to the zero X tippet.

Our equipment finally in order, I pushed the raft off the gravel bank and Tom rowed us out into the briskly flowing river. With a deep pull on the right oar, he turned us to face downstream. Embraced by the current, we drifted along at an easy-going pace. The chop of the current slapping against the raft sang a cheerful song perfectly attuned to our festive spirits. Being weak fliers, the mosquitoes were unable to home in on us while we were on the river, offering us reprieve from their odious attentions.

I leaned back, my elbows resting on the inflated pontoon, enjoying the passing scenery. Dark green spruce trees intermixed with lighter aspen and alder lined the river. A thick understory of shrubs flourished beneath the trees; being especially heavy along the banks where sunlight was plentiful. It wasn't really beautiful, but it was unmistakably wild; a place where a moose or bear or eagle could appear at any moment. An excited tingle swept through my body as the wildness enveloped me.

Our craft flexed as we negotiated some minor rapids and headed toward a bend in the river. Tom pulled hard on the oars, trying to keep us in the main current, but his effort had begun too late and we drifted into the far bank. Chuckling profanely, I tried to rescue the rods from the overhanging tree limbs with one hand and push us off with the other. Tom pulled mightily on the oars and eventually we freed ourselves. It wasn't to be our last collision with the bank, as we took turns learning to position ourselves properly in the current to avoid the obstacles before us.

Navigation practice came to a sudden halt when a silver backed salmon breached like a porpoise in the pool before us. "My God! Did you see the size of that fish? Pull over. Pull over," I exhorted. We beached the raft and fumbled excitedly with our rods. We cast our lures repeatedly into the small pool. Our attention riveted to each cast, we were sure that a strike was imminent. Hope eventually waned however as the salmon seemed unimpressed with our offerings. Gradually we drifted apart; me fishing upstream and Tom fishing down. When we were separated by about 100 yards, I heard Tom whoop and I knew he had a fish on. I waded out of the river to watch him fight the fish, when without warning his 20-pound test line snapped. Tom, who is rarely profane, let loose a string of expletives at losing his first salmon. He went momentarily limp, staring down at the river before he looked up and hollered in a matter of fact tone, "Too much drag."

Enthused by Tom's early flirtation with success, we resumed fishing with an optimism that each cast would bring a beautiful salmon. However the afternoon and early evening wore on without another strike. There was no need to become discouraged though. After all, the trip was young. We were here in Alaska. Life was too good to worry about not catching a fish. We had plenty of time.

We floated down river about half a mile until we came to a broad gravel bar where we skidded the raft well onto shore and unloaded our equipment. As we assembled the gray, two-manned dome tent, a screeching cry drifted from the sky. A bald eagle with immense, mahogany wings with outer primary feathers extended like fingers, sailed over, fifty feet above our heads. Setting his wings, he glided down and perched on a dead limb at the top of an alder almost as if posing for us. I had seen eagles many times near my home in Washington, but for Tom this was a first, and he stood awestruck at the majesty of the bird.

"Oh look!" I said. "There is another one in the same tree. It looks like they have a nest."

Throughout the extended evening, the eagles cruised the river periodically gliding back to their nest. Fishless, we cooked steaks and potatoes over our Coleman stove and enjoyed the show; A perfect Alaskan night.

Morning found us eager to reverse our fortunes so we hurriedly broke camp and resumed our float. Less than 200 yards from camp, a dozen or more salmon porpoised in a pool formed by a bend in the river. We quickly beached the raft. Once again, Tom's luck hit first. On his second cast, he felt a tug and struck, driving the hook deep into the salmon's jaw. He let out a whoop and the fight was on. The fish charged down stream with Tom running along the bank in hot pursuit. I scrambled for my camera and yelled for Tom to hang on. By the time I caught up to the action, Tom was wearing the fish down and soon we saw his shadowy form struggling just beneath the surface. The big king was easily as long as my leg.

"How are we going to land this monster without a net?" asked Tom.

"The only thing I can think is for me to step into the water when you get him close to the bank. Then, you try backing him up onto the beach while I give him a push. Make sure he's played out, though."

Our plan worked perfectly and soon a big hook-jawed male flopped on the sand before us. As we learned later, this fish was too dark, having spent considerable time in fresh water, and we should have released him. Fresher, more silver, colored fish were sure to follow, but we didn't know that at the time and we weren't about to let go of the biggest fish either of us had ever seen.

Immersed in snapping photographs, we didn't notice the trio of fishermen striding up river until they were nearly upon us. What we supposed to be a grandfather, a middle aged-son and his teen aged grandson stopped to admire our catch. They were Alaskans who had flown their tiny floatplane and landed it on a straight stretch of river a few hundred yards downstream from us. The old gent carried a rifle strung across his back for bear protection. I had debated leaving my pistol at home thinking I might be paranoid about the bear threat. Seeing the locals with firearms reassured me that I was not foolish to have my .357 on my belt, after all.

Our new friends cast their lines into the pool, and in a matter of minutes all three were into nice kings. For bait they used billiard ball-sized globs of salmon eggs. They had removed the twin, eighteen inch long, wrist-thick skeins of eggs from the females caught on previous trips, and rolled them in borax. The treatment dried the eggs slightly and toughened the membranes, which held the eggs together. Slicing a section off the skein, a treble hook was threaded into the center of the sticky, pungent, orange mass. Using no weight, the eggs were dead drifted through the pool on a taut line. A gentle tap, the only sign that a salmon had picked up the eggs, was answered with a hard strike to drive the hook into the bony mouth. We watched as the three of them hauled salmon after salmon from the dark pool.

The men shared some eggs with us, and soon Tom had another fish on. This was a smaller fish of about 10 pounds. The men told us it was a jack, which meant that it was an immature male that had for some reason swam into fresh water with the mature fish. It would not mate, but like all Pacific salmon it would die without returning to the sea. We decided to keep that fish for camp meat.

Before parting company, the grandfather sold us a dozen of the trebled hooks and several plastic bags filled with long skeins of eggs. He wished us well and suggested that we camp at a pool a few hundred yards below where their plane was tied up. He assured us that it was a favorite resting place for salmon on the journey up river.

I was beginning to feel left out as I had yet to hook my first fish. The fly rod was not very effective in casting the heavy eggs. I could not backcast as the eggs would tear off the hooks, so I was forced to strip out as much line as I could manage and simply swing the eggs into the water. For all intents and purposes, it was like fishing with a cane pole. I cursed my stupidity in not bringing another rod with me.

We floated down to the proscribed pool and skidded the raft onto the gravel beach. Tom began filleting the jack for a late lunch and handed me his spinning rod. The pool was not as large or deep as the one where Tom had caught his fish earlier. There was a narrow riffle perhaps four feet deep at the head of a pool, which spanned 75 yards.

On the seventh or eighth cast into the riffle, I felt a tap not much stronger than the strike of the blue gills of my youth. I struck hard, and a silver slab rolled in midstream. I had missed him, but my adrenalin began to pump. I immediately cast again, desperately hoping the salmon would grant me a second chance. The long-awaited tap finally came, and this time when I lifted the rod I felt the heavy weight of a well-hooked but as yet unalarmed king.

The author with his first salmon, taken in June of 1988.

I leaned back on the rod, pressuring him out of the quick current. At last realizing his predicament, the fish surged downstream causing the drag to sing as he took line. The bowed, throbbing rod sent shock waves of excitement coursing up my arms. The dream of being in an Alaskan river, fighting a king salmon was coming true and the reality was delicious. He was not a huge fish, as kings go, perhaps weighing 20 pounds, but he was the largest fish that I had ever hooked and I didn't want to lose him. Tom and I attempted the same crude technique for landing a fish without a net. On the final pull, the salmon, now just inches shy of the beach, thrashed wildly, dislodging the hook. We instantly dropped to our knees and frantically wrestled him ashore.

I felt positively triumphant holding the beautiful silver fish up for photographs. No matter what happened during the remainder of the journey, the trip was a success now. I had caught an Alaskan king salmon. We were limited to possession of two fish each in possession for the trip, so I gladly released the fish.

We spent a leisurely afternoon setting up camp while the brilliant orange salmon steaks, sprinkled liberally with salt and pepper and smothered in butter and lemon, sizzled on top of the Coleman stove. Used to the measly 6 ounce filets served up in most restaurants, we mumbled contented groans as we gorged on several pounds of fresh-from-the-river salmon. Surely no two men in the finest establishment ever ate better than we did sitting in the sand, tin plates on our laps, our backs propped against the raft, the river filled with salmon drifting past.

At 9:00 p.m. in broad daylight, we decided to sleep. With virtually no darkness, we slept when tired and traveled and fished when the mood struck us. Time seemed irrelevant. So it was when I was awakened at 2:00 a.m. by the sound of splashing in the river. I peered through the mosquito-covered screens to see a school of salmon porpoising in our pool. Quickly pulling on my pants and re-dosing myself with repellent, I scrambled out of the tent into the dusky subarctic night.

In a matter of minutes, I had hooked a truly large salmon. His powerful back rose out of the water as he motored across the pool in a furious first charge for freedom. Three times I fought to regain line and three times the salmon made fierce runs to take it back. At last on my fourth try, his strength seemed to desert him. I forced the fish toward the bank. Without the assistance of my fish landing partner who remained snug in his sleeping bag, I tried to simply walk backward and drag the four-foot-long behemoth onto the sand. He was not quite finished however, and with a tremendous surge he snapped my line at the knot and drifted back into the depths. With a net he would have been mine, but it didn't really matter, for what is a fish but a joy and a memory.

I awakened Tom, excitedly telling him what had happened and urging him to join me. There were still fish in the pool. Bleary-eyed, he came grumbling out of the tent but was soon wide awake when a salmon, equal to the one I had just fought, hit his bait. For nearly 15 minutes, he battled the great fish as I cheered him on. Together, we were able to land this fish. He was a full 48 inches long and had to weigh 40 pounds or more. In order to keep him fresh, we slipped a length of parachute cord beneath his gill plate and tied it in front of his jaw. Carrying him to a tiny feeder stream, we tethered him to the submerged root of a tree.

After breakfast, Tom went to retrieve his fish before we shoved off to continue our trip. The salmon had revived nicely in the cool flowing creek and seemed to have forgotten that he had ever been caught. As Tom led him from the creek into the river as one would lead a dog on a leash, the salmon began to leap. Tom had a look of horror on his face as the 40 pounder reached waist height before crashing with a mighty splash at his feet. Cascades of water flew in all directions, dousing Tom. The salmon jumped again, hit the water and took off a third, fourth and fifth time. With each jump Tom yelled "Whoa, Whoa!" A look of panicked determination was etched on his dripping wet face. I was no help at all, as I sat on the beach doubled over in laughter.

This third day of our float was to be the best rainy day of my life. By 7:00 a.m. the skies opened up and poured with no sign of a let up. As we hadn't traveled far in our first two days, we couldn't afford to stay tucked away in the tent. We had to cover some river miles. We donned our rain gear, packed our clothes and sleeping bags into the rubber duffels, rolled up the soaked tent and shoved off. Our faces and hands were exposed to the pelting rain, but fortunately the temperature remained in the 60s. We felt a little clammy but not cold.

The forest absorbed the steady downpour almost silently. Bonaparte gulls, their black heads glistening, seemed not to notice the rain as they stood impassively on the sand bars. Salmon porpoised in the rain splattered river as they had done since the beginning of time. Rain was an integral part of coastal Alaska and all of the creatures including myself accepted it.

My brother-in-law, Tom Wilson, and me with Tom's first salmon, taken on the Deshka River in June of 1988.

We now felt confident rowing the raft, even through the sharp curves. Miles flowed past as the current pulled us along. We took turns rowing and fishing, although we occasionally stopped at particularly promising pools where we could both try our luck. Despite having to share the spinning rod, we hooked seven salmon, landing five of them. All were in the 25 to 35 pound range.

The rain let up in the evening, allowing us to spread out our wet equipment. Fortunately the rubber duffels had kept our sleeping bags and pads dry. Once again we gorged on salmon chased by barely cool beer. We had reached the stage of our trip at which we were utterly relaxed and completely detached from our responsible lives. We sat up late into the night, too satisfied to fish, listening to the river, happy to be in Alaska.

The character of the river had begun to change as we approached its mouth. The current was slower and deeper, which slowed our progress considerably. No longer could we just steer the raft as the current carried us along. Now, we had to do some serious rowing. There were still salmon in the river however and we caught three in the first two hours of the day. Our slow progress began to concern us, as we had an appointment with the float plane that afternoon. We decided to quit fishing and each man an oar. Fan boats similar to the ones seen in the Everglades, raced up and down the river. Cabins were popping up along the banks.

We were headed back to civilization. I was sorry to see our trip end, although I was looking forward to a shower, shave and shampoo to get rid of the accursed repellant. As we beached the raft at our rendezvous point, I reflected that sometimes fantasies are actually dreams, and dreams can come true.

The author with "The Great Anja" in the field.

Chapter Eighteen

MIXED BAG

For millions of Easterners and Midwesterners who struggle through snowy winters, California is the promised land. They love the perfect climate and the proximity of mountains and ocean. I, however; spent the longest two years, five months and two days of my life in California.

There was upland bird and waterfowl hunting in California, but it was mainly reserved for two groups: people who owned their own land and people wealthy enough to pay for it. I didn't qualify in either category. I knocked on hundreds of doors searching for places to hunt pheasants, quail or ducks, and obtained permission on precisely three farms totaling two hundred acres. Landowners, deluged with requests to hunt from friends and relatives, felt they just couldn't allow a stranger to hunt. Public pheasant hunting in wildlife refuges resembled a bargain basement sale at Macy's.

Several chukar hunts each season in Nevada were all that stood between me and insanity. The hunting was fairly good, but I chafed at not being able to go more often. Since getting my driver's license at sixteen, I had hunted no less than thirty days per season. In California, I was limited to perhaps ten days.

To paraphrase Mac Davis, I let out a whoop of joy when I saw California in my rear view mirror. I had convinced my boss to allow me to transfer, and in April 1986, I moved my family to Yakima, Washington. Located in the eastern rain shadow of the Cascade Mountains, Yakima received less than eight inches of rain per year. Irrigation, however, had transformed the shrub steppe into one of the premiere fruit growing areas of the world. Famous Washington apples and sweet cherries, as well as peaches, pears and wine grapes, were grown in the valley.

The beauty of Eastern Washington consisted not only what was present, but what was absent. Only a million people lived in the entire eastern half of the state. In the forested mountains, three species of grouse flourished: blues, ruffed and spruce. In the mountainous shrub steppe, chukars and huns were plentiful. Pheasants, quail and ducks made their home in the agricultural valleys. All three habitats were less than an hour's drive from my house. I was in heaven.

Since making the switch from English setters to the versatile

German Longhaired pointers, I especially loved to combine a hunt for waterfowl, pheasants and quail. Longhairs were equally at home on land or water and were ideal for a mixed bag hunt.

My buddy Milt Cobb pulled into the drive about 8:00 on a frigid, cloudy morning. After loading my Longhair, Anja, with Milt's Longhair Cassie, we headed to the Lower Yakima Valley.

The heavy December snows had kept most hunters home for the last few weeks, but Milt and I had been enjoying the best hunting of the year. Most of the ponds had frozen up, forcing the mallards, which were thick in the valley that winter, to seek refuge in the flowing creeks and drains.

We knew of a half dozen such places where a well-executed sneak could put us within shotgun range of ducks. Parking well out of sight, we uncrated the dogs and brought them immediately to heel. The flat, shadowless light made the sky and snow blend together indistinguishably as we trudged through the calf deep snow on the mint field. Separating about 50 yards, we prepared for the final approach. We nodded toward one another as a signal, and briskly walked to the creek bank. Five mergansers burst into flight, croaking hoarsely through their thin, toothy bills. The dogs watched the ducks intently and no doubt wondered why we failed to shoot, but we wanted nothing to do with fish ducks.

We withdrew 100 yards from the bank and continued hiking downstream to a nearby bend in the creek frequented by mallards and occasionally a wood duck or two. We separated to cover both sides of a patch of streamside willows, and made our approach. The creek clearly in view, I was about to conclude that there were no ducks when fifteen squawking mallards flushed in front of me. I swung in front of a drake that seemed to be standing still as he fought for altitude. He dropped with a splash at the edge of the ice shelf. I dropped a second greenhead as he reached the willows on the far bank.

Without hesitation, Anja cracked through the ice to retrieve the first drake, which was floating downstream on the current. She struggled to break ice on the retrieve, but eventually delivered the bird to hand. I tossed a snowball across the creek to help Anja locate the second duck and commanded "fetch". She had not seen the second greenhead drop, but she trusted my command and plunged into the icy waters again. Once on the far bank, Anja used her keen nose to locate the drake and was soon swimming back to me. I had heard Milt shoot moments after my second shot, and I could now hear him commanding

Cassie to fetch.

Our next stop took us to a slough on Department of Wildlife land. Most of the slough had frozen, but on one end a warm spring kept a stretch of water open. We hiked to the north side where we could use a mass of rushes to cloak our approach. Bent double, the dogs at heel, we crept forward. A sharp-eyed hen spotted us when we were about 50 yards from the slough, and quacked an alarm as she jumped into flight. We raced forward, while an additional 125 mallards rolled from the pond in a massive wave. Skidding to a halt, we fired at the departing flock and a hen and drake tumbled out.

Milt's duck had fallen dead on the far side of the slough and Cassie quickly collected it and retrieved. My drake had a broken wing, and had hit the water swimming. It slipped into the reeds and out of sight. Anja swam in circles for several minutes, her head raised high as she tried to pick up a scent off the water. At last she did, and even began to yelp excitedly as she followed the trail into the vegetation. For several moments, all we could see was shaking reeds as she followed the trail. When she emerged, her brown fur caked in black muck, she had the still-alive mallard firmly in her jaws.

My German Longhaired Pointer, Anja, and my English setter, Gina, on a mixed bag hunt near Yakima, Washington.

Our limit of mallards in hand, it was time to try our luck on the pheasants and quail. A short distance from the slough, the Department of Wildlife had a five acre food plot planted in sorghum. We parked beneath a locust tree on the edge of the plot, and began to unload the dogs. Suddenly a covey of about 12 California Valley Quail flushed from the other side of the locust. The beautiful gray, black and bronze quail with the jaunty top knot plumes fanned out and landed in the sorghum. Fumbling to get our shotguns from the cases, we loaded up and headed after them.

Anja pointed first, frozen like a brown statue against the snowy background. Fully expecting a quail, I barely held my fire when the hen pheasant flushed at my feet. The quail were sitting tight in the snow. Milt kicked one out on his own, and dumped the cock as it streaked away. Anja pointed again in a clump of greasewood on the edge of the sorghum. Cassie slammed to a backing point the instant she saw Anja stopped. Anja was stretched out, her tail straight back, in her usual style. Cassie held her head and tail high in a classic pose.

Two quail flushed when I kicked into the brush and I dropped the hen as it flew down the fence line. Cassie got to the bird first and retrieved it to Milt. We took two more birds from the covey before deciding we had enough. There was no point shooting the covey down too low. We wanted some birds for next year. We decided to hunt on the Yakima Indian land long the river.

The cover along the riverbanks was thick with wild rose, willows and cottonwoods. There were dozens of coveys living there, but they were exceedingly difficult to hunt. We opted instead for a sagebrush flat interspersed with clumps of Russian olive trees. If we could find quail there, we had a good chance for open shots.

The first covey we located had 25 birds in it. They flushed wild from the sagebrush as we approached, and landed in the olive thickets. The dogs pointed again and again as we hunted from clump to clump. Milt and I posted ourselves on opposite sides of the trees so that one of us always had an open shot. We took eight birds from that covey before moving on toward the river.

In a young cottonwood, I spotted a young barn owl, and I called Milt over to see it. While we admired the little raptor, a rooster pheasant, unnerved by our presence, flushed wild. Reacting instinctively, we fired simultaneously. Both of us were slightly behind the bird, but he was hit hard enough to go down. He splashed into the fast flowing Yakima River. Cassie battled through the brush, skidded down the sheer embankment, and plunged into the current. A few moments later, she returned with a wet, bedraggled ringneck.

On the way back to the truck, Cassie pointed and Anja backed in another Russian olive thicket. When I kicked, one of the largest coveys I had ever witnessed came buzzing out. As Valley quail often do, they did not all flush together but came out in groups of five and ten. Three times, I reloaded before the covey had completely vacated the tangle. When all was done, we had six birds on the ground. It took several minutes for the dogs to locate them all, but eventually all were slipped onto our straps.

Dusk was beginning to fall. We were only two quail shy of our limits anyway, so we trudged back through the snowy sagebrush. It had been a great day of mixed bag hunting, but not an unusual day in my beloved Yakima Valley.

*My wife, Claudia Rohlfs, with a pronghorned antelope
taken in Montana in 1992.*

Chapter Nineteen

PRONGHORNS

A cowboy once described antelope hunting as "A real grin". I've never heard a better description. Despite tripe to the contrary, pronghorn hunting is close to a sure thing. Success rates in Wyoming and Montana run about 90 percent. Probably 5 percent of the unsuccessful hunters were holding out for record book heads, so the bottom line is that very few hunters go home without their antelope.

How do antelope compare to deer or elk or bighorn sheep as challenging game animals? About the same as dunking worms for bluegills compares to flyfishing for trout. It so happens, however, that I enjoy fishing for bluegills every once in a while, and I'm downright crazy for it if I can take a kid or first time fisherman along. Antelope are for fun, pure and simple.

My first hunt for antelope occurred in 1985, when my brother-in-law, Tom Wilson, joined me for a hunt near Miles City, Montana. Tom had hunted both whitetails and mule deer with me over the years. While Tom seemed always to bring me luck, I was unable to return the favor so he had yet to shoot his first big game animal.

We arrived the day before the season opened, and began to scout for a place to hunt. Less than two miles outside the city limits, we spotted our first band of pronghorns standing by the road. Circumnavigating the hunting area in which we held permits, we saw at least 500 antelope before dark. Virtually every rancher we spoke to gladly gave permission to hunt. The antelope, it seemed, either were tough on the wheat crop, or were an unwanted competitor with their cattle for the grass supply.

Never had I seen so many animals in a day. Therein lies one of the attractions of antelope hunting. Where else can such herds be seen outside of Africa or perhaps Alaska during caribou migrations. Pronghorns are truly handsome beasts with flanks of white and tan, and white rumps which flare to warn of danger. The males have black cheek patches and muzzles, as well as elegant two pronged horns. A band of antelope racing full out across the rolling grass hills, a cloud of dust billowing in their wake, is truly a sight to stir the soul.

Tom and I arrived at the ranch just as the sky began to brighten. The rancher had told us of a huge band of antelope that fed in his winter wheat field every night. He suggested approaching them via a series of hills to the south. We were less than 150 yards from the ranch road when we spotted our first buck. Tom bellied over a rise and shot the 11 inch buck with a single, well placed shot. He was delighted at taking his first big game animal after so many attempts and I was equally happy for him. We field dressed and tagged the animal and left it to be collected later.

We almost reached the wheat field when a truck spooked the antelope. A band of 60 animals came running up the draw directly at me. I passed up a group of yearling bucks, before spotting two mature bucks that had stopped beneath a slight rise in front of me. I flattened myself into the grass and waited. Both animals continued toward me. I decided that the trailing animal was the larger of the two and had to wait until the first one moved from the line of fire. At seventy yards, I finally had my chance, and dropped the 12-inch buck.

Our hunt was over. It had begun only 30 minutes before. By taking two average bucks so quickly, we had missed out on the most delightful part of antelope hunting: stalking and selecting large bucks. On my next pronghorn hunt I did not make the same mistake.

I was hunting with my stepbrother, Hunter Leigh, and our mutual friend, Earle Falast. Hunter had even less experience than Tom, and was, in fact, on his first big game hunt. Earle was an experienced whitetail hunter. After the long drive to Big Timber, Montana, we were determined to extend the entire experience. We paid a rancher a nominal trespass fee and camped out by an old homestead. A spring of sweet water gurgled from the ground next to the dilapidated log house where we pitched our tent beneath a grove of gnarled cottonwoods and set up a kitchen on a portable table.

We spent the afternoon before opening day, scouting the grass covered hills around camp. From each rise, antelope could be seen grazing in the distance. We knew we were in for a great hunt. As night fell, we gathered up a great pile of cottonwood limbs and got a roaring fire going. We passed the bottle as we plotted our morning strategy and renewed our friendship. Stars flooded the clear night sky, and I declined the tent, opting to sleep beneath the open heavens.

I offered to guide Hunter since this was his first antelope hunt. We climbed the hill behind camp just as dawn was breaking. We planned to spot a herd from the crest and stalk them. A stalk proved unnecessary as a band of thirty animals wandered up the draw 150 yards below us. The band included one very nice buck of perhaps thirteen inches. Hunter wanted to shoot it, but I persuaded him not to. I wanted to stretch out our hunt, at least for a little while.

Using the hills for cover and paying heed to the wind direction, we stalked to within rifle range of three more bands of pronghorns over the course of the morning. None had any outstanding bucks. The fourth band had only eight animals, but two were nice bucks. The larger of the pair was equal to the first buck we had passed up, and Hunter decided to try a shot.

As beginning hunters are apt to do, he delayed shooting so long that the animals eventually wandered around the hill. We scurried to the next rise. Hunter was in perfect position; the herd about 100 yards below him. I waited for what seemed an eternity before the .243 finally barked. The shot was slightly back. The buck staggered about for a few moments and then dropped. He was a fine buck that Hunter now has in his den at home. Despite the fact that the buck was no larger than the one we spotted at daybreak, I'm certain that Hunter prizes him more than he would have the first buck.

Earle, who had missed a buck in the morning, hunted to the north, and I hunted west in the afternoon. I stalked to within shooting range of at least 20 bucks, all of which I deemed to be too small. I then spotted a tremendous herd. Twelve mature bucks and 40 or 50 does and fawns were resting in a broad valley. Using a series of hills, I stalked to about 300 yards. I spread the legs of the bipod and cranked the scope up to 9X in order to compare the heads. One buck appeared to have horns in the 13 inch class, but they were quite massive, and I decided to take a shot.

There was no chance of stalking closer, so I had to shoot from where I was. When the .280 cracked, the entire herd, including my buck, raced off. I could see that he was hit low on the chest. Realizing I should have held higher, I raised the crosshairs above his rapidly departing rump and fired twice. The second shot broke his hind leg at the knee and dropped him. By the time I returned to camp, Earle was there. He reported that he also had a buck down. Fortunately, we were able to drive the Blazer right up to both bucks; no grueling drags in antelope hunting.

We celebrated that night by broiling tenderloin over the fire. The bucks we had shot were nice although not huge antelope. We had taken our time, enjoyed watching the herds, enjoyed the camping, enjoyed the fellowship, and concluded the hunt when it felt right. The outcome was never in doubt, and in that way it differed from other types of hunts, but it was sure a grin.

My setter, Gina, with blue grouse shot in the Okanogan Valley of Washington.

Chapter Twenty

THREE GROUSE OPENER

My wife calls it obsession. During August, that is obvious even to me. Sleep comes slowly as I plot the details of opening day: What time will I leave? Bring the big sleeping bag this year? Don't forget the stake outs for the dogs. Should I hunt Bald Mountain or White Pass first? Break in those new boots before leaving? Get propane for the lantern.

Each circuit with the lawn mower is part of a weekly countdown: three more cuts until hunting season. Early mornings are devoted to dog training. The dogs need the conditioning and I need to evaluate the success of the year's hatch. Equipment is examined and orders placed with the catalogs. Two pair of boots need replacing; a few pairs of socks; the tent should be good for another season; a new foam pad would be handy though.

For years, I opened the season with a dove hunt. Since moving to the Pacific Northwest, my tradition has changed, for the better, I think. Opening day now means grouse hunting. The Cascade Mountains offer a welcome relief from the late summer heat. Escaping the cheat grass and sagebrush to be among trees that actually grow without irrigation, is reason enough to go. Most compelling, however, is that the Pacific Northwest has the best grouse hunting in America. New England may have the tradition, but has fewer birds and fewer places to hunt. Minnesota and Michigan have lots of open country and great hunting for ruffeds, but they don't have blue grouse.

Our grouse are denigrated as stupid birds that stand in the open or land on the closest limb waiting to be shot. Granted, western grouse can be taken advantage of and often are by hunters who give the birds no respect; considering them "pot" birds to be shot on the ground or limb with a .22 rifle or pistol. The truth of the matter is that sport is what a hunter makes it.

The addition of dogs to the hunt improves the sporting experience dramatically. In most cases, all but the finest grouse dogs are a hindrance in terms of the number of grouse killed. Western grouse, especially blues, are extremely wary of dogs perhaps, because coyotes are so numerous in their habitat. Grouse frequently flush wildly at the mere sight of a dog, while they will permit a human to walk very close to them.

Dogs therefore solve the problem of the "stupid" bird that will not

161

flush. Then what of the bird that lands on a limb? To the best of my knowledge, no hunter has ever been forced to blast a bird off a limb. It is a simple matter to either flush the grouse out of the tree or simply to leave it alone and search for another bird. If a hunter shoots a bird off a limb (and I will admit to doing it on occasion), then he really shouldn't complain that the *bird* was unsporting.

With the use of dogs, and a little discretion on shot selection, the Western forest grouse make for challenging shooting in magnificent settings. Add minimal competition from other hunters and lots of birds, and you have the recipe for outstanding sport.

Bill Von Stubbe, a man at least as obsessed as I, called in mid-August. "Well, September 1 is almost here. Same place as last year? Or someplace new?" he asked in his clipped, no nonsense style. Bill is a physician, about a dozen years older than I, bright as hell, a good shot, and a cheerful companion in any conditions. He is one of my favorite hunting buddies.

"I'm ready, Bill," I answered. "I've got an idea to run by you. I'm sure we can find ruffeds and blues, but spruce grouse live in that country also. There aren't a helluva lot of them, but I ran into some a few years back. Why don't we try to collect all three species on this trip?"

"Sounds good. Pick you up at 1:00 on Friday."

We arrived just before dinner and set up camp at a lake situated at 3,000 feet elevation, where the sagebrush and forest merged. An aspen-choked stream flowed east from the lake. Aspen are a key plant in locating ruffeds, providing both food and cover for the birds. Our plan called for a morning hunt along the stream in hopes of picking up the first of our three species.

Shortly after dawn, we drove Bill's truck downstream to begin our hunt. Wanting to avoid mixing Bill's flushing Labrador with my pointing dog, we decided to split up, with me taking the main creek bottom and Bill trying his luck on the side draws. I let Gina my English setter out of her crate, as her white coloring would be easier to see in the thicket than the dark brown of Anja, my German Longhaired pointer. Anja yelped her disappointment at my selection, but her chance would soon come.

A flannel shirt proved to be ideal in fending off the early morning chill. Heavy dew soon soaked my pant legs and boots. Aspens without a hint of gold cloaked the bottom in lush greenery. Plowing through the thicket, a roar of wings thundered. A mature gray phased cock rocketed overhead in perfect view for a millisecond before disappearing through the foliage. My snap shot was in vain, but it didn't seem to matter. The long awaited season was here. The shotgun in the crook of my arm felt like a long lost friend. Birds were in the coverts once again. The dogs were joyful with renewed purpose. Dozens of days and hundreds of shots lay ahead. A miss was nothing.

Several hundred yards of walking hunched over in the tangled trees soon sent me retreating to the edge of the creek bottom and easier walking. The dog was better suited for this cover, so I tried with limited success to keep an eye on her from the periphery. My strategy paid off, as I glimpsed a white statue of a setter pointing intently into a brushy-topped deadfall. What appeared to be a juvenile bird, flushed before I could get into shooting position. Gina being staunch but not steady, dashed off after it.

I stood there bemoaning my ill fortune, when I heard a chirping sound emanating from the deadfall. Upon closer examination, I spotted the head of a ruffed grouse, its feathery crest raised, eyeing me suspiciously. At the instant of eye contact, the young bird, followed by two clutch-mates, erupted into flight. I connected with the first barrel but missed with the second. No sooner had I reloaded than two additional birds flushed, and I added one more to the bag. Family groups like this one were common during the September opener, but I was surprised nonetheless by the multiple flush. Gina returned rather sheepishly, realizing that she had run off and missed all the fun. Being the forgiving sort however, I left the birds on the ground where they had fallen to allow her the opportunity to retrieve. It wasn't exactly classic dog work, but having witnessed far worse, I could live with it.

My third and limit-filling bird came from another family group that I flushed myself. My wet boots squeaking underfoot, I headed across the pasture toward the truck. Gina cocked her head oddly, wondering why anyone would leave a grouse haven like this. I had mixed feelings about leaving myself. It was only 8:30 and I was done for the day, but aside from it being illegal I wouldn't have felt right about taking advantage of too many of the young ruffeds on their first day facing human hunters.

Gathering the keys from the rear tire, I fetched the thermos, poured a cup of coffee and stretched out at the base of a giant Ponderosa pine. The sun had risen over the mountains and the dew was evaporating in the growing, silent warmth of the late summer morning. Periodically, I heard the report of Bill's side-by-side from across the valley. An hour or so later, he appeared on the dusty road, smiling. One third of our three grouse opener was complete. Tomorrow would be the day for blues.

Blue grouse are rarely found below 5,000 feet elevation. They prefer forests with openings rather than uninterrupted trees. Even openings caused by rock outcroppings are acceptable, but patches of sagebrush or meadows of grasses and forbs are preferred. Blues are especially fond of ridges in close proximity to springs. Bill had just such a ridge in mind for our second day's hunt.

Bill elected to hunt the brushy north slope that harbored several springs, in hopes of catching blue or possibly even spruce grouse feeding on the plentiful berries that flourished there. Being a chukar hunting fanatic addicted to climbing, I continued on toward the summit. The grassy areas above timberline were typically full of grasshoppers, a favorite blue grouse food. We agreed to meet back at the truck no later than noon.

My first action came when Anja pointed into a patch of dwarfed firs just at timberline. Again, I was lucky to find a family group of seven birds that flushed in twos and threes, allowing me to take a pair on three shots. Both birds were full of grasshoppers. Blue grouse are large birds and even the youngsters are close in size to hen pheasants. The blue grouse is of course not blue at all but basically gray and white although I suppose you could stretch the point and say that they are blue-gray. The hens and juveniles are extremely drab, but their lack of beauty is more than made up for by their delicious taste.

Hoping to round out my day with a tom, I climbed all the way to the summit. The toms stay up high all year long, coming only as far down the mountain as necessary to locate water. The hens nest in the lower elevations and gradually move their broods uphill as summer and fall progress. Winters are spent in trees high on the ridges feeding on needles. Despite wintering in this harsh environment, blue grouse have some of the best winter survivorship of any game bird.

After a heart-thumping climb, I finally reached the top of the mountain where only scattered trees survived. I stooped to examine two coal black tail feathers, when a wing popping flush scarcely six feet above startled me so badly that I ducked. I was too flustered to get the gun to my shoulder let alone shoot at the fast departing tom. None of those big fellows hanging out on the ridge were fools. Three separate birds flushed a full 30 yards in front of Anja. I snapped shots at all three, with no result.

Climbing over a pile of granite boulders, I nearly bumped into Anja on point. Her head was stretched up as if trying to peer over the rocks at an unsuspecting grouse. I climbed to the top, and momentarily spotted the tom on the ground. He flushed in a roar, catapulting his big body into flight. I fired as he motored through the limbs of a lone larch and I heard a heavy thump as he crashed to the ground on the far side.

Anja returned with the bird held proudly in her jaws. The big tom was definitely larger than a rooster pheasant. Although still drab, he was considerably more regal than the hen. A yellow comb was visible over each eye and his breast more black and white than gray. His tail was completely soot-black.

Three blue grouse pulled heavily on my bird strap as I worked my way down the mountain in search of Bill. I had no difficulty in finding him, as shots were ringing from the slope beneath me. He was hunting in some thick cover where the shooting could be tough, so I didn't know how he was faring. When I finally found him, he had two blues in the bag.

Sweat had soaked through our hats, leaving irregular salty rings around the brims. The dogs' tongues lolled from their panting mouths. A lazy afternoon by the lake, a swim to cool off man and beast, and a dinner of rice, grouse breasts and Chardonnay sounded just perfect. Two thirds of our goal had been met, but the most difficult of the three species, the spruce grouse, had thus far eluded us.

Spruce grouse are quite common throughout the forested portions of Canada. The Pacific Nortwestern U.S. represents the southern portion of their range, where they are relatively uncommon. Spruce grouse prefer forests with heavy undergrowth, and like the blue grouse, prefer to live near springs. By the Fall hunting season, they are often widely dispersed and difficult to locate. Part of the reason for their scarcity is their trusting nature (some would say stupid). Spruce grouse are easily taken advantage of by hunters who shoot birds on the ground or off limbs. As a result, few are found in easily accessible areas. Because of their relative scarcity in Washington I maintain a personal limit of two spruce grouse per season, even though I could legally shoot three per day.

I played guide on our final day in the mountains, taking Bill to a favorite area. We parked at the base of a bald peak strewn with granite boulders. On the north slope was a thick stand of four-inch diameter lodgepole pines with an occasional Douglas fir towering overhead. Thigh-high vaccinium, heavy with red berries, grew beneath the trees, and numerous springs seeped from the ground, creating the only openings in an otherwise dense forest.

I was hoping to locate a male for a mount, as they are exceptionally handsome birds of deep browns and blacks interspersed with white and punctuated with a brilliant red eye comb. Being our final day, I uncrated both dogs, not wanting to leave either of them. I knew it was a mistake almost as soon as I let down the tailgate. Gina, the setter, was really a chukar specialist and her range was too great to keep track of her in such a dense covert. Several times as we side-hilled along, I heard grouse flushing ahead of us and I was certain that Gina was the culprit. I could only hope she was pointing first and that the birds were flushing before I arrived.

By the time Anja and I showed up, most of the grouse were in the trees. A half dozen times, blue grouse rocketed from overhead limbs without warning, and each time I snapped a futile shot as they disappeared through the pine tops. Bill had climbed higher on the slope close to timberline, reportedly to get more open shooting, but in reality to escape from my high geared setter. While he shot less frequently, he was having better success, as twice I heard the command "fetch" drift down the mountain. I was certain that at that elevation he must have been finding blues instead of spruce grouse.

At last, Anja located a bird that Gina had run past. She trailed it up slope for about 50 yards before locking onto point. I scrambled up hill but the grouse flushed before I could get to Anja. Fortunately, the bird flew downhill, presenting a shot which sent the big tom blue grouse crashing into the tree tops before landing with a resounding thump.

Several of my missed birds had also flown down slope, so I decided to follow them in hopes of a re-flush. I took extra time to hunt through every berry patch during my descent, in hopes that same birds might have landed on the ground. As I stepped from a rotten log, a grouse exploded directly underfoot. I instinctively swung up to overtake the bird. The instant before I touched off, I realized that something was different. The bird was smaller than a blue and it had flown in a straight-up swoop as if heading for an overhead branch. Luckily, my shot load had caught it in the head, as a body shot would have crushed it at the close range. Anja was on it immediately and before she had time to deliver, I realized that it had to be a spruce grouse. It was a hen and certainly not fit for a mount, but it was a perfect finish to a three grouse opener.

Chapter Twenty-one

PRAIRIE WINGS

Well bred gentlemen and their equally well bred dogs have long journeyed to the great northern prairies of Montana, North Dakota and the Canadian provinces of Alberta, Saskatchewan and Manitoba. While September heat sears the States, forcing most sportsmen to satisfy themselves with an occasional dove shoot, men of means have escaped to cooler climes where they have pursued the sharptail grouse and Hungarian partridge.

Professional dog trainers developing pointers for the field trial circuit flock there as well. The vast country lends itself to training from horseback, which develops the wide ranging dogs that field trial people are so enamored with. Under the heavy September prairie, Huns often sit like the bobwhites which are the trial dog's steady fare.

For years I had read about the prairie hunts, and decided they sounded wonderfully romantic. Until I moved to Washington, however, they were simply too far away. Much to his wife's chagrin, I bent the ear of my hunting buddy, Milt Cobb, until he, too, was anxious to give the prairies a try. In September, we loaded our three dogs into my truck for the journey east. Milt took Cassie, a German Longhaired pointer pup just starting her second hunting season. I brought my nine-year-old English setter, Gina, and Anja, my German Longhair bitch, who was recovering from raising a litter of pups.

A vast sea of grass once covered an expanse from Kansas north to the aspen belt above Edmonton. Much of the prairie grasslands of the American Plains had been replaced by corn and soybeans. The native sharptails had likewise been replaced by ringnecked pheasants and bobwhite quail.

Along the northern tier of states and on into Canada however, the temperatures are too extreme for corn. Wheat is grown, but much of the native short grass prairie survives. Little bluestem, June grass, needle grass, buffalo grass and wild sunflower blanket the uplands, while dwarf oaks, water birch and wild rose proliferate in the draws. Sharptailed grouse thrive in this country, as they have since long before the white man arrived. Hungarian or gray partridge were introduced into the northern prairies in 1906, and flourished as they did in the steppes of their native Eurasia. Today both species live side by side and provide some of the greatest wing shooting in North America.

Miraculously avoiding hundreds of deer along the highway, we made Great Falls by midnight and awakened the night clerk of the cheapest motel we could find. Truck engines roaring outside the window at daybreak rousted us and sent us on a search for breakfast and hunting licenses. The guru at the sporting goods store informed us that Great Falls had huns and pheasants but no sharptails to speak of; too much agriculture and not enough grass apparently. Despite the fact that pheasant season was not yet open, we were anxious to get into the field. We chose to delay our travel until after dark and hunt while we had light.   Cruising around, searching out the best cover, and following tips from locals; we at last found a ranch on the rim of a broad, wheat-covered plateau. A series of breaks above a shallow creek held enough brush to look birdy. The rancher stepped out on the porch and seemed ready to "visit". Sure, we could hunt and yes, there were quite a few huns about. But there were some cows and horses in there, too. As we began to assure him that we would be careful, he continued, "Don't you worry about them, they won't bother you." I had to grin at that one. We were clearly dealing with a different attitude here in Montana.

Anja, slowed by her still sagging teats, went immediately to work pinning a covey in a small patch of alfalfa that the mower had missed. I dropped one on the first barrel and missed on the second. Gina then bumped up a second covey. I shouldn't have shot, but she was an old dog beyond ruining and I'm a weak mortal. I completed my first brace. On a third covey, Anja performed her usual magic and pointed from thirty yards. I managed a pair from that bunch. We had covered less than a quarter of the property and visions of a limit were dancing in my head.

We continued to find birds for the next three hours. The problem was that all of the birds were pheasants and pheasant season was not yet open. Gina pointed into one cattail patch along the creek and I swear, twenty pheasants came pouring out. Roosters at varying stages of color development from squealers to mature cocks flooded from the tules. We had plenty of fine dog work to enjoy, but no shooting. After Cassie chomped down on a porcupine, both she and Anja pointed separate rattlesnakes and we decided to call it a day. We wanted to make Lewistown by dinnertime.

Lewistown, "In the heart of Wonderful Montana" as the brochures announce, is an ordinary little town of about 8,000 people situated in an extraordinary spot. The mountains end and the prairies begin (or vice versa depending on your line of travel) in Lewistown. Grasslands to the east, mountains to the west and south, sagebrush and the Missouri River Badlands to the north offer wonderful diversity for game birds and hunters alike.

The motel parking lot looked like a field trial in progress. English pointers, English setters, Gordon setters, and German shorthairs were chained to the bumpers of pick-ups with license plates from South Carolina, Georgia, Washington and California. We shuffled over to our neighbors, intent on getting the low down on the birds. Pheasants everywhere, but almost no sharptails, sage hens or huns this year, was the word on the lot. No snow last winter and no rain until July made for a late flush of grass on the prairie.

One pro trainer from Georgia growled, "When the birds were ready to nest, the prairie looked like indoor-outdoor carpet. No place for 'em to hide."

"The boy and I drove 40 hours from South Carolina and haven't killed a bird in three days," moaned another.

I've heard of trying to dissuade the competition, but either these guys were laying it on a little thick or we were in for a tough week. I had the phone number of a few ranchers who allowed hunting if they were asked. I got the same sad story from them.

"Sure as hell, they haven't gone extinct," I said to Milt. "We're just going to have to hunt harder than anybody else. We've got good dogs and if we put in enough miles, they'll find some birds."

When we awoke, it was difficult to believe it was mid-September. A cold rain whipped by a twenty mile an hour wind pelted us as we ducked into a casino for breakfast. The food was great, but the grumbling of morose hunters was as depressing as the weather. The rain was letting up as we headed east toward the town of Grass Range. We spotted a likely looking hillside and stopped in to talk with the rancher. He explained that all that ground was in Conservation Reserve Program (CRP) and that we were welcome to hunt, but "There aren't many birds". We knew.

The field, several hundred acres in size, had originally been in alfalfa. Allowed to grow un-mowed for several years, it was waist high and dense. Wanting to alternate dogs I took only Gina, and Milt took Cassie. Immediately it became apparent that we had located another pheasant mecca. Gina pinned three roosters and two hens in the first fifteen minutes. Milt was also into pheasants, as I saw several wing overhead from his position on the hill below.

When we entered a shallow draw, I heard Milt's gun crack and I spotted a half dozen sharptails flying uphill. They appeared to have landed just beyond a rise, so I ran toward them. Two birds flushed on the periphery of gun range and miraculously my skeet choke brought one down. As I called for Gina to fetch, another sharpie took wing and I added him to the bag. Gina rapidly retrieved the second bird, but the first bird had run. A beautiful tracking job through 50 yards of dense ground cover was required before Gina came up with my still alive bird.

The author and friend Milt Cobb on a hunt in Montana in 1992 for sharp-tailed grouse and Hungarian partridge.

Milt admired the beautiful, white speckled breast and tan heads and wings of the first sharptails he had ever seen. He admitted to having missed a long shot when the covey first flushed, and I could tell he was anxious for another crack at them. We continued on to where the field gave way to a series of breaks. Once again I was having all the luck. I spotted a sharpie standing bolt upright and looking back at me. To my surprise, the bird flew directly at me in order to fly with the wind at her back. I dropped my third sharpie of the day. No birds, huh?

Cassie came to Milt's rescue and slammed onto a point at the top of the breaks. Milt flushed a pair of cackling sharpies that went whipping away, with the wind at their backs. Milt's Parker scored with the left and right and both birds folded and plunged into the deep alfalfa. A double retrieve and a sit to deliver put the cap on the beautiful piece of dog work. It was difficult to tell if Milt was more excited about his first sharptails, his shooting or his pup's performance.

He didn't say but his grin spoke volumes.

In a replay of the previous day, just as our confidence was building in our ability to find birds, we found nothing but pheasants. It was a good opportunity to take some video of the dogs, but we failed to fatten our bag for the remainder of the afternoon. We elected to spend the last hour of light scouting for a place to hunt in the morning. We looped north on our return to town and drove through hillsides blanketed with brilliant yellow aspens.

"There just about have to be some ruffed grouse in those aspens," I suggested. "The sharpies and huns don't seem real numerous. Do you want to try for ruffeds tomorrow?"

"Why don't we do that?" Milt replied. "We may not take a lot of birds on this trip, but it would be fun to see if we could take several species. We already have huns and sharptails. If we could get ruffeds and sage grouse, that would make for one helluva trip."

Brilliant blue skies accentuated the golden yellow of the aspen. A gentle breeze set the leaves quaking in a shimmering ballet. My flannel shirt fended off the cool morning chill. Strolling among the scarred white trunks left me in a reverential mood similar to the feeling I'd had hiking the sequoia groves of California. Vaguely disappointed in not finding many grouse, I was nonetheless very glad we had made this hunt. One ruffed did jump up wild on Gina and landed on a limb. I flushed and shot him, for our only ruffed of the trip.

We rendezvoused in midmorning and decided to try for sage grouse in the afternoon. Both of us were interested in seeing the C.M. Russell Wildlife Refuge. Antelope, handsome in their tan and white pelage, fed by the hundreds along the roads, as we made the three hour drive north. Crossing the Missouri River, we headed east along the northern refuge boundary.

Hand painted signs announcing the presence of prairie dog towns seemed odd at first until I realized that they were invitations to shoot the varmints. The perky, little rodents were everywhere in towns stretching over hundreds of acres. Neither of us had ever witnessed such a sight, and we parked at one town to watch their antics. A never-ending series of social interactions was occurring between the residents of the burrows and I could only guess at the meaning of all the chasing and chirping.

Shortly after crossing over the boundary, we bumped into the refuge manager. He cautioned us not to shoot any prairie dogs while on the refuge. The United States Fish and Wildlife Service planned to reintroduce black-footed ferrets to the area and wanted to protect the food source for the little predators. He suggested an area to hunt sage grouse where there was a permanent water supply. Sharptails were also supposedly found in that area.

We failed to find birds of any description, despite a long hike. We did however find jackrabbits, cottontails, rattlesnakes and coyotes in plentiful supply. Anja pointed once and it turned out to be a sleeping coyote. I walked to within seven paces of the critter before he sleepily raised his head, yawned, did a classic double take, and nearly fell over himself in his panic to escape.

We eventually did spot a large covey of sage hens on our drive out, but they were unhuntably wild. They took flight and, as sage grouse are apt to do, flew clear out of sight. Despite our meager bag of one ruffed grouse for the day, we had thoroughly enjoyed seeing the new country and the wildlife.

Hoping to make our final day in Montana successful, we returned to the CRP fields where we had some luck before. We hiked for hours and again, the pheasants were driving us crazy. Mule deer (including a nice four point), bounded from the brushy draws ahead of us. We did get one point from Gina on a wild flushing covey of sharptails. Milt missed one but I had no shots. After swapping dogs, Anja pointed one lone sharptail, possibly from the same covey. I dropped that bird on a straight away.

I considered leaving but Milt prevailed upon me to try one more spot. Across the dirt road from the overgrown alfalfa field was another CRP field with much sparser grass cover. I worked the lower part of the hills while Milt hunted the top. Milt must have broken up an upland bird poker game, because I heard six shots (and Milt was shooting a double barrel). I raced uphill where he stood holding two sharptails. "There was a covey of sharptails and a covey of huns sitting right next to one another," he explained excitedly. "I've got a third bird down here someplace."

The dogs never came up with the third bird, but while we searched, a single hun flushed at my feet and I collected it. We never relocated the covey of huns, and the sharptails had flown out of sight. We were running out of light but decided to make one more swing along the hillside. Our next point was by Anja, on a porcupine. Thank heaven she was staunch on point, and I led her away.

As I reached the top of the hill on my way to the truck, Anja pointed again where the grassland gave way to a disked wheat field. Five sharptails came cackling up at my feet and I made a clean double. Anja retrieved both birds and I headed straight to the truck. I couldn't conceive of a better finale to a wonderful trip to Montana. If Montana hunting was this much fun when there weren't any grouse, I couldn't wait to see it in a good year.

Chapter Twenty-two

ELK THE HARD WAY

Deer were animals I knew how to hunt. Find some good habitat and the deer will be there; usually living and dying within one or two square miles. Of course, no one in their right mind could claim that deer hunting was easy. It took time to figure out where they bedded in different weather, what foods were available as the autumn progressed and where they went for refuge. The point is that I always knew the deer were somewhere nearby. If I stuck with it and learned the lay of the land, I would eventually locate them.

When I moved west in 1983, I was looking forward to hunting elk, but elk just plain intimidated me. Being herd animals, elk were tougher to find than the more evenly distributed deer. Those herds could hardly be called homebodies either. The elk sometimes hung out in the same vicinity throughout the summer, occasionally even in broad sight of people. However once the hunting season opened or a big snowstorm blew in, they didn't think twice about vacating a drainage and traversing 30 miles in a single night.

To make things more difficult, elk were the glamour species among Westerners, so hunters flocked to the National Forests during elk season. After the opening morning barrage, elk headed for remote country where they could stay out of harm's way. Even if I could walk into the roadless country that held elk during the hunting season, how would I, without horses, ever transport a 700 pound beast back to the road should I be lucky enough to shoot one?

For the first two years that I lived in elk country, I hoped for an invitation from a hunter who knew how to hunt wapiti. I soon learned however, that elk camps were usually family affairs or gatherings of members of long standing. It would have been easier to snag an invitation to the White House than to most elk camps I knew of. It seemed that my only hope of successfully hunting elk was to save up the thousands of dollars required to hire an outfitter to take me into the back country on horse back.

Autumn came once again and failing to have the needed funds for a guided elk hunt, I opted for a mule deer hunt. I had shot some nice whitetails but had yet to take a trophy mulie, so my step brother, Hunter Leigh and I paid an outfitter to provide us with a drop camp in the Sawtooth Wilderness of Idaho. As was often the case with drop camps, the outfitter had not taken us into the truly remote country where he took his fully guided hunters but had plunked us down about four miles from the trailhead. None the less, the jagged granite spires and crystal clear streams of the Sawtooths provided a lovely setting for a hunt, and the wall tent, wood stove, and cots made for what Hunter dubbed "condo living". Being the final week of the season, hunting pressure was low and we saw bucks every day although only one was trophy quality.

It was the elk however, rather than the deer that really impressed me. During our first afternoon of hunting, we climbed half way up the mountain behind camp. Four inches of snow had fallen three days previously but the snow only clung to the north slopes and shadows. Side-hilling along about 200 yards apart, we glassed each rock pile and glade in hopes of spotting deer feeding along the slopes. It was our ears however, which first alerted us to the presence of game. The unmistakable mewing of cow elk drifted up the mountain. A herd of 15 cows and calves climbed through the firs 150 yards ahead of us.

We crept forward a few steps and spotted a cow and a spike bull standing immobile a mere 80 yards away; their tan coats vivid against the white snow. Elk season had closed a week before but I couldn't help but think how tender that spike would have been on the table. I eventually stepped into broad sight, causing the cow to bark an alarm as she led the spike through the forest at a ground gobbling pace. The spike was not the last bull we were to see that afternoon. I spotted a four or five point on a slope about 400 yards away and two bulls trotted right past Hunter just before dark.

Snow fell twice during our week in the mountains, making for good tracking. Rarely did we hunt for more than an hour before crossing fresh elk tracks. Although I saw no more bulls, I did creep within a dozen yards of an entire herd bedded on a ridge top. For a full ten seconds, an old cow and I stared into one another's eyes. She seemed unwilling to leave her comfortable bed, but finally bounded to her feet, sending the herd charging off the ridge into the deep, north-slope forest.

The memory of those elk, particularly the spike bull that I could have so easily shot, remained with me throughout the winter and I began to plot a way to hunt them next season. The outfitter's drop camps were more expensive during elk season and I wasn't certain that it was worth the money for a mere four mile ride. I had, however, thoroughly enjoyed "condo living".

The more I considered it, the more I thought that four miles was not all that far. If Hunter and I could get one more partner and if we each made two trips in with 75 pound packs, that would add up to 450 pounds of gear. We could have all the comforts of home. Of course if we shot deer and elk it could be quite a chore getting them plus all of our equipment back out. We hoped that by boning out all of the meat, we could reduce a deer to a one-trip load and an elk to a three-trip load. The whole idea seemed a little crazy but not entirely impossible. Being stronger of back than mind we agreed to give it a try.

Most of our regular hunting partners decided that Hunter and I had definitely gone over the edge this time and minced no words in telling us so. Undeterred, we kept up our search and eventually talked Craig Collins, a business friend of mine, into joining us. Craig indicated that yes, he was crazy enough to pack in all of that equipment, but he was damned if he was going to attempt to pack an elk out on his back. He decided to hunt for deer only.

We located Craig at the trailhead on an unseasonably warm October evening. It was five days before the opening of elk season although deer were already legal game. We hoped that the deer hunting would be better before the arrival of other elk hunters disturbed the deer. The extra days of hunting would give us a chance to scout for elk.

The doors of the truck remained open; the radio playing as we cooked hotcakes and sausages in Craig's camper. The disc jockey announced the forecast of hot dry weather for the upcoming week. Even at our elevation by 8:00 a.m. it was already shirt sleeve weather. It was hardly an ideal forecast for successful hunting. We dawdled over our second cup of coffee, somehow hesitant to begin what was sure to be a difficult day. The pile of equipment scattered on the ground was daunting; an eight man tent, tarps, a two burner stove, two lanterns, a propane tank, sleeping bags, foam pads, rifles, spotting scopes, binoculars, clothing, boots, saws, flashlights and what seemed like enough food to feed an army.

When Hunter hoisted the loaded pack onto my back, my whole body shivered in revolt. Here was a healthy dose of reality. It was one thing to talk about carrying a 75 pound pack, and quite another to feel the weight compress one's entire skeleton. Sweat dripped from our brows as we trudged in line up the trail, packs creaking and gravel crunching underfoot. The weight of the packs became familiar after the first mile however, and our bodies ceased their protests. Although we rested briefly after each mile, we felt strong.

We selected a campsite several hundred yards off the main trail along a surging, crystal stream. Hunter and I unloaded the gear and set up the geodesic dome tent while Craig headed back for his second load. We had no plan to hunt on this set-up day so we took a brief siesta on the damp, cool boulders along the brook. We stripped down and stepped gingerly over the slippery rocks into the frigid, gin clear water. We sucked in our breath as we reached knee depth and whooped in delight and agony when we sat in the deepest part of the pool; submerging to our chests. We tolerated the water only long enough to wash off the sweat from our hike and then retreated shivering to the boulders. Hunter cracked open a fifth of Yukon Jack and we each took a long draw from the bottle.

Our second leg of the trip began at 2:00 p.m. during the heat of the day. We hiked in shorts alone, using rolled up T shirts under the pack straps to protect our shoulders. Our steps came more slowly as the afternoon wore on, but there was solace in knowing that we were into the final leg of our day.

By nightfall, we had the camp organized. A separate kitchen area was established under a blue tarp tied onto some lodgepole pines. We scavenged several logs that the Forest Service had removed from the trail and used them to create a table for the two burner Coleman stove. Pans, plates, cups and silverware were stacked near the stove as were cooking condiments. The double mantle lantern hung from a convenient branch above the kitchen. We built a fire ring of stones a safe distance from the kitchen and tent, and gathered firewood from the numerous trees felled by storms. Onion bags submerged by rocks in the icy stream served as a refrigerator for our meats and cheeses.

I had been determined to carry in two special luxuries. I had spent many a Fall camping trip shivering in an inadequate sleeping bag so I had purchased an obscenely heavy bag. It was Army surplus from the Korean War and had been used for keeping casualties alive on frozen battlefields. It was wide enough to insert a stretcher, had eight pounds of down and a coyote fur hood. Feeling that such a monumental bag needed a name I dubbed it "Mammy" after the character immortalized by Hattie McDaniel in *"Gone with the Wind"*; huge, soft and warm.

The other luxury was lawn chairs. Perhaps even worse than an inability to bathe on camping trips, I missed sitting in a chair where I could rest my back after a long day of hunting. The hike seemed well worth the effort, as we sat in our chairs, legs stretched before a crackling fire of lodgepole limbs, sipping our evening toddies. A prideful, warm, secure sensation embraced me as I scanned the first rate elk camp we had created. Although our camp would not be as remote as that of some of the horsemen, it would allow us to escape the majority of the hunters camped by the roads, and hopefully put us into elk country.

Hunter and I spent the first day hunting up a long, box canyon above camp where Hunter had missed the only big buck we had seen the previous year. According to the topographic map, there were several small lakes above timberline at the head of the canyon. We had failed to reach the lakes last year, so we planned to climb there and enjoy a lengthy lunch and siesta. We hoped to find some big bucks feeding on the brushy cover at timberline.

Heavy buck brush covered the slopes on south side of the stream, although spring runoff had torn scars of granite gravel through the vegetation in several places. Aspens, already golden yellow, grew thick along the stream. The north side of the stream was a mass of impassable boulders. I hunted slowly through the aspens while Hunter paralleled me on the south slope. In midmorning, we caught a glimpse of three does that Hunter jumped out of their beds but we didn't spot any deer moving on their own. By 11:00 we had reached a narrow portion of the canyon with boulders on both sides. Hunter and I followed one another along the stream, climbing over an endless supply of deadfalls. By 1:30 it became obvious we were not going to make it to the lakes until nearly dark, so we turned back. We both took stands overlooking parts of the canyon and remained there until total darkness set in. Neither of us had seen any game.

In our campfire strategy session that evening, Craig provided a more optimistic report than we were able to. Within the first twenty minutes of light, he had spotted a three point, a fork horn and two doe mule deer, but he had chosen to pass them up in hopes of killing a larger buck. He admitted however, that he had hunted hard the remainder of the day without any additional action. We all reported seeing plenty of sign, but the warm, dry weather was forcing the game to be nocturnal. Our only chance would be to catch the game moving very early or very late, or to team up to drive them from their midday refuges. Despite the day's aborted attempt, I still wanted to climb to higher elevation in hopes that the deer might be up there enjoying the cooler temperatures.

Craig had begun to kick himself for passing up the three point and decided to head to the same spot the following morning. Hunter and I elected to cross the river in the dark and make the long climb to the peaks on the east side of the river. The three of us departed camp in total darkness, crossing the camp-side stream by means of a fallen tree. Craig wished us luck as he left the trail and began climbing toward the meadow where he had seen the bucks. Hunter and I hiked for nearly a mile before reaching the ford in the main river. I had brought knee high rubber boots and Hunter had brought old sneakers for crossing. Dawn was breaking as we cautiously negotiated the quick, shin-deep water.

We stashed our footgear in the brush on the far bank and continued along the trail. A piercing elk bugle not three hundred yards away sent a shiver up my spine. I was surprised to hear a bull bugle this late in the season but there was no mistake; one just had. I caught a glimpse of a cow elk feeding noisily in thick timber only fifty yards away and I was tempted to stay and try to see the bull. I realized however that would be foolish. We knew where he was and if we slipped off unseen he might still be there in a few days when the season opened. I tiptoed up the trail but Hunter lagged behind just long enough to see a mature five point bull cross the trail behind him. The herd had been hanging out less than 300 yards from our previous year's campsite.

The hike to the top of the ridge was a grueling climb that left us sucking air like a couple of marathon runners. It was an hour past dawn when we topped out. The heat had already started to build and our flannel shirts were tucked into our daypacks. If there had been deer or elk moving along the ridge, they had probably already bedded down. We spent the remainder of the morning and all afternoon trying to push through pockets of thick timber in hopes of driving a deer to one another. We saw plenty of deer and especially elk sign but only succeeded in moving two cow elk. At 4:00 p.m., having failed to spot a single deer and facing a two hour walk back to camp, we started back passing up some of the prime hours of hunting. We realized that the ridge was too far from camp to hunt since, the only hours worth hunting were dawn and dusk.

When we returned to camp, Craig was nowhere to be seen. Shortly after Hunter carried a bucket to the stream, I heard him calling excitedly, so I walked down to investigate. Stacked on the damp boulders were four nylon sacks containing deer quarters. We searched camp and found the head of a medium sized three point wrapped in cheese cloth. A few moments later Craig came sauntering into camp smiling.

"Congratulations there cap'n," I offered. "Looks like you found that buck from yesterday."

"He was in exactly the same spot. I got him about 45 minutes after we split up. I knew you guys like deer liver so I stashed it in a plastic bag but then forgot to carry it out. I went back to get it though," he said.

Hunter, being the best cook in camp took charge of preparing dinner. Craig and I fetched a heavy rope for hanging the venison in a tree before darkness set in. We found an immense dead Ponderosa pine about fifty yards out of camp. After a few tries we succeeded in slinging the rope over a stout limb and raising the meat about eight feet off the ground.

When we returned, Hunter had sliced the liver thin and was soaking it in warm water to pull some of the blood out of it. I cut up some onions and placed them in a fry pan with water and butter, then put them on the stove to steam. In a second pan, we cooked up about half a pound of bacon. We set the bacon aside, then dredged the liver slices in flour and fried them in the bacon grease. When tender, we topped the liver with the bacon and onions. The liver was much milder than calf liver and even Craig, who professed not to like liver, dived into second helpings.

Hunter, who works long hours at his job, becomes a world champion sleeper when on vacation. No degree of cold or discomfort will keep him awake on a camping trip. After dinner, he toddled off to his down bag and we soon heard him snoring contentedly. Craig and I fed the fire for another hour or two, toasting his buck with spiked hot chocolate. When we finally retired, my exhausted body welcomed Mammy's warm embrace.

Rapidly sinking into sleep, I started spasmodically as I thought I heard a heavy breathing, snorting sound. My eyes opened but I wanted to believe it was a dream so I could drift back to sleep. Suddenly, unmistakably, there came a distinct pop. Oh, God! There was something big right outside of the tent. I sat bolt upright and shouted, "Something is out there!" Craig bounded to his feet yelling at the top of his lungs trying to scare whatever it was away. We both crammed cartridges into our rifles, grabbed our flashlights and came boiling out of the tent like riled hornets. Our beams of light cast about wildly, as we tried to spot the intruder, but we didn't pick up anything.

"I'll bet something tried to get into that meat," suggested Craig.

"Let's go check on it. I'll take a look. You keep that .270 ready just in case."

I shined the light onto the suspended meat sacks. "Look at that bag. The bottom is torn to ribbons," I exclaimed.

"Wait a minute. I think one of my bags is missing...... Dammit it is. I think it is a front quarter though. Can you believe that son of a gun got up that high? What do you think it was."

"It sort of looks like a coyote jumped up and grabbed the bags with his teeth and just hung on until one dropped."

"I don't know. Maybe a bear did it with his claws. Either way he has about ten pounds of my meat so he probably won't be back. Just in case though, let's raise these bags higher."

Together we grabbed the rope and heaved the meat a full 20 feet off the ground. When we returned to the tent, unbelievably, Hunter was still sound asleep.

At breakfast the following morning, Craig announced that he was heading home. He had his deer and he was starting to think about all the work waiting for him back at his office. Of course we would still need a lot of the equipment that he had carried in, such as the stove, lantern and propane tank so he was able to consolidate his gear into one load and the meat into a second load. Hunter and I, on the other hand, had just inherited another load to carry out.

We said our good-byes in the pre-morning darkness as Hunter and I headed out for our third day of hunting. We split up, trying to cover more ground and agreed to meet back at camp for lunch. I hunted the hillside where I had seen the elk last Fall and Hunter patrolled the river bottom near camp. Despite our best efforts, by lunch time Hunter hadn't seen a single deer and I had only spotted three does in the distance. Once again, I had seen considerable deer and elk sign but my confidence was flagging badly.

"Tomorrow is the last day of doe season," I muttered as I munched my sardines and crackers. "I didn't shoot a deer last year and I would really like to take home some venison this year. Starting this afternoon, I'm going to shoot any deer. I don't have much faith in finding elk right now due to this heat, so a doe might be all I get this year."

"I agree, but I'll tell you what, I have a feeling that even getting a shot at a doe might not be all that easy."

Hunter was right. We hunted all afternoon, returning to camp in the darkness. Neither of us had seen a thing and we were a depressed pair that evening. Despite all of our planning and effort, it did not appear that luck would be with us on this hunt. We decided that the area where Craig had shot his buck was our best chance for the morning. Once again we left camp in darkness, covering about one half mile before dawn began to break into another clear warm day. We separated a hundred yards and slowly hunted along the hillside. Stopping every five steps, we scanned each sage covered opening, hoping to catch some deer still out feeding.

Hunter and I often planned to hunt together, but ended up unable to keep track of one another. I was determined not to let that happen again, so I waited patiently to catch a glimpse of Hunter's orange hat as he slipped through the trees on the slope below me. When I was certain of his whereabouts, I would creep forward a few steps. I briefly saw Hunter slip into a patch of timber, but I waited for a full ten minutes for him to appear at the far edge. Nothing. Feeling a little annoyed by his dawdling, I was about to hunt off by myself when I was startled by the roar of his 7mm magnum. I heard Hunter cry out that he had one down. I trotted as quickly as possible through an aspen thicket and found Hunter standing over a large doe.

180

"There were three of them," he said excitedly. "They went up that draw. *If you* hustle you might catch up to them."

Craig had described this mountain to me, so I knew the top was covered with immense boulders and impassable rocky spires. My only hope was to catch up to the deer before they reached the top. I scrambled up the slope, my legs pumping as fast as they would go. Poor footing repeatedly forced me to catch myself with my hands. My lungs sucked greedily for air. I anxiously kept glancing up the slope in hopes of seeing the deer.

Finally I spotted a lone doe about 500 yards above me. She had already seen me, but stood utterly still, staring at me curiously. A careful stalk was out of the question. My only hope was that she would hesitate long enough to allow me to close ground. I put a tree between the two of us and ran toward her. Twice I peeked through branches to look at her through the scope, but decided that she was still too far. Upon reaching the big pines I sat down, not daring to get closer. I was 250 yards from her and I knew I had to shoot. The doe nervously trotted up the slope but then stopped one last time to look back at me. I was breathing heavily from the climb and the cross hairs wavered badly. I inhaled deeply three times, then held my breath and squeezed the trigger of the Remington .280. The 165 grain Nosler partition bullet caught her on the point of the shoulder. She collapsed like a rag doll, summersaulting madly as she fell down the slope.

The next day was spent boning out our meat und recuperating from an exhausting five days. Hunter and I felt lucky to take the does, considering how many miles we had walked and how few deer we had seen. Despite our success, neither of us were very confident about the prospects of finding a bull elk. We had, in fact, become so pessimistic that we spent opening morning of elk season packing our venison back to the truck where we had several large coolers jammed with ice.

I knew of the perfect place to refresh our bodies and to renew our spirits. We drove along the river for a few miles and parked the truck at a pullout along the dirt road. Seeping from the rocky river's edge, a hot spring bubbled steaming water. Previous bathers had created four rock pools to capture the hot water just before it entered the cold river. We stripped down and tested the temperature in each pool. Some springs can be dangerously hot, but none of pools were intolerable. We selected the second warmest and slipped cautiously in.

Despite the algae that flourished on the rocks in the warm water, the pool felt luxurious beyond comprehension. We slid down, submerging to our necks, groaning in delight. In trance-like ecstasy, we watched as the crystal water of the river shimmered in the sun light. Massive Ponderosa pines stood statuesque along the far bank and pine siskins winged in tremendous flocks overhead. The hot water therapeutically penetrated our pores, unknotting every muscle. The relaxation of our bodies was so total after our half hour soak, that we scarcely felt capable of standing. We forced ourselves to step over the pool wall into the surging, icy stream. Warmed to the bone, the cold felt refreshing rather than painful.

The hike back in with empty pack was nearly effortless, and we arrived back in camp at 2:00, ready to give the elk hunting our best shot. It was too late in the afternoon to go far from camp. We had seen the week's only bull in the thick timber along the river. Unfortunately, a group had set up camp close to where we had spotted him, so we knew he must have moved on. We decided to cross the river and try the thick, black timber along the river, down stream from the other camp.

The woods were too dry and noisy for us to have much chance of sneaking up on a bedded bull in the heavy timber, so we once again planned to hunt parallel to one another in hopes of moving an elk past the other. The bottom was strewn with fallen trees, making it impossible to hunt silently. I had been practicing with a cow elk call and now seemed a perfect time to try it. Perhaps I could fool an elk into thinking that the noise I was making was made by another elk. If nothing else, it would allow Hunter to keep track of me.

Any reservations that I might have held over the selection of our afternoon's hunting place quickly vanished. There was more sign in this bottom than I had seen all week. In thirty minutes, I came across a half dozen saplings rubbed bare by the rutting elk. Glistening, black elk droppings less than a day old were scattered everywhere. My entire system was on full alert; my confidence back in force. Predatory eyes shining, ears pricked for the slightest sound, I slipped through the forest.

A click. Just a click. A hoof hitting a deadfall perhaps? I scanned the forest to my left and there he was! Drifting ghostlike through the timber, not a cow but a big bull. My rifle snapped to my shoulder.

There! In the scope. Too many branches. Don't want to miss. Gone.

Catch up to him but don't make too much noise. Blow the cow call. Hurry up.

There he is again. Still walking. Maybe he suspects something but he isn't sure. Still too many branches. One chance is all there will be. An opening! Squeeze the trigger.....Wait. No. Gone again. Hurry up. Run on tiptoes, but run. Blow the damned cow call. If he clears the bottom and starts up the slope, maybe I'll get my chance. Get to the edge fast! OK, I'm out of the bottom. Where is he? He might be long gone. No wait a minute. I can smell him, pungent as a barnyard bull. He can't be far. Oh my God! There he is on the slope above me. In the open but not for long. Standing still. It is now or never. No time to get a rest. Got to shoot off hand. Hurry, but be sure. Only going to get one chance. The cross hairs won't settle down. Got to shoot now. Just do it.

The rifle roared and the bull raced at unbelievable speed into the timber. Chambering a round frantically, I shot again at the disappearing bull.

Damn it! I blew it. I just know I blew it. Got to check for blood anyway.

Short of breath from the climb. No pity, you jerk. You blew it. He was standing right here.

"Hunter! Hunter! Come help me look for blood."

Wait a minute. Blood! A lot of blood there on the clump of grass. Halleluah! "Blood, I've got blood, Hunter. Hurry up."

All right! More blood right there. What is that? An antler? By God it is! There he is! There he is! Dead as a doornail.

"YEEEEHAH!"

God, look at the size of him. Look at that body. Look at those huge, thick jointed legs.

How many points? Five on a side. There may be bigger bulls out here but he'll do just fine, thanks.

By the time Hunter arrived, I was in full celebration. Dancing a jig while belting out "Happy Days are Here Again". Hunter stared at me somewhat indulgently when he arrived puffing from his climb. As soon as he saw the bull, he understood my reason for celebration. "Whoa!, Man!, He's huge," he gushed. "Way to go, Mitch," he said as he extended his hand in congratulations.

I was finally beginning to calm down with that realization that always comes when a big animal is down. Now the work begins. I wanted to have the head mounted, so Hunter and I stripped down to our T-shirts, unsheathed our knives and began skinning the neck. We were careful to take plenty of skin for the taxidermist to work with; starting behind the forelegs and getting ample skin around the brisket. We detached the skull at the last cervical vertebrae and set the head away from the carcass.

Eviscerating the beast was next on the agenda. The slope proved helpful in sliding the innards out, although I repeatedly lost my footing on the broken limbs, loose rocks and blood. It turned out that I had hit the bull right in the aorta, killing him almost instantly. Darkness was nearly upon us, so Hunter suggested that he return to camp to get a lantern, some pack frames and some rope. It looked like we had a long night ahead of us. I remained with the carcass, a flashlight clenched between my teeth, skinning.

It was a longer trip back for Hunter than I had imagined, and I labored alone in the dark for hours. Fatigue started to set in, but I refused to rest. Mechanically I pulled skin and stroked with my knife until the exposed side of the bull was skinned. The skin on the side touching the ground was left intact in order to keep debris off the meat while I began boning the top half. The cool evening air had turned my bare, blood-caked arms cold to the touch, but the exertion prevented me from feeling the chill.

By the time Hunter returned, I had the boned meat from one side and was ready to roll the animal over. The lantern was a welcome relief after having a flashlight in my teeth all evening. Hunter's helping hands allowed the boning job to go faster. Within a few hours, we managed to remove all but a few scraps of the meat and stash it into the cloth sacks.

After our incident with Craig's venison, I wanted to be certain that our elk was not going to be scavenged. We couldn't possibly carry out 200 pounds of boned meat plus the 60 pound head and neck skin in one trip. I was particularly concerned that the head survive unscathed. We decided to hang 100 pounds of meat in a tree. The meat sacks were cheap cheesecloth, too weak to withstand the heft of the suspended meat. Lashing the sacks to one of the pack frames and suspending the frame from a limb seemed the only solution. The warm, boned meat, however, was an amorphous mass that defied our attempts to secure it to the frame. Reaching the point of exhaustion, we were infuriated each time the meat bag slipped from our ropes. Repeated effort proved

The author packing out his elk from the Sawtooth Wilderness Area in Idaho, October 1991.

successful however, and we finally succeeded in fastening the meat and lifting it high into a tree.

The moon was well above the horizon as we entered the home stretch. Hunter muscled the pack frame containing the remaining one hundred pounds of meat onto his back and toted the lantern in one hand. I used the antlers as shoulder supports to carry the head. So much neck skin trailed from the head that it dragged on the ground. I was forced to roll the pungent skin into a ball and pin it between the severed head and my neck.

The return to camp necessitated crossing the black timber of the river bottom, as well as fording the river itself. Multitudes of deadfalls, scattered throughout the river bottom, had been relatively easy to step around during the daylight. By lantern light however, we were unable to discern a route beyond the illuminated ring of light. Time and again we found ourselves surrounded by fallen trees with our only option being to climb over them. Encumbered by our heavy loads, maintaining balance was a supreme challenge. Using the moon and sound of the rushing river to guide us, we doggedly fought our way toward camp.

At long last we reached the river, only to waste a half hour trying to find our river crossing shoes, the location of which we had marked with flagging tape. Struggling onward deeply exhausted, we faced another two dozen climbs over fallen trees before at last crossing the trail which ran past camp. We reached the cutoff from the trail that lead to the tent. Only 100 yards to go; but where was it? I began wandering in circles utterly out of gas. Sitting heavily on a log, I swore. "We're right here and I can't find the bloody camp." Hunter, equally exhausted, maintained his orientation well enough to lead us to the tent. It was 1:30 in the morning. It didn't seem possible that the hike to the truck with the venison had occurred that morning.

"Mammy, Mammy. My dear, dear Mammy!"

Neither of us budged from the sack until 9:30 the following morning. Although we both would have loved a lazy day in camp, work remained to be done. One hundred pounds of meat was sitting in camp and another 100 pounds was hanging from a tree. The heat was rising, and all of it needed to be put on ice. Hunter hauled his load from last night to the truck, while I re-crossed the river to retrieve the remainder. By mid-afternoon the meat was safely stored and we headed for a well deserved soak in the hot spring.

Hunter still hoped to fill his elk tag so I took up life as a full time pack mule. There was still an elk head and three hundred pounds of gear to move. I hauled the elk head to the truck the following day. The head was one load I didn't mind carrying. I admit to a swell of pride as I walked past several horse pack trains with my bull lashed to my packframe. When I had almost reached the trailhead, I noticed something on the trail before me. A beer, fallen from one of the horse packs, lay unopened and still cool before me. I popped it open, looked skyward, and said, "Thanks, Big Guy."

That afternoon marked my first return to civilization in more than a week. I drove to a local grocery and restaurant where I bought more ice for the meat. The lady at the store sold me several pounds of salt which I rubbed into the elk cape to prevent the hair from slipping before I could get it to the taxidermist. I chowed down on a cheeseburger and caught up on the news. Tennessee Ernie Ford had died that morning and the waitress, who was a big fan, had known him. She was slightly sop-eyed as she served me lunch.

As long as Hunter didn't connect on an elk, life as a pack mule wasn't too bad. I headed out of camp each morning about 8:00, weighed down with about 70 pounds of unneeded gear, arrived at the truck by 10:30, where I unloaded and headed for a soak in the hot springs. By 2:30, I was back in camp where I cooked, tended fire and washed dishes for Hunter, allowing him to concentrate on the hunting. While I was hoping Hunter would get his elk, I can't deny being relieved that he didn't. While he certainly gave it a shot, he didn't hunt exceptionally hard. He, too, must have had reservations about going through another hell night.

As I sit in my trophy room and see that beautiful elk on the wall, I realize that he wasn't the biggest elk that ever lived. He was however, an elk I truly earned. He will live forever in my memory as the elk I got the hard way.

Chapter Twenty-three

NAMIBIA

African hunting exists in the American psyche as a vague recollection of Stewart Granger stalking through the Kenyan bush in the 1950s movie, *"King Soloman's Mines"*. For most Americans, the thought of actually going to Africa themselves to hunt, seems preposterously inconceivable. After all, hunting is a sport pursued with Dad and Uncle Fred in the mountains a few hours drive from home. Dreams of an Idaho pack trip for elk and mule deer might linger in the back of the mind; but Africa, don't be ridiculous.

The thought of hunting in Africa first occurred to me when I was 12 years old. I had just finished reading Robert Ruark's, *The Old Man and the Boy* for the tenth time, and I decided to explore some of his other work. I tagged along with my mother on her next trip to the library and located *The Horn of the Hunter.* Ruark didn't disappoint me. I felt that I was sitting in the Land Rover with him and Harry Selby as we crossed the plains of East Africa. I could see the vast herds of zebra, wildebeest and impala that he described. I agonized with him on his quest for kudu. I celebrated with him when he shot his black maned lion.

I became hopelessly infatuated with the idea of hunting in Africa. For several months, I plowed through the African hunting shelf of the library that included Hemingway, Hunter and Bell. My daydreams were filled with hot, dusty rides through the veldt. I longed to hear the rumble of roaring lions reverberating through camp; to stalk kudu and eland; to see a bull elephant in the wild.

As with most boyhood dreams, the discovery of girls pretty much obliterated my African fantasies. For twenty years, those thoughts lay dormant; sleeping, but apparently not dead. Peter Capstick's vivid and humorous descriptions in *Death in the Long Grass* reawakened that sense of excitement and adventure that I had felt as a boy.

There was a fundamental difference this time around however. At 36, I wasn't a kid any more; while I wasn't rich, I wasn't student-poor like I had been for so many years. I began to devour magazine articles on African hunts. The 30-day, tent camp safaris for the Big Five, like the ones I had read about as boy, remained clearly out of my price range. There were, however, some Ranch style hunts in South Africa,

Namibia and Zimbabwe that were moderately priced and seemed within reach. I realized that I would need to commit myself to a multi-year savings program, but any dream still alive after 20 years deserved to be fulfilled,

When my plane took off for Windhoek, Namibia, I was 39. I felt 12 years old again. For the previous six weeks, I had counted the days, just like I used to do before the opening of pheasant season. Thoughts of my safari never left my mind, and I prattled on about it until even my daughters thought I was acting childish. I had been packed for a full month.

My hunting buddy, Dr. Terry Truhler, in Namibia, 1993.

My partner was Terry Truhler, a next door neighbor, who in a moment of wine-induced weakness had offered to join me. Terry was a medical doctor with a quiet, but not uncommunicative manner. Although he was certainly no jokester, he enjoyed a laugh and smiled easily. Perhaps it was the years Terry had spent practicing emergency medicine, or perhaps it was simply his nature, but he was utterly unflappable. Although we had never hunted together, we had been fly fishing buddies for several years. I was confident that we would make equally compatible hunting partners.

On the afternoon of our third day of travel, we emerged bleary-eyed from the 15 hour, New York to Johannesburg flight. One more travel day lay before us, but at least we had finally arrived in Africa. We stowed our gear in the bright, modern, hotel room and made a beeline for the bar. A wrought iron grating separated the lounge from the bar area, where a black bartender dressed in a red jacket was serving some businessmen. Looking around, I couldn't help but imagine hunters from a previous era who stopped, on their way to safari, in similar watering holes in Nairobi. Johannesburg, I supposed, had become the Nairobi of the 90s.

We ordered one of the local "Castle" beers. Terry proposed a toast to, "The rest of the world; the poor bastards." I drank heartily to those sentiments. The first of many pleasant surprises of our trip was the favorable exchange rate from dollars to rand. Unable to pass up a bargain, I feasted on twin filet mignons for only seven bucks.

One final, two hour flight landed us in Windhoek where the outfitter had a car and driver waiting for us. The hunting area was a three and one half hour drive north. Since this was an infrequent trip into town, the driver had a laundry list of errands to accomplish before we could start back. He dropped us downtown with a promise to retrieve us in a few hours. Windhoek was a surprisingly modern city of pleasant shops and busy, car-filled streets. Although the town was interesting, we were, after four days of travel, ready to get to the ranch.

Despite getting the overloaded Volkswagon van stuck in a sandy riverbed, we arrived at the ranch about an hour after dark. The lodge was a stucco-sided complex with six guest rooms. Terry and I were directed into private rooms, complete with queen sized beds and hot showers. Roughing it, was apparently, not in the equation. Dinner was waiting in a circular dining room called a lappa. A domed roof with a round opening covered the structure, allowing smoke from the central fire pit to escape. A bar and grill was situated along one wall and a series of red, linen covered trays was arranged in a semicircle opposite the bar.

Six people were enjoying a sundowner when we arrived, and we went through introductions. Two other hunters and one of their wives were, we learned to our amusement, from Spokane, Washington, a mere 150 miles from our home. These men had just completed their hunt. Their sense of relaxation was palpable and contrasted with our own nervous excitement.

Natie, one of the professional hunters, was a muscular 5 foot 9 inches, with blond hair and blue eyes partially obscured by rimless spectacles. His smile was imp-like and made him look younger than his 26 years. I guessed that he would be easy to get along with over a ten day hunt. Natie's wife, Cornee, was a petite, trim woman with dark hair, a gentle face and a joyful laugh. We soon learned that she was also a wonderful cook, when her assistant, Macarios, served her superb gemsbok cordon bleu.

Steve, the other professional hunter was, to my surprise, an American; the only American P.H. in Namibia. He had been in Africa for 18 years, however, and spoke fluent Afrikans. He was a six footer, just slightly overweight at 200 pounds. He had an unruly head of light brown hair that stuck out beneath his hunting cap, and a broad, intelligent face. Everything about Steve was intense. He spoke with a booming voice while gesticulating vigorously with his hands. Steve was clearly a guy with opinions, and, in fact, reminded me a lot of my brother. Being rather animated myself, I was certain I could get along well with Steve. Terry, on the other hand, was the antithesis of Steve and I couldn't really see them as a team.

I awakened hours before dawn, my internal clock a shambles after the 10 hour time difference. I lay in bed listening to all varieties of birds crying out in voices strange to me. Finally at 5:00, I wandered into the kitchen where Cornee and Marcarios were already preparing breakfast. She poured me a cup of steaming black coffee which I carried to the patio. Dawn broke slowly over the lake and the first day of a dream come true.

We had sighted in the rifles before leaving home, but we wanted to double check them after the long trip. A heavy wooden table equipped with sand bags was located a short distance behind the lodge. My .375 Holland & Holland was still an inch high at 100 yards, but my .280 Remington was shooting four inches left and needed adjustment. By

9:30, we were ready to go hunting.

When we returned to the car, my tracker, a lean, sloe-eyed, black man in his early thirties was waiting for us. Dressed in a neatly pressed, camoflauge shirt, tan cap, with binoculars draped around his neck, he had a prosperous and confident manner. He was from the Ovambo tribe, but spoke fluent Afrikans and enough English to introduce himself as Naftali. Sitting between his legs was Steve's little fox terrier. Foxie, as he was called, had an alert, aggressive air typical of his breed.

A rich, earthy, powerful aroma filled the air as we drove down the deeply rutted, road. Soil, reddish yellow in color, was still damp from the previous afternoon's downpour. Much to the relief of the P.H., the rainy season was extending into April, leaving the ground covered with knee high grasses and forbs. The terrible drought which had caused the deaths of many of the ranch's older animals, was now safely behind them. Acacia trees of various types grew thickly throughout the rolling ranch land. A large, green, Sphinx moth caterpillar had defoliated one species of tree causing whole areas of forest to appear dead. Closer inspection, however, revealed that new leaves had already started to appear. While most of the green caterpillars had pupated, a second species of caterpillars was now feeding on a different type of tree. These fellows were especially nasty; with sharp, barbed hairs which stung like nettles if they touched the skin.

Less than 15 minutes from the lodge, we spotted our first game. A herd of 75 springbok spread across a meadow blanketed with yellow daisies. Light tan, with a bold stroke of black across the flanks, the little antelope only weighed about 60 pounds. A herd of black wildebeest, which had been grazing nearby, swished their prominent white tails and bolted away. Within minutes, we spotted a small band of red hartebeest bulls moving warily away from the truck. Rich red in color, with elongated faces and thick, upright, S-shaped horns, they were the most unusual beasts I'd ever seen.

We passed three herds of gemsbok in rapid succession. Beautiful, boldly marked faces crowned with dagger straight horns, stared at us for a long moment and then dashed, in unison through the trees. We climbed a kopje, to gain a vantage point over the countryside. Hundreds of thousands of acres of bush veldt spread below us. Mountains, less than ten miles off, rose up to the west and north. A herd of giraffe, to the south, stood statuesque above the bush. Sixty Birchell's zebra trotted below followed by a band of twenty eland. A huge bull eland, as big as a Brahma bull, followed the cows and smaller bulls.

191

Steve explained that it was nearly impossible to kill a big eland out of a large herd like that. By the time you caught up to them, they were invariably in thick bush. It was then very difficult to locate the bull you were after before being spotted by the cows. The strategy for eland was to find the track of a lone bull and follow it. The spectacle of wildlife surrounding us held me in such awe, that I was unprepared to shoot anything, for the moment at least.

We returned to the Suzuki and continued our tour. Although I never road hunted in the U.S., the use of vehicles to locate game is standard operating procedure in Africa. While it would be quite possible to take almost all the species by foot, it would require considerable luck to locate trophy quality animals. By using the vehicle, we would be able to look over hundreds of animals before selecting the ones we wanted.

The Suzuki four wheel drive was admirably suited for the job. Stripped down of all frills, the car was equipped with everything necessary to do the job. Light in weight, it was able to ride on top of the wet, river sand without miring down. Roofless and with a fold down windshield, it was possible to shoot directly from the car if needed. The raised, back seat offered Naftali a good vantage for spotting game, and a two way radio allowed us to remain in contact with the lodge.

My sense of direction was totally confused as the mid-day sun shone in the north rather than the south as in the Northern Hemisphere. Even the steering wheel of the car was on the right rather than the left side. I hadn't the slightest idea of where the lodge was until we pulled into the driveway. Cornee had an immense lunch of ham and cheese filled crepes prepared for us, after which we retired to the sitting room for a siesta.

Midway through our afternoon hunt, I started to become accustomed to the sights of strange and beautiful herds parting before us as we drove. Remembering the reason I had come, I began to view the animals as potential trophies. Steve drove over a rocky ridge toward an area where he had seen a good gemsbok recently.

We spotted waterbuck, roan and finally several bands of gemsbok. Gemsbok cows and calves also have horns, with cow's horns often being longer, but not as thick as a bull's. I was unable to differentiate a big gemsbok from a small one or a bull from a cow. They all looked huge to me. We did spot one lone bull that Steve said was a good one, but he galloped away leaving us a view of his black, horse-like tail disappearing through the acacias.

As we drove into an open meadow, we came upon another herd of springbok. We glassed them, but none of the rams were mature enough to shoot. When we had driven less than a half mile from the herd, Naftali spoke rapidly to Steve, in Afrikans, and pointing into the bush. I immediately identified the lone springbok, which he had spotted.

"A good ram," Steve informed me. "Do you want him?" I wanted a springbok, and I had to take Steve's word on size, so I quickly assented. "He sees us," he warned "and if you get out of the car, he will bolt."

I was torn as to what I should do. I had never shot from a vehicle before. There was nothing illegal about it in Namibia, and I knew that some clients shot all their animals from a car. The question I had to answer was how I would feel about it. I decided that there was no fundamental difference between bailing out to shoot from the ground beside the car and shooting from the seat. I certainly did not plan to shoot all my game from the vehicle, but if a quality animal offered me a shot from the car, I was not going to pass it up. Ethics being what they are, another man may have made a different decision. I don't apologize for mine.

The crosshairs settled on the forward edge of the springbok's black flank patch. They wavered for an instant, and then came firmly to rest as I concentrated on the trigger pull. The .280 boomed and the springbok reared up momentarily before racing out of sight. Foxie, leaped from the back seat and went charging after him. "He ran like hell," said Steve. I couldn't believe my eyes. The hold felt perfect, but how could a 60 pound animal take a 150 grain Nosler bullet behind the shoulder and run off. Could I have flinched?

When we arrived at where he was standing, Naftali pointed out where the antelope's tracks dug deeply into the ground as he bolted. Naftali walked briskly forward, his eyes scarcely glancing at the ground. Such tracking was child's play for him. After fifty yards, he pointed toward a splash of bright red blood. My confidence started to trickle back, but my stomach remained in knots.

One hundred, two hundred yards later and still no springbok. I began to believe that I had only wounded him, but Naftali broke a smile and patted me on the back. He raised one finger, cocked his head to listen and said, "Foxie gottem".

Then I heard it as well. The frenetic growling of the little terrier emanated from a ditch just ahead of us. When we arrived, Foxie was chewing ferociously on the hind quarters of the dead springbok. He was a graceful, beautiful animal with telescoping horns that curved inward to form a heart shape. Steve pulled a tape measure from his pocket and began measuring the horns. "Fifteen and a half," he announced, "very nice, very nice. He will make the book easy." I never cared much for record books but it was somehow satisfying to know that he was a better than average, mature animal. He would make a lovely mount.

My shot had pierced the left lung and angled back through the liver. The bullet had entered exactly where I had aimed. If a 60 pound springbok could take that sort of punishment and run 300 yards, I wondered what a 500 pound gemsbok or a 2,000 pound eland would do. Steve tied the front and rear legs together and draped the rope over the spare behind the rear seat. He tied up the head so it wouldn't drag, and we headed back to find the skinner.

The skinning and butchering shed was functionally perfect. Built as an open-ended garage, we were able to back the car right into the tile walled room. Foxie had become very possessive of the springbok and he yapped ferociously at the skinner. The blacks considered Foxie to be hilarious, and howled in laughter as Steve tried to convince the little devil to allow us to remove the antelope. Meat hooks were lowered on a chain suspended from the ceiling and the springbok was hoisted into the air. As darkness descended, we left the skinner to his work and headed back to the lodge.

A more somber than usual Terry was waiting for me with a stiff scotch on the rocks. He graciously congratulated me on my springbok before confiding his bad news. He had also shot a springbok, hitting it right through the neck with a 180 grain Nosler. The animal had dropped instantly, but then got up and ran away. They tracked him for two hours before the bleeding stopped and the tracks became hopelessly intermingled with those of a large herd. It seemed impossible that the bullet could have failed to hit the vertebrae or the trachea or at least a major artery, but that apparently was what had happened; A stroke of bad luck and another testament to the toughness of African game.

I watched Terry closely, trying to read his mood. He had not done much hunting for several years and I worried that he might lose confidence in his shooting. A particularly difficult deer season, a number of years back, had taught me how intertwined confidence and good shooting could be. He seemed disappointed, but not disheartened, and over dinner we discussed his plans to resume his search for the wounded springbok in the morning. Hopefully, he would get some assistance from the vultures.

The author with a Kalahari springbok taken in Namibia in April of 1993.

DAY TWO

I planned to spend the day hunting kudu. The kudu was, to my eye, the most magnificent of Africa's antelopes. Nearly elk sized, with a striped gray back and long spiral shaped horns, a bull kudu was the epitome of grace and beauty. Steve met me for a predawn breakfast, and then we drove to a nearby cattle ranch. Several small bands of kudu, including several medium-sized bulls, passed in front of the car in the pink morning light. In the midst of the ranch, a range of rocky mountains rose 2,000 feet from the surrounding bush which, itself, was 4,000 feet in elevation.

I had considered myself to be a good climber, but Steve and Naftali scampered ahead of me. I plodded along at the slow pace that I found comfortable in the mountains.

Periodically, I caught up to the guides when they stopped to glass the hillsides. Not wanting to run his client into the ground, Steve cast concerned glances back at me, as he tried to gauge my fatigue. He eventually came to realize that although I was slow, I was not really tiring much, and he quit worrying about me.

We hunted slowly along the spine of the ridge, glassing as we went.

The first animal we spotted was not a kudu at all, but an old gemsbok bull bedded only 30 yards in front of us. I raised the rifle, but Steve stopped me. "Too short," he declared, "as big as they come in the body, but short. Good eyes though." As if not to be outdone by the client, Naftali pointed to a hillside at least a mile away and claimed that he saw a big bull kudu. Neither Steve nor I could even make out the animal much less determine its size, but we took the tracker's word and began a stalk.

Before we could close ground on him, we stumbled into a pair of bedded bull kudu. They bounded along the ridge and then stopped in a little saddle about 250 yards away. One had horns 46 or 47 inches long and was shootable, but Steve was convinced that the one Naftali had spotted was larger. The bigger bull watched us for several minutes before drifting over the ridge. The smaller one trotted in the direction of the bull we were after, and effectively blocked our stalk by stopping half way between us and him.

Our only alternative was to wait until one of the bulls moved. We sat in the growing heat for an hour and a half, listening to the baboon's aggressive barking from the rocks above us. The bulls had moved closer together, but were now standing immobile in a thicket of trees. Had we not already known where they were, we never would have been able to see them. It appeared that they would remain there until evening. Unwilling to wait them out, we attempted a stalk.

Using the ridge to block their vision, we stalked to within 300 yards. When we re-emerged over the spine, we could no longer see either bull. We knew where they were however, and we began a painstakingly slow approach toward their position. We closed ground to 200, then 100, then 50 yards and still we could not see them. Finally at 15 yards, I found myself looking directly into the face of the big bull. The brush was so dense that his face was all that was visible.

Naftali attempted to step aside, to allow me to shoot, and when he did, a rock rolled under his foot. The bull leaped instantly out of sight and I could hear both bulls bounding down the rocky slope. They reappeared for an instant as they ran through an opening 150 yards away. I got the bull in my scope, but the thought of Terry's wounded springbok jumped into my mind. I didn't want to wound such a magnificent animal. I held my fire and watched him go.

The rocks had grown hot in the midday heat as we made the long climb down. My boots were well broken in, but the heat from the ground was beginning to cook the soles of my feet. Moleskin, applied at that moment, would have prevented further damage, but I foolishly had left it back at the lodge. I had a five mile hike in front of me, and with each step, I could feel fluid oozing into blisters. By the time we reached the car, there were silver dollar sized blisters on both feet.

My face was crusted with salt, and I was parched. Steve unpacked the cooler with the lunch, but I couldn't eat anything until I gulped down my eighth glass of water. Shadows were long by the time we returned to the lodge, so I headed for a shower. I doctored my feet by piercing each blister and draining the fluid. In the morning, I would drain them again before applying moleskin.

Darkness had fallen and Terry and Natie still had not returned. I was just into my third scotch when their car pulled in, and I hobbled out to greet them. "I did it right this time," Terry's reported cheerfully. "I shot a nice impala just before dark. He dropped like a stone at the shot." It was my turn to pour drinks as the entire camp breathed a collective sigh of relief. All of us had been concerned about how Terry's bad break the day before might have upset him, and we celebrated his triumph.

DAY THREE

My feet were not yet up to another climb up Kudu Mountain, so the plan was to remain in the flat country for a day in search of a gemsbok, an impala or a hartebeest. At first light, a bull gemsbok seemed anxious to play along with our plan. We spotted him from the vehicle and made a stalk through the acacias. The bull cooperated perfectly and stopped in the open a mere 75 yards in front of us. I dropped to a sitting position, and began to squeeze, when I heard Steve's voice. "Hold it. He really isn't all that big. Maybe we should hold off." Frankly, he looked huge to me, and it took all my will power to pull the rifle from my shoulder.

The bull walked serenely away as if he knew we wouldn't hurt him. He never knew how close he had come. Steve began to examine the ground and called Naftali over. An eland track, as big around as a dessert plate, looked very fresh. It had to be a bull and he was apparently alone.

"This is the situation we've been looking for," said Steve. "Are you feet up to doing some eland tracking?"

"Momma didn't raise any weanies," I answered. "I'll be damned if I'm going to let a few blisters stand between me and an eland."

Steve smiled and turned to Naftali and said, "The man wants to go eland hunting. Let's go."

The bull was not far ahead of us, and we quickly found several glistening, fresh, droppings; horse-like but slightly looser. The tracks meandered along, showing that the bull was feeding. Several times, he crossed rocky ground. Steve and especially Naftali were absolute wizards at remaining on the track. They were forced to spend most of their time examining the ground, so my job was to keep my eyes trained ahead of us, in hopes of spotting the eland before he spotted us.

For two hours, we stayed on his track; never far behind him. My nervous system was on red alert as I constantly scanned the bush. Suddenly, we heard a crash off to our right. We whirled around but could not see anything. The bull had not grown large by being stupid. He had bedded downwind of his back trail just in case anything followed him.

We hoped that he wasn't badly spooked and continued following his trail. Over the next hour, we did manage to walk up on a very large warthog, which I did not want to shoot, as well as a small herd of cow and calf gemsbok. The eland however was onto us. Plowing into a tremendous thicket, he waited; all the time watching his back trail. He bolted the instant we came into view, offering us a brief glimpse of his tawny hide before he disappeared into the brush. There was no point in following the bull any further, so I limped back to the car.

During the afternoon, we had two unsuccessful stalks on hartebeest before turning the car toward home. Around a bend and THERE!, in the dusky meadow stood our bull eland. His body was massive, his horns looking like giant loaves of French bread twisted in the middle. As he trotted seamlessly away, the silver colored dewlaps at his throat swayed ponderously from side to side. He was too far for a shot and it was too late to track him. We scuttled plans to return to Kudu Mountain and vowed to be on his track at dawn. Hopefully, he would bed down during the night and we could catch up to him.

DAY FOUR

A heavy dew coated the grass and soaked our pant legs as we followed the tracks through the early morning mists. Hopes were high for the first hour. The track cut through soft ground and we followed along at a trot. Three hours later, we still had not found where the eland had bedded. His tracks began to cross through those of another herd of eland, and we lost time at each juncture.

Naftali and Steve circled in order to determine where the bull had left the herd. Naftali had started tracking his father's goats when he was three years old, and his ability was pure genius. Despite his awesome display of tracking, luck was against us. The bull had traveled all night under the full moon. After five hours of tracking, we were no closer to him than when we started.

We accepted defeat and headed back. I had switched to tennis shoes in hopes of preventing further damage to my feet. It turned out to be a poor choice. The dew drenched my socks causing new blisters to form on the toes of my left foot. By the time we returned to the car, the blisters had ruptured, staining my socks with blood.

Impala and hartebeest were supposedly easy animals to take. By day's end, however, I still had not seen a ram impala on the entire trip, and every hartebeest I approached galloped off the instant I raised the rifle. Gemsbok were everywhere, but finding a big one that would stand still long enough for a shot seemed an impossibility. Of course, the cows and small bulls seemed intent on suicide, but that didn't help.

I was getting frustrated and I began to think that I had shot the most expensive springbok in history. As we made our way toward the lodge in fading light, I was ready to drop my trophy standards by a considerable margin to prevent going home empty handed. Steve was adamantly against it. "We just don't shoot animals that aren't fully mature," he said firmly. "We still have six days to hunt. Hang in there. Our luck will change." I wasn't so certain, but he was the professional. I just had to trust that he knew what he was doing.

"Well, I say to hell with the eland. If we get everything else and still have any time left over, we can try for one at the end," I responded, somewhat petulantly, I'm afraid.

No sooner were the words out of my mouth, than the very same eland, big as a house, raced across the road 150 yards in front of us. By the time we skidded to a halt and I got out, he had crossed into a ravine. He reappeared 500 yards away, still running.

"I still say the hell with him," I said defiantly. "Tomorrow, let's go back after kudu."

DAY FIVE

Bad luck seemed to have found me and moved in like an obnoxious relative at Christmas time. A few more days with this hex and my trip would be over. Luck can change rapidly during a hunt and I fervently hoped this would be my day. Mists hung close to the ground as daylight crept across the veldt. We planned to hunt another area, flatter than Kudu Mountain, where Terry had seen several nice bulls. As we rounded a bend in the road we spotted a huge herd of hartebeest. Uncharacteristically placid, they appeared to be very huntable. I suggested we sneak up a nearby ditch, pick out a bull and end our drought right then and there.

"Morning is prime kudu time," Steve reminded me. "If we want to get a kudu, we may have to stay after them every morning from here on out. We could blow the whole morning getting a hartebeest skinned, and another day would be shot. We've got time to get a hartebeest later."

I wanted to whine like a four year old in the grocery checkout line when his father denies him a candy bar. Steve, however was the pro. He had 18 years experience, and I had to respect that. I accepted his decision, with a simple "OK", but he could tell I was losing confidence in his assurances.

A cloudburst during the night left the normally dry riverbeds boiling with brown water. The flat ground we were hunting was blanketed in sheets of water, and even the light, little Suzuki barely made it through. There was no place to glass the terrain, so we were forced to drive along the ranch fence lines in hopes of finding a kudu out feeding. We saw a few 43 and 44 inch kudu that morning, but even I wasn't desperate enough to want to shoot them yet.

The ranch also ran a tourist lodge catering to people wanting to view wildlife. The tourists usually enjoyed the opportunity to eat wild game, and all of the meat shot on the game ranch was used at the lodge. Terry and I had, thus far, shot only a springbok and an impala, and the meat supply was nearly exhausted. We received a plea over the radio to shoot something, preferably a gemsbok, no later than tomorrow evening.

I would not be charged for any nontrophy, meat animal that I shot. I recognized an opportunity to kill two birds (or in this case, gemsbok) with one stone, so I offered a suggestion. We could spend the afternoon looking for gemsbok, but we still would not shoot a small one. If a medium sized bull or large cow presented itself, we would take it. In that way, if we failed to take a big gemsbok later, I could pay for the one we shot, and take him home as my trophy. Steve agreed, and the hunt was on.

The gemsbok must have smelled my eagerness. Those same average sized bulls, which had offered themselves up to be shot just the previous day, suddenly became hopelessly wild. At the first sight of the vehicle, they broke into a gallop and disappeared into the bush. Even the cows and calves raced off.

Steve cursed in frustration, probably thinking that his client just might be hexed after all. The gemsbok had been acting calmly at dusk, so we continued our search until dark. We saw at least 100 gemsbok, but had no chance for a stalk or a shot.

Terry had also been suffering through a dry spell. Cornee did her best to keep up our spirits with her cheerful laughter and another superb meal. She was only partly successful however, and a creeping gloom filled the silences in the conversation. I overheard Steve and Natie talking quietly at the bar, and even they were getting a little concerned. These were men with a lot of pride, and they felt that their reputations were on the line.

DAY SIX

Hope springs eternal in the hunter's heart and we headed back to Kudu Mountain. A pink dawn portended a magnificent African day; a day full of possibilities. Early indications were promising, when a pair of one and three quarter curl kudus crossed the road in the dim light. I passed them up, my heart still set on a bull with two complete curls.

We parked in the same place that we had used on our first kudu hunt, and began the climb to the ridge. My original blisters were improving, although the new ones still had me limping along. It seemed, however, that once the nerve endings realized that I was going to ignore them, they quit screaming and retreated to a sulky throb.

Steve, Naftali and I had developed a rhythm to our hiking. They were faster than I, but I was steady and didn't tire easily. Rather than try to restrict themselves to my slow pace, they moved ahead, and glassed the surrounding hillsides until I caught up. Just shy of the ridgetop, I relocated them sitting on a rock outcropping. Rapid Afrikans accompanied by pointing arms told me that they had something spotted. I settled down on a flat rock and tried to find the object of their interest.

Nearly at the bottom of the mountain, at least 1,500 yards away, stood eight kudus. At least two were bulls. Hesitant to give up our hard earned elevation for another mediocre bull, we spent almost a half hour trying to size them up. Naftali and Steve were locked in an incomprehensible discussion on the size and shape of the horns. How it is possible, with 10 power binoculars, to separate a 45 from a 50 inch kudu from a distance of a mile is beyond me. Finally, however, Steve announced that one looked like a big bull.

The wind was in our faces, and we could use a knob on the

mountain to shield our approach. A successful stalk seemed likely. We bounded downhill, braving loose rock and ankle clutching brush in hopes of closing ground before the bull wandered off. At last reaching the knob, we peered over the top. The bull was still there, but we had misjudged his distance from the knob. He was still 500 yards away. The wind remained in our favor, so we could try to sneak up on him. Once we lost the advantage of height, however, he would be much more difficult to keep track of.

It seemed to be our only option, and then that option also closed. A band of baboons appeared, feeding between us and the bull, and a herd of gemsbok were also drifting toward us. If we spooked either group of animals, the kudu would vanish. We decided to wait things out and hope the kudu would feed toward us. He did not, and in fact was starting to feed away from us. One last ditch hope remained.

If Naftali could circle around the bull and intentionally give him his scent, then perhaps he would run toward us. A half hour passed before we once again saw Naftali through our binoculars. He was not quite directly downwind, but was nonetheless headed directly toward the brush where the bull had disappeared. The muscles in my shoulders and chest tightened as I expected to see the bull dash from cover at any moment.

My eyes darted between openings in the trees. He had to pass through one. My heart pounded. At last my chance would come. I had to make it count. Time passed and the thrill of anticipation ebbed; first replaced by confusion and finally by the realization that the kudu was gone. Somehow he had slipped off unseen. Steve exploded in a tirade of profanity. He was thoroughly disgusted and frustrated. Now it was my turn to offer reassurances. "Hey, it was a good try; our only option really. We'll get a kudu tomorrow or maybe a gemsbok this afternoon. Nothing sadder than a starving tourist, you know," I joked.

We lunched under a windmill before heading back toward the ranch. We did not siesta long, but continued our hunt through the heat of mid-day. Insects droned lazily in the hazy sunshine. The bush itself seemed to be sleeping. Except for the giraffe, which were unable to hide, and the dimwitted ostriches, we saw no game for several hours.

A long ridge, only a few hundred feet high, traversed the north end of the ranch. We picked our way over the top on a rugged, boulder-strewn road before dropping down into a dry river bed. Acacias grew thickly along the banks, but the flowing water had scrubbed the ground almost bare. Terry had shot his impala in just such a spot, and we were all straining our eyes as we crept the car along.

Steve spotted the impala before the rest of us. They had been bedded in the thicket and had stood up when they spotted the car. It was a band of five rams; golden brown in color, with dainty thin legs, deer-like faces, and graceful curved horns. Two were definitely larger than the rest. The rams weren't badly spooked, but they did trot back into the thicket a short distance.

Steve pulled the car off the road, drove into the bush a short ways, and turned off the engine. The impala trotted about 50 yards further and stopped. Steve told me to keep my eyes on the last ram as he was definitely a good one. When they stopped, their heads were obscured by brush but their bodies remained in view. Perhaps because they could not see us, they thought that we could not see them.

I had a steady hold just behind the shoulder and didn't waste any time. The .280 boomed and the impala bolted without showing any sign of a hit.

"I didn't hear the bullet strike," said Steve.

"That animal is going to be stone cold dead when we find him," I answered confidently. "There is no way I missed him."

Although we were unable to find blood for 50 yards, my confidence was unshaken. Once again Foxie came through. We heard him growling from a ditch, worrying the dead impala. The ram was a beautiful animal; golden brown on the back and honey colored on the flanks and belly. His jet black horns had that same telescoping appearance as the springbok's, but they were 22 inches long, seven inches longer than the springbok. He also would qualify for the Safari Club Record Book.

Naftali seemed more thrilled by the impala than I. Smiling from ear to ear, he patted himself on the chest and repeated over and over, "Me happy, happy. Five day, nothing. Today, me happy."

The drought was over at last. A sense of relief spread through me like a shot of whisky. Everything was going to be all right. My bad luck had run its course and I just knew that luck would break my way for a while. I continued to feel that way two hours later, even after I flat missed a monster gemsbok at 50 yards.

We had spotted three gemsbok crossing the road in front of us. We bailed out and stalked into the bush, hoping the animals would curve back and cross our path. I was behind Steve and Naftali when we first spotted them. If they continued in the same direction, they would cross a thirty foot wide clearing just in front of us. We still were not sure if there was a bull in the group, or if there was, how big his horns were. I

The author with his impala and professional hunter Steve Tors and tracker Naftali.

made a foolish error of not getting into shooting position just in case.

The first two animals that crossed the opening were cows. Then a monster bull stepped into view. Steve frantically signaled me to shoot. In order to freeze him, Naftali gave a lowing cry like a calf in distress. I stepped forward and dropped to one knee, which has always been a poor shooting stance for me. The crosshairs floated wildly about the bull's chest, but I was afraid he was about to run. I should have realized that the bull was looking directly into the sun and probably didn't see me clearly. The instant the .375 fired, the bull ran and I knew I had missed. Steve and Naftali said they heard the bullet tearing through the brush. We followed his tracks for several hundred yards anyway, but the gemsbok was unscathed.

Naftali patted me on the shoulder in sympathy and Steve offered condolences, as he had undoubtedly done hundreds of time during his 18 years of guiding. I hated to let them down after the super effort they had been making for me. I didn't feel depressed however, as I might have had I not killed the impala earlier, but I did feel a little stupid.

Terry's drought also ended on day six. He shot a second springbok late in the day, killing it cleanly with a shot through both shoulders. The mood at dinner was considerably brighter as we celebrated long into the evening.

DAY SEVEN

I had grown to love hunting on Kudu Mountain. The climbing was invigorating, we always saw kudu before they saw us, and we were able to make challenging stalks. It reminded me of elk hunting in Idaho, except there were more kudu in Namibia than elk in Idaho.

After finding the big bull near the base of the mountain on the previous day, we only climbed high enough to give us a good vantage point. We glassed and hiked for almost two hours before spotting a nice bull. The wind was in our faces, and he was slowly feeding towards us. All we really needed to do was sit tight and let him feed into range.

Steve and Naftali were locked in an animated conversation, none of which I could fathom. Eventually Steve said, "He is pretty decent, but I think we can still do better." I would have been willing to shoot that kudu, but I was also willing to pass him up. I had a feeling that even if we never saw another kudu as large, we would be able to find another nearly as big.

As we walked off, Steve confided, "Naftali hated to leave that one." Now I understood their argument.

White and billowy clouds had been drifting in from the east; just a few at first, lonely in the azure sky; then a few more and then more, until they ran out of room and began colliding; building themselves into huge thunderheads. In a heartbeat, the dry riverbed could turn into a torrent powerful enough to float a car downstream in a heart beat. None of us had any desire to be stuck in an open topped car during a thunderstorm. We hustled back to the car and made a run for it.

Giant drops splattered on the hood just as the lodge came into sight. A deafening crash of thunder exploded behind us and Steve poured on the gas. We skidded the car into the garage just as the heavens opened, unleashing sheets of rain. We sneaked into the kitchen and absconded with a couple of beers and plates of Cornee's lunch. In the twenty steps from the kitchen to the sitting room, we were nearly soaked. Nothing cheers a Namibian as much as a good rain, and Steve chatted away happily.

One hour, and an inch and a half of rain later, the thunderheads had deflated into flat, gray, rained-out vapor. We collected Naftali from the tracker's lodge and resumed our hunt. The rain seemed to have calmed the game. Herds of springbok and black wildebeest stared at us blankly as we drove by. A herd of cow and calf hartebeest walked slowly through the brush. "Women and children," Steve called them.

Four bull hartebeest, were tucked back in the bush. Steve stopped the car, and pulled up his binoculars. "They're all pretty decent bulls," he said. They know we're here but they don't seem all that concerned. They strolled off and we followed, trying to keep up. We closed to within 300 yards, but they wouldn't let us get closer. Several times, I raised the rifle, but each time they melted into the brush, forcing us to give chase. "All of them are shootable," said Steve. "If any of them gives you an open shot, take it."

The bulls were walking through the acacias on the edge of a narrow meadow. I had them in my scope, but at 300 yards, I wasn't going to attempt even a walking shot, if I could help it. Then one bull stopped, only his shoulder clearly visible through the thorns. That was all I needed, and I fired the .280. The bull bucked when the bullet hit, and took off in a tear.

"God, I didn't expect you to shoot," said Steve holding his ear.

"I had an open view of his shoulder for just a second. You did tell me to shoot if I had the chance."

"Oh, definitely," said Steve. "You did the right thing. It looked like a damn good shot too."

Naftali grinned broadly as he pantomimed the bull's reaction to the shot. He kept repeating "Good! Good! Dead sure."

The bull's tracks were easy to follow in the soft mud, although there was no blood. We didn't see the first drop for 100 yards and then found the dead bull twenty yards further on.

"You sure can plant 'em in ditches," Steve laughed, as he pointed to where the bull collapsed.

Naftali understood Steve's comment and went into another silly pantomime of animals running and collapsing. "Springbok," he said. "Ditch. Impala Ditch, Hartebeest. Ditch."

While I dug into my duffel for my video camera, Steve pulled out his tape. Naftali pinched the tape to the horns as Steve measured the length. A disbelieving smile crossed his face. Naftali started to laugh.

"This bull has 23 and 1/2 inch horns," exclaimed Steve. When they measured the bases, Naftali clenched his first excitedly and grunted, "Yes, Yes."

Professional hunter Steve Tors with my monster Red Hartebeest.

"Unbelievable," said Steve. "His bases are over 13 inches. This guy will probably be in the top 20 in the S.C.I. book. And, you know what? I don't even think you shot the biggest of the four."

I couldn't have cared less. I was ecstatic with the bull I had on the ground. His horns, which were shaped like an "S" with twist in the middle, were massive and rose straight up making his already long face appear even longer. He was brick red in color with a yellowish rump and a black blaze on his face. His ears were narrow and pointed. Unlike my first two trophies, he couldn't be called beautiful, but he had an exotic look that, to me, was the epitome of Africa.

At 350 pounds, the hartebeest was too large to carry in the Suzuki, so we radioed back to the skinner to bring a bigger truck. He showed up with three helpers, and they heaved him into the bed and hauled him back to the always hungry tourists. By the time we returned to the lodge, it was nearly dark. Terry was already "home" having taken a magnificent 36 inch gemsbok bull earlier in the day. We were on a roll and we knew it.

DAY EIGHT

Voices, hoarse from sleep, echoed from the patio into my room, gently awakening me. I sorted through the stack of freshly laundered clothes and quickly dressed. My blisters were nearly healed and I only needed a moleskin protection on one toe. Single bulbs dimly illuminated the tables where Steve, Natie, Cornee and Terry sat hunched over their coffee. None of us were big breakfast eaters and, Cornee had finally given up on her offers to cook; merely spreading cereal, juice and coffee on the table. I bid everyone good morning and poured myself a cup.

The strategy of only climbing part way up Kudu Mountain had nearly paid off yesterday, so we planned the same approach, this time starting a mile farther north on the mountain. For the first time all week we didn't see a single kudu on the drive in. We reached the top of a knoll shortly after first light, and settled down to glass. We had been systematically scanning the bush for about 20 minutes when Steve spotted a bull about 1,000 yards away.

He directed our eyes to the spot and soon we were all staring at the bull. I then noticed a second bull and Naftali identified a third. We examined them for a long time as Steve tried to compute the length of horn. He particularly concentrated on the direction that the tips were pointing and the depth of the spiral. Tips that pointed out were usually just shy of two curls and would almost certainly be less than 50 inches. The only exception to this rule was if the bull had two and one half turns, and those bulls were obviously monsters. The depth of the spiral was critical, as the deeper the curvature, the longer the horn.

He finally decided that none of the bulls were exceptional, and suggested we keep hunting. We dropped back to the car in order to drive a mile north to another lookout. We would end up driving very close to the three bulls, but we were no longer concerned about spooking them. Naftali, hopped out of the truck to unlatch a gate, when suddenly his head dropped and his shoulders hunched. A bull kudu, bigger than the three we had been watching, strolled between the acacias only 100 yards away.

We froze and watched as 7 bulls appeared and began trotting slowly up the hill. It spoke volumes about the camouflage of kudus that three people had watched them for nearly 40 minutes and had only spotted three of seven bulls.

"I think there are two shootable bulls there," said Steve. "They haven't smelled us and aren't badly spooked. They headed uphill which is to our advantage because we can keep an eye on them better."

Steve pulled the car through the gate to an opening about 50 yards away. We parked and turned off the engine. We could make out the bulls stopped on a bench below a knoll. They were about 350 yards away. We could see the bodies of five of them including the two biggest ones. The head of one big bull was obscured by branches. We wanted to identify the biggest of the two if at all possible, and we suspected that the kudu with his head hidden was the one we wanted.

I rested the rifle on a sand bag on the hood of the car giving me a dead solid hold. It was a long shot, but I was confident that I could pull it off. We waited for a half hour for the bull to move. All he needed to do was take one step and we could be certain. My neck muscles began to tire from staring through the scope, and I had to pull back every few moments to rest.

When he finally moved, he went through the opening too fast for me to chance a shot. He had indeed been the biggest one. I had had his exposed shoulder in the crosshairs for all that time. We would have to get to the knoll above them somehow, and try a shot from there. Steve backed up through the gate, and we drove away from them until we were out of sight on the far side of the knoll.

Once we were completely downwind, we began the climb. We reached the top without incident, but when we looked over, we could not see down into the bench. We had to get closer, but a single rolling rock or cracked limb would spook them. We sat on the slope and tentatively scooted on our rears down the hill. We inched to within a hundred yards, when we first spotted them. Steve whispered to me, "I can't see all of them and I want to get the biggest one. Give me a few minutes."

The wait seemed interminable. I could clearly see one bull bedded down and several others standing near him. Naftali and Steve discussed the merits of each bull in nearly inaudible whispers. Then a bull that had been bedded behind some brush, stood up. I could see Naftali's excited, silent exhortation to Steve. Steve looked at me with a sly grin. He crooked a finger in my direction, as if to say, "See I told you I'd find you a good one."

"Do you see that one walking right there?" he whispered. "That's him. Scoot down to that stump and use it for a rest...

I didn't dawdle. I forced myself to ignore his horns and concentrate on where I would place the shot. There are the crosshairs. A couple inches forward. There. They're steady. Am I sure? Yep. Bang! The bullet struck with a tremendous whopping sound and the kudu leaped completely off the ground. He ran forward twenty yards, crashed through a fallen tree, did a complete summersault and fell dead.

I let out a war whoop as we walked up on the bull. He was magnificent. Steve said, "You know, when you can get a stalk like that, a 45 inch kudu is a real trophy." I was overjoyed with him and didn't care how big he was, but that didn't sound right. I crinkled my eyebrows, cocked my head, and looked first at the bull then at Steve. He broke into gales of laughter. "I'm just teasing you," he said. "That bull is at least 53 inches. Congratulations."

After a round of handshaking and backslapping, I said to Steve. "I want to thank you. I know I've been pushing you to let me shoot, but you stuck to your guns until we found this bull. I really appreciate it. You're a real pro."

The meat from the kudu belonged to the rancher who owned the land where we were hunting, so Steve headed back to fetch him and his crew. Naftali and I just sat with the bull, admiring his thick double spirals, his white chevroned face, his huge ears, and his gray hide striped with white. Here was the animal that I'd come half way around the world to find, and he was worth it.

Steve had complained of having a fever that kept him up most of the night, so I suggested he take the afternoon off to get rested up. I didn't want to dilute the glow of my kudu by more hunting, anyway. He protested that he was okay, but I insisted.

The author with his hard-sought kudu.

DAY NINE

When Steve arrived for breakfast, he had two day's stubble on his chin and a weary, drawn look. He claimed to be feeling better, although he admitted to feeling feverish again last night. I suspected that his claim had more to do with his determination to see his job through, than with fact.

Gemsbok hunting wasn't particularly rigorous, however, and I thought Steve would make it. Gemsbok were common right near the lodge, so there was no need to hit the road an hour before dawn as we had been doing. We enjoyed a third cup of coffee, before daylight began creeping into the patio.

We had been so busy chasing kudu or eland each morning, that we hadn't hunted gemsbok before noon. The difference in their behavior was striking. The sense of security that animals felt at night seemed to remain with the gemsbok during the first light of day. Less than a mile from the lodge, a group of five, including a 30 inch bull, stood staring at us from the road. A few hundred yards further and a 32 inch bull stood equally placidly.

They scarcely seemed like the same species that two days before had bolted at the first sight of us. I raised the .375 on both bulls and peered at them through the scope but wasn't ready to shoot. I was still feeling a glow from the kudu and a gemsbok was the final animal I really wanted. I had two days left to get one. It was going to take a big gemsbok to get me to pull the trigger this morning. Little did I realize, that that big gemsbok would appear in less than two minutes.

When we stopped the car to watch the gemsbok standing on the edge of a meadow 150 yards from the road, we saw only a pair of cows. One had horns of 36 inches, but I was determined to shoot a bull. I liked the masculine, broad face and the thicker horns of the bulls. The rifle was still in the gun rack and we were just enjoying the nature scene. Suddenly, out of the brush stepped a monster bull.

Simultaneous gasps came from both Steve and Naftali. "Oh, God!" Steve gasped. "OK, OK! Do you see that big one that just stepped out? Shoot him."

I might have been a poor judge of gemsbok horns, but even I had no trouble telling which one to shoot. I yanked the rifle out of the rack and brought it quickly to my shoulder. I would have preferred not shooting this bull from the car, but I had successfully hunted dozens of gemsbok on foot already. I had just chosen not to shoot them. This was a once in a lifetime bull, and I didn't spend two seconds wondering if I should shoot. He was quartering toward me, so I aimed at the point of his forward shoulder. When the .375 boomed he began to run and Foxie bailed out of the back seat to give chase.

"It looks like his front leg is broken," said Steve. "It's OK though, a gemsbok is too heavy to run far on a broken front leg. Foxie will bay him."

"I'm sure that he's hit better than that," I countered. Foxie immediately identified which gemsbok was wounded and raced behind him. The feisty terrier looked like a bounding black and white ball as he repeatedly leaped into the air and nipped the gemsbok on the hamstrings. We ran behind and soon saw the bull, his back to a bush, and his head down as he tried to fend off the dog. His wound was too severe to put up much of a fight, however, and he sank to his knees then rolled on his side. I ran toward the bull.

Steve called to his dog to get him out of the line of fire, and I put a finishing shot into the bull's heart. The first shot had been perfect. It had struck the shoulder, passing diagonally through the lower chest, which is why Steve thought I had broken a leg. That bull had run 200 yards after being hit with a 300 grain Nosler bullet; a truly amazing feat.

No sooner had I touched his eye with the rifle barrel to be certain that he was dead than Steve rushed in with a tape measure. "Thirty nine! Thirty nine!" he crowed. "That would have been the third largest bull out of 60 that we shot all of last year. Man! When your luck turns around, I mean, it really turns around!"

Naftali kept jumping into the air. "Big. Good gemsbok." Then he stopped for more a moment and became more serious. "Same bull, him miss," he said in broken English before switching to his much better Afrikans.

"Naftali said that he thinks this is the same bull you missed the other day. Where you missed him is less than a quarter mile from here, and these bulls are territorial."

The author with his outstanding gemsbok.

He was a magnificent beast. He weighed about 500 pounds, with a neck so massive that it just blended into his shoulders without even a hint of where the throat stopped and the brisket began. Coarse tan hair covered his body and his face was distinctly marked in black and white. His horns were spear-shaft straight and needle sharp. They extended over his head an impossibly long way. The jet black tail looked identical to a horse's.

It was so early in the day, that we had to wait until the sun came up in order to take pictures. The skinner had not yet arrived at work, anyway, and we needed him to bring the big truck out to pick up the bull.

"Cornee has been offering to make breakfast all week," I said. "What do you say we go back in and take her up on the offer? This gemsbok hunting has given me an appetite."

There is nothing like a good old American breakfast of eggs, sausage and hash browns, washed down with black coffee, to fill a man up. We needed to decide what we were going to hunt next. There was eland or blue wildebeest or perhaps mountain zebra. I didn't have much confidence in our ability to track down an eland in the time remaining, and I was starting to worry where I was going to put all those heads. The kudu and gemsbok were going to take up a lot of wall space, but an eland would dwarf them.

"I think you would really like mountain zebra hunting," suggested Steve. "You like to climb and stalk and that's how zebra are hunted. They live in rough country and Namibia is the only country that has free ranging herds that can be hunted. They're an animal you may never get another chance to hunt."

Like a lot of people, I had never quite thought of zebras as game animals. Basically they were wild, striped horses. Steve's arguments however made a lot of sense and I decided that any aversion I had to hunting zebra was irrational. The ranch where the mountain zebra were hunted was two hours west of our lodge in a drier zone of rugged mountains. We wouldn't be able to get there until morning.

"You still don't look like you're feeling too well. Why don't you go on home and go to bed," I said.

"I can make it. I'm OK," he insisted. "We can go out around here and see if we can find an eland. Its your trip; your call."

"I just made my call," I said. "Go home to your wife and let her take care of you."

"Well, I'll tell you what. I'll come back around 4:00 and we can go out and take some more video for your film."

I agreed and then shooed him out of the lodge.

Terry and Natie returned for lunch, and before I said a word, congratulated me on my gemsbok.

"If you two have already seen my gemsbok, you must have made a trip to the skinner yourself. What's going on, boys? Fess up."

"I finally got my kudu," Terry admitted with a smile. "He was a beautiful, old animal; very dark in color, with one horn sort of broomed down."

The morning of our ninth day filled in the final pieces of the puzzle. Kudu and gemsbok were the animals we had dreamed of taking. Those dreams were now fulfilled and my heart soared at the accomplishment. But then a tinge of regret seeped through the joy. There would never again be a first kudu or a first African safari. Our hunt was one day from being over and I was already starting to mourn.

When Steve met me to take the video, he was shivering and clutching his jacket collar to his throat. It was 85 degrees. It was pretty obvious to me that Steve had malaria. He must have contracted it in the Caprivi Strip in the northern part of Namibia, because the area we were in was not supposed to be malaria country.

Jan Oelofse, the owner of the game ranch and Steve's boss, stopped by for a drink late that afternoon. Jan was a wonderful gentleman in his early fifties. Although not a large man, he had a vigorous appearance of someone who had lived in the bush all of his life. A cheerful smile seemed never to leave his face for long. He sported a trim moustache and wore a jaunty safari hat over his balding crown. I liked him immediately.

Jan explained that he had moved to central Namibia twenty years before without a penny to his name. He had built the ranch from scratch, even capturing all the wildlife, which had been used to start his herds. A man of many talents, he piloted his own plane, had once served as a stunt double for John Wayne in the movie *Hatari* and had trained a number of the animals used in the film.

I told him of my suspicions about Steve's malaria. I described his symptoms, which Jan, a malaria sufferer himself, knew all too well. He immediately got Steve's wife on the radio, and told her to keep him home tomorrow so she could take him to the doctor. I could hear Steve protesting in the background, but Jan would not take no for an answer.

"I can guide Terry tomorrow and Natie can take you after the

215

mountain zebra," he suggested, "and after our hunt, I'd like you and Terry to come to my home for a farewell dinner."

The late Natie Oelofse and his lovely wife (and great cook), Corne.

DAY 10 – THE FINAL DAY

Natie, his tracker Phillipoos, and I had a two-hour drive to zebra country, so we were on the road long before daybreak. Driving northwest, we wound our way into a mountainous area south of Ethosha National Park. The countryside was drier, with less grass cover than the area around the lodge. The trees were more scattered and the acacia trees largely replaced by mopane, which looked something like scrub oak. The terrain didn't fit my image of zebra habitat.

I was so thrilled with the trophies that I had already taken, that I was hunting more to enjoy the change in scenery than for any burning desire to shoot a zebra. I was, however, looking forward to hunting with Natie.

Natie and I had to go through the process that Steve and I had long since reconciled, of getting accustomed to our different walking paces. I assured him that I was fine and he eventually believed me. My feet were 100 percent healthy for the first time in a week, and I enjoyed the climbing in the cool, dry morning air. The adaptable baboons barked at us as we passed, and three kudu bolted ahead of us, sending shale clattering down the slope.

The .375 would probably have been the better choice for zebra, but I didn't want to lug it up the hills all day. I reasoned that the .280 could do the job, if called upon. We reached the top of the ridge where we were able to glass the slopes below; we spent fifteen minutes in each spot before moving on. I was in no hurry as I wanted to savor every moment of my last day.

Luck was still with me. Natie spotted a band of seven zebra on an opposing ridge. As Hartman's Mountain Zebra go, that was a large group. They were feeding on a saddle of the ridge, crosswind to us. We hoped they would feed over the crest, so that we could stalk directly at them.

After a half hour they were still in sight, so we planned a more circuitous stalk. We ducked below a rock ledge to get out of sight and hiked downwind for about a quarter mile. A knoll between the two ridges shielding us from view and allowed us to eventually reach the ridge where the zebra were feeding. Sound traveled well in those mountains, and falling rocks could easily betray us. Natie's crepe soles were quieter than my Vibram, but I tried to place every step on solid rock to keep noise to a minimum.

"When we reach the next knob, we should be above them and about 150 yards away," whispered Natie. "They've got to still be there."

Suddenly, Phillipoos dropped into a crouch and Natie froze as he extended his hand behind him in a signal for halt. Then I also heard them; A clattering of hooves right below us. A gust of wind carried the strong odor of horse to my nostrils. The entire herd was only 15 yards away, but they were screened by an impenetrable thicket of mopane trees.

"Shoot one," mouthed Natie. I took two steps forward and Natie grabbed my shirt to stop me.

The zebra started to trot and I caught the briefest glimpse of stripes. One was a baby, and I wanted to be certain that I didn't shoot him. Natie signaled me and we ran forward ten steps. We were counting on the clatter of the zebra's footsteps to mask our sound. When we stopped, we could make out patches of zebra hide through the branches.

"That big one. Shoot," whispered Natie, as he pointed moving only his finger.

I raised the rifle, but for a moment was unable to find the patch of hide through the scope. Even three power was too much magnification at 15 yards. I at last found a hole through the branches where I could squeeze a bullet through. I knew the crosshairs were somewhere on his chest although I wasn't certain where. I pulled the trigger and immediately heard the sound of running hooves.

Natie and I ran forward, bounding across the loose rock. One lone zebra, stared at us. He was obviously wounded or he would have run off with the others. All I could see of him this time was his face and neck. I shot and he crashed to the ground; his neck broken.

Natie stuck out his hand and said, "You've got your mountain zebra. Good job!"

The zebra was a stallion and much bigger than I had anticipated. His coat was absolutely striking. The stripes, especially over the haunches, were much closer together than those of the Birchell's plains zebra that we had been seeing. I had a twinge of discomfort at having shot him. He was so much like a horse. I refused to dwell on the feeling. It had been an exciting hunt in wonderful, new country and he would make a gorgeous rug for the wall.

I caught up with Terry late that afternoon and joined him on his search for a waterbuck. We had seen a lot of waterbuck, but nothing mature enough to be considered a trophy. This was to be my farewell tour of the ranch. I tried to sear every sight and smell into memories to retrieve and cherish as years went by. I missed my wife and daughters and would be glad to return to them, but I was overcome with a sense of poignancy as we turned toward the lodge for the last time.

Jan's home was beautiful, with a garden and waterfall in the central foyer. Steve was there looking better rested. He did indeed have malaria, but had received some medication from the doctor. A delicious meal of gemsbok and lamb was placed before us as we sat around a large round table. As we served ourselves, an odd rumble, almost like a locomotive, could be heard in the room. We stopped, serving spoons hovering in mid air. "Lions. Do you hear the lions?" asked Jan. Wonderful Africa was giving us a farewell treat. The lions were saying goodbye.

As we drove back to the lodge under the star filled skies, I looked up and saw the Southern Cross; a constellation only visible from the Southern Hemisphere. I wondered how long it would be before I would see it again. I vowed that I would have to return to this majestic continent of my boyhood dreams.

The author with professional hunter Natie Oelofse and his big Hartman's Mountain Zebra stallion.

The author with the black bear he took on Prince of Wales Island, Alaska, in September of 1994.

Chapter Twenty-four

THE YEAR OF THE BEAR

My transformation from being a hunter of deer, elk, and antelope – herbivores all – to becoming a hunter of the omnivorous bear, was a tortured journey. While rarely having a moment's doubt about the propriety of shooting a deer, at a visceral level, the idea of shooting a bear left me uneasy. Intellectually, I could not explain my concerns. After all, bear populations were strong throughout most of the continent, and the meat from bears was quite edible.

Still, there was something holding me back. A kinship between men and bears, recognized since the Stone Age, was heard as a whisper from a distant, anthropological conscience. Beyond being a beast of great intelligence, the bear was a symbol of mystical power. I must also admit that the idea of eating a bear left me feeling oddly cannibalistic.

Despite those concerns, there remained a desire to enter the bear's world; to experience the age-old dance of hunter and hunted; to glimpse the soul of a bear as no camera-toting park visitor ever could. For 25 years, the battle raged in my mind; one side winning and then giving ground before victory could be claimed.

While in Africa, I spoke with men who hunted lion and leopard. They were as fascinated by these beasts as I was with the bear, but they were at peace with themselves; viewing the hunting of the great predators as entirely natural. The big cats were fascinating and at times dangerous game, which gave no quarter and expected none in return. I found the certainty of these men reassuring and I felt the impasse in my mind settled at last. In my heart, I at last knew that I could hunt a bear and not place undue weight on my conscience. The battle had been won; the decision made; I would hunt bear when I returned home.

The next decision revolved around the method of the hunt; spot and stalk, bait or hounds. Spot and stalk hunting, generally recognized by all but the most zealous anti-hunters as a sporting hunting method, requires knowledge of the bear's habits and habitat, ability to read sign and most of all patience. It is also the method with the lowest success rate and is only practical in areas where visibility is good and where the bears are concentrated by some major source of food. A spot and stalk hunt was the method that I most wanted to try. Finding the right location where I could try such a hunt was going to represent a challenge, however.

Baiting for game birds, illegal almost everywhere, has conditioned many hunters to view baiting of any animal as an unfair tactic. I have never accepted that criticism. Bears are not white-tailed deer that have set patterns of travel that can be studied and used to the hunter's benefit. Bears are wanderers that cover many square miles in their normal travels. Without a means of bringing a bear to the hunter, a hunter has very little realistic chance of ever shooting a bear in the heavily forested country that blankets much of the continent.

Besides, baiting is not nearly so easy as it sounds. A hunter or his guide must repeatedly tote foul offerings into the forest over a period of weeks, and then continue to monitor those baits until they are hit by a bear. Then the waiting game begins. The bear, especially if he has been baited before, will often only feed at night. Even a less educated bear will generally only appear at dawn or dusk, and the slightest hint of human scent will send him racing away. Patience and perseverance are critical if a hunter is to succeed in taking a bear over bait.

My reservations about hunting over bait had nothing to do with a lack of sportsmanship, but simply my aversion to spending long hours in a tree stand. I was capable of it as I had proven over my years hunting Alabama whitetails, but it was not my favorite way to hunt.

The other option was a hound hunt. In this case, sportsmanship was the issue. Clearly, a man who spent years training a pack of hounds to hunt bears was involved in a very sporting venture which required serious commitment to his sport and provided tremendous satisfaction when his pack succeeded in treeing a bear. My doubts centered around the hunter who hired a houndsman to use his pack to tree a bear which he could then shoot.

I had nearly dismissed the idea of a hound hunt until I read Craig Boddington's book _Campfires and Game Trails._ Boddington, an author and hunter for whom I have tremendous respect, suggested that most hunters who criticize hunting bears with hounds have never tried it. Based on that endorsement, I decided to also try a hound hunt.

My Year of the Bear began in September, 1994. After considerable research, I decided that the coastal islands of Alaska would be the ideal location for my spot and stalk hunt. Bear populations were high and the presence of salmon caused the bears to concentrate along the streams and tidal areas. Since I was a nonresident, hunting unguided, I was only permitted to hunt for black bear. I didn't relish having a close encounter with a giant brown bear for which I would have no license. I therefore elected to hunt on Prince of Wales Island which had a plentiful population of blacks, but no brownies at all.

My brother-in-law, Tom Wilson, who had been salmon fishing with me in Alaska several years before, was anxious to join me, although his goal more was salmon fishing and deer hunting. Tom, an experienced private pilot, who if truth be told, liked to fly even more than he liked to hunt or fish, volunteered his Bilanca four-seater for the trip north. We crammed a week's worth of camping and hunting gear into the plane, fueled up, and took off, leaving a worried wife and sister wondering if she would ever see either of us alive again.

The flight up the inland passage at a mere 4,000 feet altitude was breathtaking. Once we cleared the northern tip of Vancouver Island, we looked down upon a virtually uninhabited coast of rocky harbors; isolated, lonely beaches; and rugged, boulder strewn islands. It was a wilderness hard to fathom in the late 20th century, when all the world seemed overwhelmed by humanity. Vast forests of fir covered the steep peaks, which rose straight from the ocean, proud sentries at the western gates of a great continent. This pristine wilderness, which could be terribly unforgiving during winter, looked almost benign in the brilliant sunshine of September.

Our only company on the trip were cruise ships ferrying people to the cities of Coastal Alaska. Dropping low, we buzzed a pair of them as they motored powerfully through the straits; close enough to see the passengers sunbathing around the pool. It was simply a gorgeous day to fly.

Gorgeous that is, until we approached Ketchikan late that afternoon. A massive bank of fog, visible from 30 miles away, hung like soaked wool over the entire coast. Our goal was to fly all the way into Prince of Wales Island that night, but we had to refuel in Ketchikan. While the local air service tended to the plane, we made a quick check with the guys in the tower to determine the advisability of continuing on.

Conditions were deteriorating rapidly and were likely to remain bad for the foreseeable future. It definitely would not be any easier to fly in the next morning. We discussed possible routes to the strip and decided to give it a try. We had a truck rented in Klawock if we could make it. Our approach was through a long inlet, and then over the top of a ridge and into the strip.

After some indecision, we located the prescribed inlet and flew

223

hopefully in. When, we reached the end of the bay, the clouds had dropped to only 300 feet above the water, completely obscuring the peaks. We would have to fly up into those clouds and then come back down blind.

I had never been in such a situation, and I just had to trust in Tom's experience. If he thought we could make it, then so be it, but if he decided to go back, then that was okay too. Tom circled around the inlet for a full ten minutes weighing the decision as I quietly considered what it would be like to die here on this lonely island. I wasn't crazy about the idea, but at least it would be better than dying at work.

Perhaps if Tom had been familiar with the island, he might have braved an attempt, but he decided that the risk was too high. As he told me, "There are bold pilots and old pilots, but there are no old, bold pilots." We hightailed it back to Ketchikan, flying a mere two hundred feet above the sea and depending heavily on Tom's global positioning unit to guide us to the airport.

During all of our turns and twists, I began to suffer my first airsickness of the trip. To my horror, I discovered that there were no airsickness bags on board. My only choice was a hospital urine bottle that had already been utilized earlier in the flight; a grim dilemma if ever there was one.

So grim in fact, that I ceased all worry about life or death as I doggedly concentrated on holding onto lunch. Never was I any happier to feel wheels hit pavement.

We arranged to rent a different 4x4 truck in Ketchikan and take it to Prince of Wales on the ferry. The man renting us the truck apparently knew more about the roads on the island than we did, and demanded a handsome deposit before giving us the keys. Having accomplished all we could that evening, we set out through the rain in search of a hotel and a good meal.

Ketchikan facing its livelihood the sea, clung to the coast at the base of a fir-covered slope. Despite the anomalous McDonalds and Super 8, the town was vintage early 1900s. What had Alaska been like then? It still seemed a virtual frontier. As we sat in the bar of our 80-year-old hotel, toasting our arrival and survival, the ghosts of gold miners and sea otter hunters surrounded us.

The three hour ferry ride seemed extraordinarily long considering that it had only taken 15 minutes to fly to the same place the previous evening. The rain that fell in sheets during the entire crossing, shrouded the forested islands along our route with a primeval gloom. Visions of bears padding silently through the mists filled my thoughts.

Hollis, our port of arrival, was a tiny collection of rough homes and even rougher mobile homes. Our cabin was on the west side of the island, about two hours drive away. Lumbering on the island was being conducted at a tremendous pace, which was somewhat disheartening to see. The good news was that lots of lumber trucks meant gravel roads, which were able to stand up to the constant rains. Although the heavy truck traffic caused the roads to be terribly washboarded, they were at least solid.

We spotted our first bear on the drive, standing in the middle of the road, and looking for all the world like a black angus. We closed to within a hundred yards before he raced down the road and plunged into the dense second growth forest. My hopes soared as I envisioned seeing dozens more and simply picking the biggest bruin from which to make my rug. Such thoughts always bring bad luck, and deep down I knew better than to think them.

Our cabin was situated along the tidal area where a sizable creek joined the sound. Surrounded by old growth timber, it was an ideal setting, and the half mile walk from the road was just enough to give us a sense of privacy. The cabin itself was tiny but sound. Inside there were four bunks, a table and a kitchen counter. A porch was attached to the front and there was a picnic table in the "yard". The better part of the first afternoon was spent carting our gear from the truck and setting up shop.

A journal, left on the table, made for some interesting reading. It was filled with everything from tips on how to keep the mice at bay, to fishing advice and wildlife sightings. I noticed that bear sightings were commonly reported throughout the summer, but that no one had spotted one since the first day of the hunting season some two weeks earlier. Still hope springs eternal in the hunters heart, and I scrambled to assemble my gear for an evening hunt while Tom opted to try his luck with the salmon.

Bear sign was everywhere. Scats and half eaten salmon were scattered along streamside. Bear trails were worn deep in the soggy ground. Perhaps no one had seen any bears, but they were there someplace. Despite the plentiful sign, I did not spot any bears that evening. I did, however, see a forkhorn sitka blacktail deer, which I chose not to shoot.

The rain continued unabated throughout the night and into the following day, but undaunted, I was out before dawn in hopes of spotting game. No bears were out and about, so after several hours I returned to the cabin for a mid-morning breakfast. Tom and I needed to go into town to purchase some No.1 diesel fuel for operating the cabin's heater. It wasn't so much the heat that we needed as a means to dry out gear. I was also anxious to gleam some pearls of wisdom from the locals on the best approach to finding myself a blackie.

Our Forest Service cabin on Prince of Wales Island, Alaska.

As luck would have it, the man at the fuel depot had two outstanding blacktail deer heads and a bleached, polished bear skull in his office. Being anything but shy, I struck up a conversation. His advice was that our cabin was in a good area and that I should concentrate my efforts to the periods of low tide. As the tide receded, spawned out salmon would be left stranded in pockets along the shore. The bears should smell them and come out of the forest to feed. He was kind enough to show me his tide table, and I left with renewed hope and a plan of attack.

For the next two days, I hunted each dawn and dusk as well as for two hours on either side of low tides. Eagles, seals, waterfowl, and gulls were my constant companions as I slipped silently along the tidal zone; but not a bear was seen.

On the third day, I foolishly followed a narrow stream from the coast where I hoped I could surprise a bear. The map showed the stream leading to a road from which I could hike back to the cabin. Unfortunately, the stream soon degenerated into a trickle and old growth along the coast gave way to ten-year-old second growth. I found myself in a thicket from Hell. Chain saws, the ubiquitous sound of the island, directed me toward the road, but as hard as I struggled I seemed to get no closer.

Frustration became despair and was finally replaced by the only emotion capable of extricating me from this brushy prison: anger. I threw myself against brush in order to create a path; grabbed anything, including devil's club, that would allow me to pull myself another three feet forward; and shinnied along slippery deadfalls that offered a rare opportunity to rise above the jungle. Three hours later, exhausted and with new-found respect for coastal rain forests, I reached the road which had been less than a mile from the start of my ill-conceived trek.

I was feeling somewhat disheartened, as I took an evening stand overlooking the tidal grass. The forkhorn buck from the first evening showed up, feeding cautiously at the edge of the timber. Determined to come home with some venison at the very least, I shot him and dragged him back to the cabin.

While I was butchering the buck, some fishermen passed by and stopped to chat. They were local men, somewhat discouraged over the many pink salmon, but few silvers in the river. When I asked for their advice on bears, they suggested a drive up to the north end of the island. Fewer people and bigger, less nocturnal bears, they assured me.

As if to verify their comments about the local bears; when I checked the deer gut pile at dawn, it was completely gone, devoured during the night by a bear. The bears were indeed still present, but were almost unhuntably nocturnal. It was time to change scenery; to make the long, kidney-jolting drive north. We only had two days left to hunt.

Tom accused me of being driven by an "Always get my man" mentality. I mulled it over and decided that while that would have once been an accurate description of my feelings while hunting, it wasn't true anymore. At one time, failure to kill game was considered a ruined hunt. Now, I could accept that hunting and killing **were not** the same. What I could not accept was that hunting and giving up **were** the same. I now viewed a true hunter as one who used all his physical and mental powers to understand the game's habits and utilize them in his pursuit. If the Hunting Gods chose to smile on him then he gratefully accepted their gift. If they did not, he accepted his fate, satisfied that he had given his best effort.

We arrived at the bay at noon, the worst possible hour to hunt. Bear sign, however was absolutely thick especially where the stream poured into the salt water. We made ourselves as comfortable as possible on the downwind side of the tidal flat and began the long wait for dusk. The plan was that if a buck showed up first, then Tom would shoot. I had the only bear license. Fortunately, we had some books along and we took turns reading while the other man kept watch. For the first time in a week the rain had lessened to a rare sprinkle.

Six hours later, during Tom's watch; a bear appeared ambling across the flat about 250 yards distant, heading upstream. My heart jumped in my throat, but I forced it down. This could be a sow with cubs, which would be illegal to shoot, or even a young adult, which I promised myself I would not shoot. The animal was too far off and too obscured by the tall tidal grass to be sure. I needed a closer look. I dropped down on hands and knees and crawled forward hoping to intercept the bear along its route. Biting gnats poured out of the grass and covered my face, driving me mad.

The bear was now entirely out of my sight, although Tom could continue to spot it occasionally. He served as my guide, keeping an arm pointed in the direction he had seen it last. Tom began to shake his hand violently, pointing almost directly toward me, and I gathered that the bear and I were on a collision course. I rose to one knee and there it was, still walking steadily but now less than 80 yards away.

There were no cubs, and the animal appeared to be heavy bodied with a deep sagging belly. I wasted no time in raising the .375 H&H to my shoulder. Grass still obscured much of the body, and I was hesitant to risk a deflection by shooting into it. Memories of the density of the timber remained fresh in my mind and I truly had no desire to trail a wounded bear into such a place. I had to attempt a spine shot and hope that the big 300 grain Nosler would do the job if the bullet placement was slightly off.

The big magnum boomed, the bear fell to the ground and rolled onto its back, frantically kicking for an instant. I hurriedly threw another round into the chamber, and crept forward; the rifle still mounted on my shoulder. I stood there for several minutes; all senses on alert out of respect for what a wounded bear was capable of even if he did appear to be dead. Nervously, I touched the barrel to an eye, and there was no blink response. I had succeeded! I had come to Alaska; hunted without a guide; figured it out on my own; made some mistakes, and I had done it! It was a truly proud moment.

The bear turned out to be a very large sow; incredibly fat, with worn, chipped teeth. She would square 6½ feet and we estimated her weight at more than 300 pounds. There were undoubtedly bigger bears on the island, but I was mighty proud of the one I had on the ground.

PART II

My hunt with hounds turned out to be a lot closer to home, and took place only two weeks after returning from Alaska. Initially arranged as a hunt for two, I did not feel the desire to kill another bear so soon after the first, but I was quite anxious to experience hound hunting. I was perfectly content to go on the hunt but allow my friend Ron Britt to do the shooting.

Ron runs an agricultural research and consulting business in Yakima, Washington, where I also live, and I had been a client of his for many years. He is a small, sturdily built man a few years my senior, with eyes that twinkle when he teases people, which is often. We had not hunted together before, but I was reasonably certain that we would be compatible partners.

We met Dave, the houndsman, at a gas station in Kettle Falls. He wasn't hard to find; a mountain of a man, substantially overweight, sitting behind the wheel of a new Chevy pickup crammed full of hounds. He lead us back to the campground that he called home during the Washington bear season. Dave had warned me over the phone, "I'm no hunting guide. I won't set up camp for you or cook for you, but I do have some damn good hounds and I'll take you hunting. You can camp with us if you want to." That was good enough for us.

Dave was quite reserved, and retreated to his own campsite while we set up our beds under the cap of the pickup and arranged the Coleman stove, lantern and other kitchen paraphernalia on the picnic table. I grabbed a six pack and headed for Dave's campsite. Dave struck me as a nice person who was simply a little bit shy. I began admiring his hounds; mostly Walkers and a few Plotts that were staked throughout the woods at the end of the campground. Immediately, Dave opened up; telling me about the exploits of Sam his strike dog.

At dawn, we assembled around Dave's truck as eight hounds were loaded into a plywood box that covered the entire pickup bed. On the hood of the truck was a pad with two short chains attached in the middle. Sam, the big Plott strike dog, and Judd, a Walker hound and the best chase dog, were clipped onto the leads on the hood. Dave, his young son, and friend, Carl, rode in the truck with the dogs while Ron and I followed in our truck.

Slowly, we cruised along the dirt forest road past yellow alders and emerald firs. Unlike in Alaska, rain had been in short supply in Washington, and dust billowed up behind us. As we crossed a narrow creek, Sam began baying frantically. It was a deep, melodious voice that told us in a sure tone that a bear or perhaps a cougar had crossed the road here sometime during the night. Despite the dry conditions, Sam's magnificent nose had detected the faint scent even while perched on the top of a moving truck.

Dave unhooked Sam to see if he could unravel the scent. Silently, he ran along either side of the road for several minutes sniffing deeply. Through some sort of canine ESP, he deciphered the bear's direction of travel, and began climbing the mountain. After trailing for about 100 yards, he bayed again, announcing to all of us that he had the trail. With every bark, there was bedlam at the truck as each dog, dying to join the hunt, howled in excitement. Judd, whose eyes had remained riveted on Sam's every move, now strained his ears as he kept track of the race. When Dave finally released his chain, Judd dived off the hood and streaked toward the chase.

The two hounds soon were out of hearing range. Dave pulled his tracking antenna from the truck and slowly scanned across a 180 degree angle. The dogs each wore transmitter collars, which were invaluable when the chase went out of ear shot as it was now or when searching for lost dogs. A steady beeping was emitted from the receiver each time the antenna was pointed southeast.

We scrambled into the trucks and headed up a road that led to the top of the ridge. Dave was absolutely flying on the rough dirt road and it was all Ron and I could do to keep his truck in sight. Once at the top, Dave unlimbered his antenna once again, but try as he might, couldn't pick up a signal. Thinking that the chase may have crossed the ridge, we retraced our route and drove back out to the highway. Again, we got no signal.

There was nothing left to do but return to where the chase had started. Sure enough, we could still pick up a signal where we first detected it. The sound of the beep was now a double beep rather than the steady single tone we had heard before. Dave explained that when the collar was held at an angle beyond 45 degrees, the tone changed.

Usually that double beep meant that the dogs had something treed.

Ron, Carl and I would have to climb the mountain. Presumably the dogs had the bear treed in a small canyon and we would need to hike along the ridge until we could hear them. We reached the top, gasping for breath, thankful at last for the opportunity to stop and listen. Nothing. We had hiked along the ridge for about two hours when Dave called on the walkie talkie to report that the dogs had returned. We climbed down, not at all disappointed. Neither of us had wanted the hunt to end so quickly.

It was impossible to know what had gone wrong. Dave guessed that the bear had never been treed, but had perched himself on a cliff face where the dogs couldn't get at him. He then gave them the slip through some sort of rear exit. It was as good an explanation as any.

We tried to get another chase going, but the heat began to build and any nighttime trails were now cold. We returned to camp, planning to try again the next morning. Ron and I tried some dogless grouse hunting in an abandoned orchard that afternoon. Although we didn't find any grouse, we did notice plentiful bear sign beneath the old apple trees.

A nighttime thunder storm cleared the air and a cold front had blown in over night. The temperature had dropped from the 60s to the mid 30s, and a stiff north wind had picked up. The entire forest swayed rhythmically in the breeze, causing the yellow larches to begin the annual shedding of needles. It felt like the first true day of fall.

Scenting conditions were helped by the overnight rain and cooler temperatures, but staying in touch with the dogs was going to be difficult in the noisy wind. We had driven for perhaps an hour when Sam cut loose. Sam and Judd charged into the forest and in a matter of minutes were baying wildly. Dave and Carl scrambled to release three more dogs.

"Hear that?" asked Dave. "They caught him down there in that bottom."

"You mean he's in the tree?" I asked.

"No, I mean they caught him and they are chewing his butt. They're going to need help from these other dogs. The only way that bear is going to tree is if the dogs force him to go up. You guys better get down there. This bear might not tree at all, but you have a chance to get him on the ground. Carl, be careful of the dogs. You hear me."

Ron scrambled to load his rifle and we charged toward the chase.

We were too late. The bear made a run for it. Soon, the dogs were racing through the forest and within 10 minutes were barely in hearing range. The chase got spread out with the better dogs far ahead of the less experienced hounds. From the sound of their voices, Carl and Dave could identify each hound, allowing them to know who was leading the chase.

Two youngsters were so far behind that we managed to catch them as they crossed a dirt road. The older dogs then began to return one by one.

"We've chased that bear before," said Dave. "He never trees, and he turns on the dogs, concentrating on one at a time. The dogs, especially the younger ones, can get a little unnerved when a bear keeps chasing them, so they come out. The older dogs eventually realize that they can't get the bear up a tree by themselves and then they come out too."

"I had always thought that a bear treed when the dogs started to get close. I didn't have any idea that dogs had to actually fight a bear and force him to tree," I said. "That takes one hell of a courageous dog to walk up to a bear and bite him."

Dave answered with a smile and a nod.

"Somebody ought to invent a helmet camcorder for those hounds," I suggested. "Boy, I would love to see what went on during those tussles."

It was late morning by the time we had retrieved all the hounds, so we returned to camp. Over lunch, we reported the bear sign at the old orchard to Dave. He suggested that we give that a try in the afternoon. Sam was the only strike dog on the hood as we worked our way up the twisted, rutted road past the gnarly old apple trees. Sam's nose again proved itself and we had another chase going within the hour.

As the dogs reached the top of the ridge, the pitch of their barking escalated and I knew that they had made contact with the bear. This time Dave let all eight dogs go, two at a time; holding each dog's head in the direction of the chase before he released him. The intense caterwauling suddenly changed to a series of double barks. The bear was treed.

We were lucky. The bear had chosen a huge old pine, only 100 yards from the dirt road. The dogs looked as if they were trying to climb the trunk themselves as they repeatedly threw themselves skyward, barking joyfully. The bear was about 100 feet off the ground, standing on two thick limbs. His head swayed back and forth; slobber dripping from his jaws.

Ron wasn't worried about shooting a record book bear, but he didn't want to shoot a small one either. One of the advantages of hunting with hounds was the ability to really look over the animal before deciding to shoot. Bear size can be easy to misjudge so we took our time, before deciding that this was indeed a good-sized adult.

"Carl, get these dogs on a leash," Dave ordered. "I don't want any dogs squashed under this bear when he comes down. Ron, I want you to try to make a good shot. I'd like this bear to come down dead. If he doesn't, you are going to have to be very careful not to shoot us or the dogs. Okay, go ahead."

Ron seemed a bit nervous as he tried to line up the shot so as to avoid hitting limbs. After several moments of indecision, the .30-06 boomed and the bear came crashing down, breaking limbs as he fell. Carl released the dogs and they swarmed the bear, which by this time was completely dead; shot through the heart. The bear turned out to be a 320 pound boar with a good, thick pelt, and a very nice trophy for Ron.

It seemed to me an odd way to end a hunt. In most hunting, the outcome was not obvious until the moment the rifle is fired. In this case however, the hunt was over as soon as we saw the bear in the tree. The shooting was anticlimactic and felt somewhat like an execution. Still the overall experience had been enjoyable. Just seeing the hounds in action had made the hunt worth doing.

My year of the bear had shown me what an interesting game animal the black bear was. After comparing the two hunting methods, I found that I enjoyed both and would do either again. The spot and stalk method was more challenging and in the final analysis more satisfying, although I must admit that at times the long waits proved tiresome. The hound hunt, on the other hand, was more plain old fun, with great camaraderie and lots of action.

Dr. Bill VonStubbe with his Dall ram taken in August of 1995.

Chapter Twenty-five

REDEMPTION

The iridescent colored breast, the white neck ring, the impossibly long tail seemed close enough to touch as the rooster pheasant cackled into flight. Snow flurries drifted through the gray November sky, as I excitedly mounted the new 12 gauge pump to my shoulder. The rooster curled around the chest high spruce trees and shifted gears as he headed across the recently harvested cornfield. Three hurried shots later, he was still flying, out of danger and forever into my memory.

The weak sun of a December afternoon reflected golden off the calm waters of the Chesapeake. Thousands of Canada geese had gathered in a noisy raft 300 yards off shore. In hopes that some birds might head toward their nighttime feeding fields a little early, I hunkered down in the honeysuckle thicket on the bluff overlooking the bay. For two hours I waited, with the geese tantalizingly close. Just before dark, a flock of about a dozen birds took off and flew directly toward me. Scarcely twenty yards high, they honked in amazement when I rose up to shoot. I had never been that close to geese before. How then, did I miss three times?

Frost coated the pasture sedges, and the oak trees stood in naked silhouette in the January dawn. Alabama's whitetails were just coming into rut, and I had taken a stand along an old fence line. A line of eight does stepped daintily through the pasture edge and disappeared into the loblolly pines. A few moments later, a six-point buck, his head held low, walked deliberately up the same trail, grunting like a love sick billy goat. Although he was only 80 yards away, I missed him.

Misses which occurred decades before, had somehow remained seared into memory on a kind of intercranial video tape. They still hurt a little, but for the most part I had come to accept them. The dozens of pheasants, geese and deer that I had taken since those misses had gone a long way to remove the sting of failure.

There was one miss in my hunting career, however, that remained a constant source of regret, an open sore in my memory; missing the Stone ram on my high school graduation hunt. Even at the time, I knew that I had just missed a shot that I would never be able to live with. As I rode soaking wet and dejected down the mountain, I swore that I would hunt sheep again someday.

Twenty-four years passed before I honored that vow. The price of Stone sheep hunts had skyrocketed from $1,100 in 1971 to $11,000 in 1995. Even something as important as a chance at redemption had to be accomplished within some sort of budget. Reasoning that a sheep was a sheep, regardless of color, I gladly settled on a Dall sheep hunt for about half the price.

When my hunting partner, Bill VonStubbe, arrived in Fairbanks, I was more than a bit glad to see him. Three weeks of solitary travel in the 49th state had left me anxious for a friendly face. Bill and I had hunted chukars, pheasants and grouse together for years, and I was certain that even though we would be sharing a guide, we would get along fine.

Bush plane travel being the unrefined science that it is, we suffered innumerable delays before arriving in base camp on the evening of August 8th; two days before the season opened. Our outfitter, Terry Overly, looked like an Alaskan Hell's Angel with shoulder length, curly black hair, thick drooping moustache and black jacket. His appearance was, at least temporarily, matched by his demeanor. Highly agitated, he briefly welcomed us, before turning his wrath on the hapless pilot who had been stranding his hunters at airstrips throughout the day.

Bill and I stood there uncomfortably wondering what to do next, when an absolutely jolly, young cowboy in a crumpled Stetson, torn blue jeans and missing front teeth stepped forward and shook our hands.

"Let's get your gear stowed in the bunkhouse and then I'll show you around," Clint offered, his eyes twinkling impishly. He loaded our gear onto a wagon pulled by a three wheel motorcyle. Bill and I piled in on top of our duffels for the ride.

The bunkhouse was a solidly built, plywood-sheeted building with three bedrooms and a small sitting room. Several other hunters, all of whom had been stranded with us during portions of the day, were already there swapping stories. Next to the bunkhouse was a shower house with a concrete floor and a large stove for heating water. There was even a green house for growing vegetables.

The main lodge was also Terry's full time home. It was a huge log structure, two stories high. Electricity, supplied by a series of diesel generators, allowed the house to have all the modern conveniences, right down to the satellite TV. The decor, however, was clearly that of a hunting lodge. The entry way was dominated by a full mounted grizzly bear holding a ground squirrel in his jaws. Wolf skins of various hues hung from pegs, along with fox and lynx pelts. Numerous sheep mounts hung on the walls, engendering anticipation of the hunt.

After dinner, we retreated to the bunkhouse. It is sometimes remarkable to see how hunting can transform serious, busy men into happy, excited kids. Within minutes, we felt that we knew each other well enough to toss jokes back and forth. We talked late into the evening before retiring, and even then sleep was difficult to come by.

Immediately after breakfast, the guides lead all of us down to the range. Two sheep silhouette targets were set up, one at 100 and the other at 250 yards. I desperately wanted to avoid embarrassing myself in front of the other guys. I didn't care about shooting better than anyone else, but I at least wanted to feel I deserved to be in their company.

When my chance came, my momentary nervousness passed as the .280 locked into my shoulder, and I went through the shooting mechanics that have become second nature through the years. I laid my shots in a three-inch group, 2½ inches high at 100 yards and about two inches low at 250; not spectacular, but adequate.

The packhorses must have sensed that the hunting season, their season of labor, was about to begin. Like kids on a final fling before the start of school, they had departed for parts unknown during the night. The guides and wranglers were able to catch most of them, but seven horses remained at large. If they weren't located soon, some of the hunters would be stuck in base camp for another day.

Bill and I hung around the corrals for several hours while three groups of hunters packed up and rode out; each being blessed by Charlie the guide with a prayer that ended with the plea that there be "steaming gut piles in the snow."

Rather than become frustrated over the delay, Bill and I grabbed his fly rod and headed down to the Chisana River. More than a half mile wide, with a hundred, braided channels separated by strips of gravel and quicksand, the river ran gray with suspended silt. The channels closest to the bank ran much clearer than the remainder of the river, and it was there that we found the grayling. They were gorgeous, speckled fish with tiny, oval mouths and fabulous dorsal fins reminiscent of Siamese fighting fish. Several exceeded 14 inches, which was rather decent size for grayling.

Meanwhile, Terry had flown the Super Cub in ever expanding circles until he had, at last, located the escaped stock 11 miles away. The remaining guides and wranglers had caught the horses, but not without several mad races through spruce forests thick enough to decapitate a rider.

Returning to base camp with ripped clothing exposing bloody scratches and bruises, the guides were exhausted after fourteen hours in the saddle. They silently wolfed down dinner; their normal, youthful boisterousness momentarily subdued. Before staggering off to their bunks, they promised that we would hit the trail first thing in the morning.

We were to be guided by Terry's son, Stryker. Movie star handsome with light blond hair and a drooping moustache similar to his father's, Stryker was a man of the bush. Born and raised in the wilds, years often passed between visits to even a small city. He started helping his father guide when he was 14, so despite his still youthful 24 years, he was an old hand at the guiding business.

Stryker's apprentice was our gap-toothed friend, Clint. Clint, a former rodeo bull rider, was so determined to learn the guiding business that he volunteered to work for the first year solely for tips. Delightfully friendly, he answered nearly any suggestion with a high-pitched, drawn out cry of "Meeeee Tooooo!"

Our ride across the Chisana River made us instantly grateful for the horses. At least 30 times, the horses plunged through belly deep channels, and I shivered thinking about wading in hip boots. Clint warned us to keep our horses directly in the tracks of the one in front of us, to avoid the quicksand which could bury a horse up to the saddle horn in a heartbeat.

As we reached the junction with Notch Creek, we heard a sound that left no doubt that we were in the wilderness: the spine-tingling howl of wolves. I had a wolf tag, so we unmounted and waited on the river's edge in hopes that the wolves would appear. They remained in the timber, so we rode on for about a mile. Suddenly, Stryker jumped off the saddle and motioned me frantically to move forward.

I kicked Nutmeg, my ancient, knobby-kneed mare, but she scarcely reached a trot. Stryker's was motioning ever more emphatically, so I jumped off the mare, grabbing my rifle as I went, and ran the final 75 yards.

"Wolf. On the far side of the river. Do you see him?"

"No."

"He is starting to run."

"Yup. I see him."

He was at least 300 yards off, loping along at a steady pace. I lay on my stomach using Stryker's daypack as a rest. I fired, kicking up gravel right behind him. The wolf shifted into high gear. I continued firing until the rifle was empty but never caught up with him Somewhat disappointed, I recognized that it had been an extremely difficult shot, and chose not to let it bother me. At least I had seen my very first wolf.

Thoughts of the wolf were quickly displaced about a half hour later when we spotted the first Dall sheep of the trip, tiny white dots, far up the mountain. We unsheathed the spotting scopes and Stryker determined that the spots were rams and one was close to full curl. There was no way to stalk him, so we left, marking the spot for future reference.

Unused to riding, my thighs and butt were starting to ache as we approached the mouth of Ram Creek where we would camp. I had had the good sense to lead my horse from time to time to keep my muscles loose, and was therefore not doing too badly. Nonetheless, I was really looking forward to a toddy and a couple of Advils.

Rather than heading straight into camp, however, Stryker lead us to a vantage point where we could view Ram's Hole. What we saw was enough to warm the heart of any hunter. We spotted more than 20 lambs and ewes on a grassy meadow far up the canyon. Above them on a rocky point sat seven rams, and an eighth was resting on another ledge a few hundred yards away. From the distance of a mile, it was hard to tell how big they were even with the 30 power scopes, but Stryker thought that one or two were probably full curl and therefore legal.

All thoughts of camp were erased, and I was anxious to charge up the hill. Stryker, showing the patience of a veteran sheep hunter, stopped me. "It is too late to start after them today," he stated. "They'll still be there tomorrow."

Since Bill and I were sharing a guide, we had to make an arrangement about who would shoot first. We decided to use an alternate day plan whereby one man would get the first opportunity on odd days and the other man would have the even days. We knew that there would be rams to stalk in the morning, and I wanted Bill to have the first crack. I was more than a decade younger and a stronger hiker. Certainly, Bill would make it up the mountain, but could he do it day after day? I knew that I could.

The rams were right where we left them when we rode to the vantage point. Stryker and Clint laid on the gravel bar staring through the scopes for what seemed like hours. My eagerness to be on with it was nearly overwhelming, but somehow I managed to hold my tongue and allow the guide to do his job. At last, Stryker straightened up and announced the plan of attack.

"The ram by himself is definitely full curl," he stated, "and he is stalkable. I can't see all 7 of them, but I think there is at least one good ram in that bunch. They will be impossible to get up on unless they move. So, I think we should try for the lone ram. If we kill him, and if the others stick around, we might get a chance at them too."

"We will be forced to be within sight of the rams some of the time," he continued. "So we need to make use of the willows along the creek, and we need to move very slowly."

"I'm ready. Let's go," replied Bill.

"Meeeee Toooo," Clint chimed in. "I want to eat sheep meat."

When Stryker said we would move slowly he meant it. For eight hours we inched up the creek bed. Twenty yards, and then sit for five minutes. Twenty more yards, and sit again. The rams remained in place, not having moved in 18 hours. We dipped out of sight for a moment, and when we returned, the ram we were stalking was gone. Convinced that we had not spooked him, we were certain that he had simply moved behind some nearby rocks.

We inched the final few yards into range of the rocks where we thought he was, when suddenly the ram trotted out of the creek bed not 30 yards in front of us. Bill quickly chambered a round. The ram seemed befuddled by our miraculous appearance and had slowed to a near walk, still only 50 yards away. Bill fired twice in quick succession. We were close enough to see the entry wounds on his brilliant white fur. The ram stood transfixed, his great head pointed skyward for a moment and then collapsed.

Bill stifled a victory whoop not wanting to spook the other rams any worse than they already were. He flashed a huge smile, and we gave each other emphatic thumbs up signals.

The first ram was ours. He was a magnificently beautiful animal. He had a full curl 34 inches around, with good mass; An animal to be proud of.

After the obligatory photo session, Stryker and I climbed up the ridge. At the shot, the seven rams had trotted around the point and out of sight. We hoped that they had stopped up there somewhere. As we scrambled across a slide area, a ram peeked over the rocks 100 yards above us. He had us pinned in the open, so we dropped to the ground and froze. The ram was a 7/8 curl with the thin horns of a less than mature animal.

Hoping that the curious ram might lead the rest of the group into sight, I set up the bipod and scooted into shooting position. We weren't that lucky, however. The ram decided that he had seen enough and trotted around the corner. We jumped up and ran to the edge in hopes of catching up with the other rams before they all spooked.

There they were. The entire group trotted nervously away, still within range. Stryker immediately pointed out the biggest ram; a heavily broomed 38 incher. I dropped to my belly, and extended the bipod once again. A familiar, almost transcendental calm covered my excitement, like ice over a flowing river. I had a steady hold and I was confident that I was about to shoot my ram.

I had one significant problem however. A 3/4 curl ram was running shoulder to shoulder with the big one, effectively shielding him. Twice they stopped to look back, but still I could not shoot. At about 350 yards distance, they stopped a third time, but finally the big ram stepped clear. I went into autopilot, locked the crosshairs right behind the shoulder and squeezed like I had done a hundred times before.

As soon as the rifle fired, I was certain that he was mine. When Stryker shouted that I had missed, I was incredulous. The hold had been rock solid. Surely, he was dead. The fact that the ram was racing full tilt up the canyon was indisputable testimony that he was most definitely alive. My shots at a running ram proved no more effective than my shots at the running wolf. We last saw him topping out over a ridge two miles away, still running.

After 24 years, I had had my chance at redemption, and I had failed again. A nausea swept over me as I sat with my head in my hands, too embarrassed to even look Stryker in the face. I kept mumbling that the hold had been perfect, and I could feel my confidence draining away.

"Where did you hold?" Stryker asked.

"Right behind the shoulder," I answered.

"Yeah, but how high?"

"About six inches above the brisket," I answered, and immediately realized what I had done wrong. I had been so intent on waiting for the ram to step clear that I had simply held the crosshairs where I always did and had failed to compensate for bullet drop on the long shot. I had shot under him.

Bill didn't deserve to return to a sulky camp on the night of taking his wonderful ram, so I tried with partial success to concentrate on his good fortune rather than my failure. I returned to camp while Stryker,

Bill and Clint carried his ram off the mountain. By the time they returned, I had dinner ready and drinks poured all round to toast Bill's ram. I secretly hoped that we would be toasting a second ram before the trip was over.

Our weather, which had been beautiful had started to turn on us as we rode into the mouth of Star Creek. We wanted to let Ram's Hole rest for a day or two while we explored new country. It didn't take long to spot more sheep, and we soon had a couple of 7/8 curls and several bands of lambs and ewes in the scope. We watched them for a while, before riding on. At last we spotted a full curl ram feeding with some lesser rams in a meadow, almost in the bottom of the canyon.

He was not huge, maybe only 33 inches, but I was not prepared to pass up any full curl rams. It appeared to be a simple stalk in which we could hike up the bottom of the canyon and come over a knoll, which would put us within 50 yards of the ram. About then the rain began to fall in earnest, and all the sheep within sight began to move. The full curl ram and a buddy headed up a long moraine that ran at the base of a mountain that Stryker called the Fortress because it was impossible to hunt.

We tiptoed up the moraine, expecting to come upon the rams each time we reached the top of rocky mound. For three hours we continued without so much as a glimpse of our quarry. At last there they were, still 800 yards away and running. Apparently a wind eddy had allowed them to smell us, and the jig was up.

Rain beat down on the tent all night, but had stopped by the time we were eating breakfast. The fog however hung heavily over the ridges, making sheep hunting impossible. I paced in camp trying to will the fog to lift, while Bill calmly read a novel by the wood stove.

By midafternoon, the weather showed signs of improving, and Stryker had grown weary of watching me pace like a caged tiger. We saddled up and rode out in search of the ram, which we had spotted on our ride up Notch Creek several days before. Amazingly, we located him only a few hundred yards from where we had last seen him.

Stryker spent close to a half hour staring at him through the scope before declaring him to be slightly short of full curl. We rode back to the vantage point where we had first spotted Bill's ram. To our surprise, we couldn't spot so much as a ewe in the canyon. I suspected that the six shots which Bill and I had fired in the canyon, had spooked all of the sheep into a quieter refuge.

Stryker was not prepared to give up so quickly, and wanted to ride as far into the canyon as possible for a better look around. My old mare was laboring as she lugged me up the mountain, and I finally took pity and led her. Clint and Stryker were stretched out on top of a rocky knoll when I arrived. I slithered up beside them and spotted the snow white rams instantly.

There were two groups of four rams only 800 yards away. Through the 36 power scope, I could clearly see that one ram was much bigger than his buddies. His horns extended for several inches beyond the bridge of his nose and flared dramatically at the tips. I wanted him more than I had ever wanted an animal in my life and I said so to Stryker.

"Well, if you want him you are going to have to be patient," he advised. "The only way that we could get to him would be to climb all the way to the top and then come down on him. That would take four or five hours and we don't have that much light. If we rush him and end up spooking him, he will run completely out of this canyon and we will never find him. He should still be there in the morning."

Although I hated to hear that advice, I had grown to trust Stryker's judgment. We slipped back to the waiting horses and mounted up. Old Nutmeg and Sage were not the strongest horses, but they soon showed us how much mountain savvy they had. As we descended a steep, shale-covered slope, both horses planted their feet and slid sideways down the mountain while Bill and I hung on in wide-eyed amazement.

I awoke to the cheerful sound of horse bells as Clint drove the hobbled horses back to camp. The weather showed signs of improving, with occasional patches of blue peeking through the swirling clouds. Bill needed a day of rest, so he volunteered to do the breakfast dishes and allow us an early start.

Within a couple of hours we were back to our lookout knoll. Sure enough, the rams were right where we had left them. Then the fog dropped in over both us and the rams. We tried to wait until it lifted, but finally decided to use the fog as cover to cross the open ground between us and the rams.

We moved painstakingly slowly, placing every step as if we were crossing a minefield. We didn't want to stumble right into their midst and be forced into another running shot. Tense as a violin string, I expected the ram to appear any second. I strained my eyes to pierce the fog. At last it dawned on me. We were standing right where the rams had bedded. They were gone.

The fog began to rise once again, and we spotted a ram 1,000 yards away. We couldn't tell if this was one of the rams which had been with the big one or not, and the big ram could easily have been nearby, but out of sight. Either way, he had us pinned down and we were afraid to spook him by exposing ourselves. To my amazement, Clint and Stryker stretched out on the jagged rocks, and despite the steady rain, fell sound asleep.

I, on the other hand, was on the threshold of hypothermia. I located a flat area of about 20 yards where I could move about and remain out of sight. For an hour, I paced, did jumping jacks, and stretched in an attempt to keep my body temperature up. At last, Stryker and Clint showed that they were indeed human, and woke up shivering mightily.

We took a chance and moved closer to the 7/8 curl ram. It turned out that he was entirely alone. Now we were stumped. The big ram seemed to have vanished into the fog, yet we were convinced that he remained somewhere within the canyon. I suggested that we climb all the way to the top of the ridge and try to relocate him.

The climb was easily 45 degrees and the slope was not only devoid of vegetation, but completely composed of loose shale. It was truly a case of two steps forward and one step back. At least the struggle forced our bodies to warm up. It was impossible not to make noise during our climb and we had to trust that sheep were not overly sensitive to falling rocks.

We reached the summit just as the snow began to fly. Our vision was reduced to less than 100 yards, forcing us to once again wait. Every ten minutes or so, the snow would let up for a while. We used those breaks to pick our way along the ridge, peering down each side canyon as we went.

At last we spotted four rams and our spirits soared until we realized that all were 7/8 curl rams. I was bemoaning my poor fortune, when I saw Stryker drop to the ground in front of me. I scooted down to his position behind a small outcropping. There, 300 yards away was my ram, standing with a 3/4 curl buddy.

Stryker told me to take the shot, but I was hesitant to try. It seemed like a long shot, and I asked Stryker if they might not come closer. He answered cryptically, "They will if you shoot."

I rested the rifle over the rock outcropping, and flipped off the scope covers. The snow instantly plastered the lens, making it difficult to clearly see the ram. Perhaps it was the awkward shooting position, perhaps it was the cold, perhaps my confidence had eroded from my previous miss, or perhaps I realized that this would be my last chance at redemption, regardless I could not hold the crosshairs steady.

Still, I had to shoot soon or I would be unable to see at all through the snow smeared scope. I tried to control the cross hairs so that although they still wobbled, at least they wobbled around the chest. I squeezed the trigger.

"You hit him! Shoot again!" Stryker yelled.

I at last realized what Stryker had meant when he said that the ram would come closer if I shot. The rams were standing on sheep trail heading in our direction. They could not tell which direction the shot had come from so they ran up the trail and closer toward us.

I missed on the second shot as the ram ran, but then he stopped 200 yards below us, his left front leg dangling. Stryker urged me to shoot, but I could no longer see the ram through the scope. I frantically tried to wipe the lens, but nothing helped. I was about to totally lose my composure, when I realized that the scope was still set on 9 power. I cranked it down to 3. Amazingly the ram had not spotted us yet and was still standing below us. I could now vaguely make out the ram through the scope.

I had moved into a sitting position with my elbows on my knees. I could make out the blurry white shape of the ram. Again the crosshairs wobbled, but I forced myself to steady down. At the shot, the ram collapsed like a rag doll, his spine broken. He rolled for nearly a half mile before coming to a rest.

A strange collage of emotions swept over me. Certainly, there was joy at taking a magnificent ram; but also sadness for the end of a beautiful animal; regret for having shot poorly and caused suffering; and perhaps most of all, relief that after 24 years I could put to rest a miss that had haunted me. Redemption at last!

The author with his Dall ram.

Epilogue

PASSING THE BATON

There is no way to logically end this book, because the end of my journey is hopefully many years away. Even more hopefully, I believe the best is yet to come. Certainly, I have no shortage of unfulfilled hunting dreams. I therefore choose to end with the story of helping another hunter's journey begin.

When I married, I dreamed that one day I would have a son; a robust, active, bright lad with muddy knees and frogs in his pocket. He would follow me into the fields and forests where I would open his eyes to the magic of nature and to the thrill of the hunt. Like a parched sponge placed below a dripping faucet, he would thirstily absorb every drop of knowledge I had accumulated through decades of hunts and decades of education.

My first child, born in 1981, was a beautiful, happy, bright little person that we named Charlotte. Our second and final child, born in 1983, was a vivacious, funny, sweet child that we named Gretchen. Although the "son" part of the dream didn't come true, I saw no reason to give up on the entire dream.

Instead of picture books, we looked through hunting magazines. Pheasants, quail, deer, elk and moose were first recognized and eventually became among the first words in their vocabularies. We took walks and trees were not just trees, but oaks; not just oaks but white oaks; not just white oaks but *Quercus alba.* Our bird identification started with the bright species like cardinals and blue jays and continued to the drab house finches and titmice. Game shot and brought home was reason for lessons on beaks and claws and feathers and even some impromptu crop dissections.

Our first hunting trip, when the girls were six and four years old, was a walk down an abandoned logging road in northeastern Washington. Gretchen quickly fell back and picked flowers with her mom, but Charlotte stayed up for nearly an hour; long enough to see me both miss and shoot a ruffed grouse.

You can lead a horse to water but you can't make him drink, and Charlotte just wasn't turned on. She went along a couple of times until she was about ten, but the interest wasn't there. She was much more involved in her dance and music, her swim team, her friends and school. My efforts weren't totally in vain. I think that she will always see things in nature that others overlook, and who knows if she will find those early lessons valuable later in life. A hunter, however, she will never be.

Gretchen on the other hand was truly fascinated. She loved to hear stories of my hunting trips as I tucked her in at night. She would dig into a chukar's crop with her bare hands and gleefully examine defunct grasshoppers. When she was seven, she wanted a BB gun, and we practiced gun safety and marksmanship in the back yard. When she was nine, I took her jump shooting for mallards. When she was ten, she took the first official step to becoming a hunter in her own right when she registered for the state's hunter safety course; a prerequisite to buying her first hunting license.

She loved the class, and took the whole thing very seriously; eventually getting a 90 percent on her final test. I wouldn't allow her to actually hunt that first season. As I told her, "You've passed the State's test, but my test says that you have to walk along for a year, before you carry a gun." During that year of tagging along, she learned the most important lesson of all: Becoming a hunter took more than just wanting to. It took hard work.

Boots get heavy, brush gets thick, thorns scratch hands, and toes get numb. That is just the way it is. I suspect most boys would be able to cope with the hardships better than most girls, and feminism to the contrary I had to take it easy. Training her as I would a young puppy, I neither coddled her, nor paid much attention to whining. I did however make every effort to make sure we had fun. We hunted places that had plenty of game, but were not overly difficult to navigate, and we kept our trips on the short side, usually ending by noon.

For Christmas, I rewarded her effort by giving her a youth/ladies model 20 gauge Browning pump gun. Some would say, too nice a gun for a kid, but I wanted her to have something that would last a lifetime. She was dying to shoot it, so that Christmas evening we went to a local field and lined up a few pop cans. It was almost dark and flame shot out the barrel when she fired; pulverizing the can.

Her nervous laughter couldn't disguise the fear in her eyes. Torn between not wanting to disappoint me, and doubts about why she had ever wished for a shotgun, she fought to maintain her nerve. This was no BB gun and the explosion of the shot and the kick had turned her knees to jelly. I couldn't allow her to be defeated by her fear, and all of my powers of persuasion were required to cajole her into shooting two more shells. Conquering her fear of the gun took most of the spring. We would go clay pigeon shooting and she would only manage 5 or 6 shots before calling it quits. Slowly, she became more comfortable as spring turned to summer, and finally broke her first clay target on the fifth trip.

Her first actual hunt was for doves on a hot September afternoon. The field had been hunted for the previous two days and most of the birds had been either shot or scared off, but at least we had the field to ourselves. An occasional bird made a nervous pass over the disked wheat field and we had some shooting. Gretchen, unaccustomed to having to shoot quickly, allowed several birds to sail directly overhead while she laboriously raised her shotgun too late. She did manage three shots fired, but no birds. Still it was a start, and she absolutely loved it.

Upland bird hunting was even more of a challenge for her. Our first attempt was on a stocked pheasant farm, where we had no competition from other hunters and plenty of tight sitting birds. My German longhaired pointer, Anja, locked up on a pheasant, moments after we left the truck. Gretchen walked into make the flush as if she were a member of the bomb squad; a feeling to which even experienced hunters can relate.

When the bird finally burst into the air, Gretchen tilted back on her heels, completely paralyzed. Anja was in top form and pointed another dozen birds, but Gretchen only managed to fire twice. At that moment, I knew she was in for a long season. These birds were easy, pen-raised birds flying across an open field. Wild birds were rarely so cooperative.

On our first day after wild pheasants, a huge gaudy rooster erupted directly beneath Gretchen's feet. I glanced at her to see if she would shoot, and saw a look of slack-jawed terror. Hoping she would get over her paralysis, we continued hunting every weekend. I tried to give her all the best opportunities, but she just wasn't getting the gun to go off. It was time for a change of tactics.

We started jump shooting ducks on some of the local creeks and irrigation drains. Gretchen liked the way the mallards leaped from the water and seemed to hang suspended for a moment before they gained speed. On our very first attempt, Gretchen had a perfect opportunity as a dozen mallards took off ten yards in front of her. She shot and missed, but at least she shot. We were making progress, and she was gaining confidence.

On the following weekend, we headed out in the dark toward a favorite creek. I was almost certain that ducks should be resting on a big bend where the water pooled up. We sneaked through the frost covered weeds, with Anja at heel beside me. Just as I planned it, 15 ducks leaped out of the water most of them in front of Gretchen. A half dozen teal swung downstream toward me and I dropped one. I heard Gretchen shoot from behind me.

"Did you shoot that duck," she asked, her voice quaking.

"I got this teal over here," I answered.

"Well, the duck I was shooting at fell across the creek," she answered as she slowly recognized what she had done. "I got one. I got one," she repeated as she leaped, joyfully into the air. Anja first retrieved the teal, and then I sent her across the creek to find Gretchen's duck. Minutes passed as Anja swam back and forth along the bank trying to pick up the scent. Gretchen's elation had turned to concern, and I began to wonder is she might have imagined the entire event.

Anja climbed up on the shore and into a huge willow thicket. For several minutes she crashed through the thick brush, as Gretchen continued to fret. Then we heard a frantic flapping of wings, followed by a loud quack. A moment later, Anja emerged with a still-alive drake mallard in her jaws.

Gretchen was beaming, proud almost to the point of bursting. Her effort, which had begun in that hunter safety course a year and a half before had come to fruition. She had reached the first milestone in her own hunter's journey. This father felt the same emotions as most fathers would at such a moment, of a dream fulfilled, of pride in her, of joy at bestowing a precious gift, of tradition passed on, and of the privilege of witnessing a coming of age. I can only wish her and my reader a long and joyful journey.

Good Hunting!

My daughter, Gretchen Rohlfs, with her first duck and our great German longhaired pointer, Anja, in December of 1994.

LISTING OF BOOKS

Additional copies of *COTTONTAILS TO KUDU* by Mitch Rohlfs and many other of Stoneydale Press' books on outdoor recreation, big game hunting, or historical reminisces centered around the Northern Rocky Mountain region, are available at many book stores and sporting goods stores, or direct from Stoneydale Press. If you'd like more information, you can contact us by calling a Toll Free Number, 1-800-735-7006, by writing to the address at the bottom of the page, or contacting us on the Web at www.stoneydale.com. Here's a partial listing of some of the books that are available.

Historical, Hunting Reminisces

The Trail of a Sportsman, By Duane Bernard. Follow the author on a life-long quest to hunt big game across the world and to achieve what is called Oregon's "Super Slam" on a working man's budget. Go with him on adventures to Montana, Idaho, British Columbia, New Mexico, Alaska, Quebec, South Africa, Zimbabwe and Namibka, as well as in his native Oregon. 6x9-inch format, 154 pages, many photographs.

Cow Range and Hunting Trail, By Malcolm S. Mackay. An expanded new edition of the early-day Montana classic first issued in 1925 written by legendary rancher-outdoorsman Malcolm S. Mackay and illustrated by famed cowboy artist Charles M. Russell. 256 pages, 35 photographs, a new long-lost chapter added to marvelous stories of ranching and big game hunting in the West, this book is a reprint of a national best-seller from 75 years ago.

Copenhaver Country, By Howard Copenhaver, the latest collection of humorous stories. Contains rich humor and studied observations of a land Howard loves and the people he met along the way in a lifetime spent in the wilds. 160 pages, many photographs.

They Left Their Tracks, By Howard Copenhaver, Recollections of Sixty Years as a Wilderness Outfitter, 192 pages, clothbound or softcover editions (One of our all-time most popular books.)

More Tracks, By Howard Copenhaver, 78 Years of Mountains, People & Happiness, 180 pages, clothbound or softcover editions.

Mule Tracks: The Last of The Story, By Howard Copenhaver. As one of Montana's most revered storytellers and honored outfitters, Howard spent years leading his mule packstrings through the Bob Marshall Wilderness. Read here of his adventures, misadventures and other wild tales of mules in the wild country. 176 pages, hardcover and softcover editions.

Indian Trails & Grizzly Tales, By Bud Cheff Sr. A wonderful collection of stories taken from a lifetime outfitting in Montana's Bob Marshall and Mission Mountain Wilderness areas, by a master woodsman. 232 pages, available in clothbound and softcover editions.

70,000 Miles Horseback In The Wilds of Idaho, By Don Habel. Don Habel worked as an outfitter in the Idaho wilderness for more than forty years and has put together a wonderfully detailed and sensitive, as well as occasionally humorous, reminisce of his adventures in the wilds. 180 pages, softcover.

The Potts' Factor Versus Murphy's Law, By Stan Potts. Life story of famous Idaho outfitter Stan Potts, lots of photographs. 192 pages.

Mules & Mountains, By Margie E. Hahn, the story of Walt Hahn, Forest Service Packer, 164 pages, clothbound or softcover editions.

Dreams Across The Divide: Stories of the Montana Pioneers, Edited by Linda Wostrel, Foreword by Stephen Ambrose. Stories and photos of the first pioneers to settle in Montana. 448 pages.

Hunting Books

The Packer's Field Manual, By Bob Hoverson. Featuring use of the Decker Pack Saddle, this manual written by one of the top experts in the country will literally provide you with every detail necessary to successfully pack with the Decker Pack Saddle. 6x9-inch softcover format, 192 pages, many photographs and illustrations by Roger Inghram.

Hunting Chukar, By Richard O'Toole. This authoritative and detailed guide to hunting the West's most elusive game bird, the chukar, provides both experience and knowledge taken from 35-plus years of experience. Chapters on locating birds, tactics used in hunting them, gear, the choice and use of dogs, and many photographs. 6x9-inch format, softcover, 12 chapters and an appendix.

Solving Elk Hunting Problems, By Mike Lapinski. Subtitled "Simple Solutions to The Elk Hunting Riddle," this book, in 15 chapters and more than 80 photographs tells you now to cope with specific problems you'll encounter in the field – a hung-up bull, changes in elk behavior under heavy hunting pressure, peak rut activity, and so on. 6x9-inch format, both softcover and hardcover editions.

High Pressure Elk Hunting, By Mike Lapinski. The latest book available on hunting elk that have become educated to the presence of more hunters working them. Lots of info on hunting these elk.192 pages, many photographs, hardcover or softcover.

Bugling for Elk, By Dwight Schuh, the bible on hunting early-season elk. A recognized classic, 164 pages, softcover edition only.

A Hunt For the Great Northern, By Herb Neils. This acclaimed new novel utilizes the drama of a hunting camp as the setting for a novel of intrigue, mystery, adventure and great challenge set in the woods of northwestern Montana. 204 pages, softcover.

Ghost of The Wilderness, By James "Mac" Mackee. A dramatic story of the pursuit of the mountain lion, the Ghost of The Wilderness. A tremendous tale of what Jim MacKee went through over several seasons in his quest for a trophy mountain lion in the wilds of Montana. 160 pages, softcover.

The Woodsman And His Hatchet, By Bud Cheff. Subtitled "Eighty Years on Wilderness Survival," this book gives you practical, common sense advice on survival under emergency conditions in the wilderness. Softcover.

Memoirs of An Idaho Elk Hunter, By Jens Andersen. This big book captures the vitality and romance of a lifetime spent hunting elk in Idaho and Montana. A superb read, many color photographs and illustrations. 216 pages, hardcover only.

Coyote Hunting, By Phil Simonski. Presents basics on hunting coyotes as well as caring for the pelts, 126 pages, many photographs, softcover only.

Predator Hunting Handbook, By Phil Simonski. The basic primer on hunting all predators – coyote, bear, mountain lion, lynx, bobcat, crows – with solid info from a nationally recognized expert. 6x9 inch format, many photographs, 140 pages.

Elk Hunting in the Northern Rockies, By Ed Wolff. Uses expertise of five recognized elk hunting experts to show the five basic concepts used to hunt elk. Another of our very popular books, 162 pages, many photographs.

So You Really Want To Be a Guide, By Dan Cherry. The latest and single most authoritative source on what it takes to be a guide today. This book is an excellent guideline to a successful guiding career. Softcover edition only.

Hunting Open Country Mule Deer, By Dwight Schuh. Simply the best and most detailed book ever done for getting in close to big mule deer. The ultimate mule deer book by a recognized master, 14 chapters, 180 pages.

Taking Big Bucks, By Ed Wolff. Subtitled "Solving the Whitetail Riddle," this book presents advice from top whitetail experts with an emphasis on hunting western whitetails. 176 pages, 62 photographs.

Radical Elk Hunting Strategies, By Mike Lapinski. Takes over where other books on early-season elk hunting leave off to give advice on what the hunter must do to adapt to changing conditions. 162 pages, 70 photographs.

Western Hunting Guide, By Mike Lapinski, the most thorough guide on hunting the western states available. A listing of where-to-go in the western states alone makes the book a valuable reference tool. 168 pages, softcover.

Quest for Giant Bighorns, By Duncan Gilchrist. Comprehensive overview on hunting bighorn sheep everywhere they're hunted; detailed how-to, where-to with lots of photos. 224 pages, softcover.

Quest for Dall Rams, By Duncan Gilchrist. The best source book ever put together on the beautiful Dall sheep, it's crammed with solid how-to and where-to information on hunting Dall sheep. 224 pages, 88 photographs, many charts, softcover format.

Montana–Land of Giant Rams, Vol. III, By Duncan Gilchrist. The best source and most acclaimed book available on hunting bighorn sheep in Montana. Updated and expanded from his earlier volumes on the same subject. 224 pages, many photographs, softcover format.

Successful Big Game Hunting, By Duncan Gilchrist. For more than four decades now, Duncan Gilchrist has hunted across North America as well as in Africa and New Zealand. This book touches every aspect of what it takes to be a successful hunter. 176 pages, 82 photographs, both softcover and hardcover formats.

Field Care Handbook, By Duncan Gilchrist and Bill Sager. The most comprehensive field guide available for the care of big game, birds, fish and other species. Illustrated by many of Duncan's photographs taken in the field. 168 pages, many photographs and illustrations, comb binding so it will lay flat while you use it.

Cookbooks

Camp Cookbook, Featuring Recipes for Fixing Both at Home and in Camp, With Field Stories by Dale A. Burk, 216 pages, comb binding.

That Perfect Batch: The Hows and Whys of Making Sausage and Jerky, By Clem Stechelin. Detailed instruction on techniques of making sausage and jerky at home from wild game, beef, etc. 116 pages, many photographs, comb binding.

Cooking for Your Hunter, By Miriam Jones, 180 pages, comb binding. Healthful recipes using wild game as well as domestic meats.

Cooking on Location, By Cheri Eby. Exhaustive content for cooking on location in the outdoors, from menu planning to camp organization, meal preparation, and recipes for all sorts and styles of dishes. 139 pages, color photos and illustrations, comb binding.

Venison As You Like It, By Ned Dobson. A manual on getting the most from game meat, with over 200 recipes and instructions on using a variety of cooking methods. Detailed index, softcover.

STONEYDALE PRESS PUBLISHING COMPANY
523 Main Street • Box 188
Stevensville, Montana 59870
Phone: 406-777-2729
Website: www.stoneydale.com